U0504619

国际教育专家论“早教”

INTERNATIONAL WORKING GROUP'S RESEARCH ON EARLY CHILDHOOD EDUCATION

来自哈佛大学、卡尔加里大学、
华东师范大学的研究

A volume contributed by Harvard University, the University of Calgary, East China Normal University

上海三联书店

高迪安 & 哈佛大学教授国际合作教育科研中心 主编

御珑幼儿园艾琳娜广场实景

真爱手心

御珑幼儿园彩虹操场，天然草坪

儿童游乐场

专业篮球场、网球场

英国皇家礼仪培训

宫廷里的下午茶

宫廷里的下午茶

香梅和平御园马术训练

香梅和平御园马术训练

御珑宫天光泳池

三大人文艺术瑰宝（海马龙、海马凤、艾琳娜）在联合国展出

9·9世界名人廊

图片注解：

一、多元化学习环境，提供丰富体验感

御珑幼儿园艾琳娜广场实景

真爱手心

御珑幼儿园户外彩虹操场，天然草坪

儿童游乐场

专业篮球场、网球场

二、国际化课程设置，培养自信世界观

英国皇家礼仪培训

宫廷里的下午茶

香梅和平御园马术训练

御珑宫天光泳池

三、个性化人文瑰宝，彰显独特艺术性

三大人文艺术瑰宝（海马龙、海马凤、艾琳娜）在联合国展出

9·9世界名人廊

小天使在艾琳娜雕塑及和平许愿池前许愿

前言

早期儿童发展对儿童来说是一段至关重要的时期，同时也是头脑发育的高峰。联合国可持续发展目标四，即“确保包容和公平的优质教育，让全民终身享有学习机会”，明确地将早期儿童教育放在了重要的位置，计划在2030年之前确保所有男女童获得优质幼儿发展、保育和学前教育，为他们接受初等教育做好准备。办好学前教育，关系亿万儿童的健康成长，关系千家万户的切身利益，关系国家和民族的未来。

为了响应国民需求、与国际先进教育接轨，高迪安集团把早期儿童教育的国际化作为战略规划的重中之重，于2015年成立了“高迪安集团早教研发中心”（以下简称“研发中心”），于2016年与哈佛大学教授团队展开合作并成立“高迪安&哈佛大学教授国际合作教育科研中心”。“研发中心”的建立旨在与世界领先的大学、组织及机构建立多边战略合作伙伴关系，从国际早教领域吸收更多超前的教学理念及经验，围绕儿童社会、情感、认知及身体需求的全面发展展开科学研究，为其终身学习及健康成长打下基础。“研发中心”所有的研究成果将会首先落地于艾琳娜双语幼儿园和人文艺术中心，使之成为全球儿童早教领域的风向标。

合作至今，美国哈佛大学、加拿大卡尔加里大学、中国华东师范大学教授团队已携手“研发中心”展开了许多有特色的学术研究项目。每位教授基于自身学术专长及研究兴趣，围绕学前儿童双语教育、早期儿童认知发展、儿童心理学、教育公平性及包容性、多文化教育、语言发展、阅读发展及识字教育、儿童社会发展与教育、中国学前儿童英语学习等话题进行研究。三年来，通过“研发中心”在艾琳娜双语幼儿园持续不断的实践与试点，他们逐渐将丰硕的研究成果汇聚成了《国际教育专家论“早教”——来自哈佛大学、卡尔加里大学、华东师范大学的研究》一书，并以中英文的形式发行，旨在为全球的教育工作者、家长及教育理论研究者提供早期儿童教育指导性读物。

本书共分为十个章节，通过有趣的案例分析、严谨的理论框架，打开了国际儿童早期教育的新格局。为本书提供支持的教育名师包括：哈佛大学教育学院 Patricia Albjerg Graham 荣誉教授凯瑟琳·E·斯诺教授；哈佛大学教育学院 Roy E. Larsen 教育与人类发展及哈佛大学医学院精神病学部心理学教授罗伯特·L·赛尔曼；加拿大卡尔加里大学副教授、原哈佛大学博士赵旭；世界学前教育协会中国区主席、华东师范大学教育学资深教授周兢。

良好的早教可以为世界培养出关爱他人、德才兼备、认真负责的全球公民。我们坚信一个国家若是对早教进行投入，那么其在推动人力资源发展、宣传性别平等、增强社会凝聚力等方面将会事半功倍，同时也降低了日后补救措施的成本。多年来，高迪安集团一直为推动早期儿童教育的发展而不懈努力。 无论是硬件还是软件，高迪安集团都竭力整合最好的资源。“工欲善其事，必先利其器。”我们衷心希望这部《国际教育专家论“早教”——来自哈佛大学、卡尔加里大学、华东师范大学的研究》可以为全球的早教事业带来福音；希望有一天不论国籍或性别，所有的孩子都可以接触到最优质的早教启蒙，体会到真爱的人文精髓。

高迪安集团早教研发中心

高迪安集团有限公司

序

钱文忠

“从婴幼儿降生的第三天开始教育，就已经晚了两天。”

著名心理学家巴甫洛夫说的这句话，是对“早教”重要性的极而言之。

“早教”，是早期儿童教育（Early Childhood Education， ECE）的简称。 这是从启蒙运动时代开始兴起的概念，一般是指从出生到6 岁所涉及到的婴幼儿教育和养育。

著名“早教”著作《卡尔威特的教育》一书中写道：“对于孩子来说，最重要的是教育。 在孩子智力曙光出现的时候尽可能早、尽可能多、尽可能正确地开发孩子的智力，这样孩子就能成为优才。”

教育的本质，是尊重生命、珍爱天性、激发良性、唤醒灵性，也就是一句话： 呵护孩子内心的那颗种子。

由成人对婴幼儿实施的“早教”，乃是人生的启蒙教育，具有奠基的意义。 如同穿衣，扣对第一粒钮扣，就规正了。

这些年来，我应邀在中央电视台《百家讲坛》解读《三字经》等经典，就是想把我的心，交给孩子，交给启蒙，交给教育。

所以，获悉《国际教育专家论“早教”——来自哈佛大学、卡尔加里大学、华东师范大学的研究》即将出版，甚感欣然。

翻阅书稿，亦饶有兴味。比如，从“绘本的使用”入手，论述跨学科、跨语言的教学框架；从“幼儿读物的选择”切入，分析不同类型孩子的不同互动；从双语教育、脑发育研究、儿童社会意识的发展等角度，纵论“优秀、快乐、成长”的目标培养，等等。这些“早教”命题，不是泛泛而谈的空洞说教，而是契合实际的具体引导。

只有“具体”，才有“生动”，才会“深入”。《国际教育专家论“早教”——来自哈佛大学、卡尔加里大学、华东师范大学的研究》是一本具体、生动、深入的启蒙教育书。

可喜可贺的，不仅是这本书的即将问世，更是本书编著机构“高迪安＆哈佛大学教授国际合作教育科研中心”的令人瞩目。

据了解，高迪安作为中国香港的一家企业集团，曾在联合国总部获颁“世界和平贡献奖”。多年来，高迪安始终在“真爱人文”的道路上砥砺奋进，在“人文教育”的事业上孜孜以求。在精进鸿业的同时，高迪安还用心独创了海马龙、海马凤、艾琳娜“三大人文艺术瑰宝”。特别是五年前开创性地倡导成立了全球第一个以“真爱人文”为主题的“艾琳娜9·9国际真爱节”，被联合国教科文组织协会主席巴纳格尔先生盛赞为“诺贝尔式的努力与贡献”。

这是宏阔的格局，这是人文的气象。

而携手哈佛大学教授设立国际合作教育科研中心，把科学的“早教”理念付诸实践于“艾琳娜双语幼儿园”这块“试验田”，则开拓了“真爱·人文·教育”的一方新天地。

世界上一切的追问，归根到底，是人文的追问。

世界上一切的求索，归根到底，是生命的求索。

从居住空间到生活方式，从天地之间到思维方式，“人文”是活水源头，“生命”是不息脉动。

生命是一条大道，人文是一种实践。

由此看来，《国际教育专家论“早教”——来自哈佛大学、卡尔加里大学、华东师范大学的研究》这本书，乃是“真爱 · 人文 · 教育”理念的水到渠成。

生命之道，人文之旅，漫漫修远。

祝愿直抵“生命大道”的“人文实践”，行稳致远。

是为序。

（作者系著名人文学者、复旦大学教授、央视《百家讲坛》主讲人）

目　录

凯瑟琳 · E · 斯诺

斯诺教授是国际著名的学前教育专家，她的研究特别聚焦双语和低收入家庭儿童。 斯诺教授是哈佛大学教育学院 Patricia Albjerg Graham 荣誉教授，同时担任美国国家科学院三个分院主席，领衔撰写了影响深远的大型研究报告：《预防阅读困难： 早期阅读教育策略》（1998 年，中文版已出版）；《儿童评价：评价的原因、内容和方法》（2008 年）以及《科学的读写： 概念、内容和影响》（2016）。 斯诺教授是美国科学院院士、美国社会科学院院士，曾担任美国教育学会主席。

罗伯特 · L · 赛尔曼

罗伯特 · L · 赛尔曼（Robert L. Selman）是哈佛大学教育学院 Roy E、Larsen 教育与人类发展学教授，也是哈佛大学医学院精神病学部心理学教授。 他致力于提升儿童与青少年的社交意识，并将其与学业成就、道德发展、心理健康、青少年跨文化参与，以及数字媒体相结合，更好地帮助儿童与青少年社交认知的发展。

他也是美国心理学协会、心理学科学协会、美国矫正精神病学协会和美国教育研究协会的成员。 同时，他曾获美国国家心理健康研究所授予职业科学家奖项，并曾任德佛罗高级行为健康机构的受托人，以及 Russell Sage 基金会（Russell Sage Foundation）的高级研究员。

1. 跨学科跨语言(CDCL)教学框架：以图画书《抱抱》为例

罗伯特·L·塞尔曼、凯瑟琳·E·斯诺

哈佛大学

I. 跨学科跨语言(CDCL)框架概述

为了帮助那些有志于促进学龄前儿童早期双语、双文化发展的教育者，我们提出了“跨学科跨语言”(Cross-discipline Cross-language Instruction Framework，CDCL)教学框架概念模型。我们希望能够帮助教育者思考，如何在儿童开始学习双语的同时，也学习、发展他们的社会和科学知识。

在本章的讨论中，我们将聚焦中国的汉语-英语双语项目。需要说明的是，儿童学习母语之外的其他语言时，甚至在不同的社会环境中学习同一种语言时，教育者都需要关注、调整一些非常关键的细节，我们提出的框架并非放之四海而皆准。在此基础上，我们提出一些原则和方法，希望它们具有普遍的适用性。

我们的总体框架由一系列教学策略和课程活动构成。这些教学策略和课程活动强调了早期儿童发展中至关重要的六个“内容和技能”领域，中国教育部具体定义了这六大领域的内容，它们分别是健康、社会、数学、语言、艺术、科学（见图 1）。CDCL 框架具体说明了如何分别应用这六个领域，以确保在两种语言的学习中培养对儿童未来的发展起着至关重要作用、在儿童早期的生活中处于中心地位的技能——社会技能（和社会意识）。这个框架使用故事和讲故事的方法，不仅为课程奠定了基础，也为所有儿童提供了参考话题，使他们能够彼此讨论对相同经历的理解，并理解这些话题对于自己的意义。这些故事为儿童（以及他们的教师和父母）提供了需要密切关注的、关于社会关系的描述。在共同理解的基础上，儿童可以学习更多内容，同时练习与其他五个领域相关的技能。

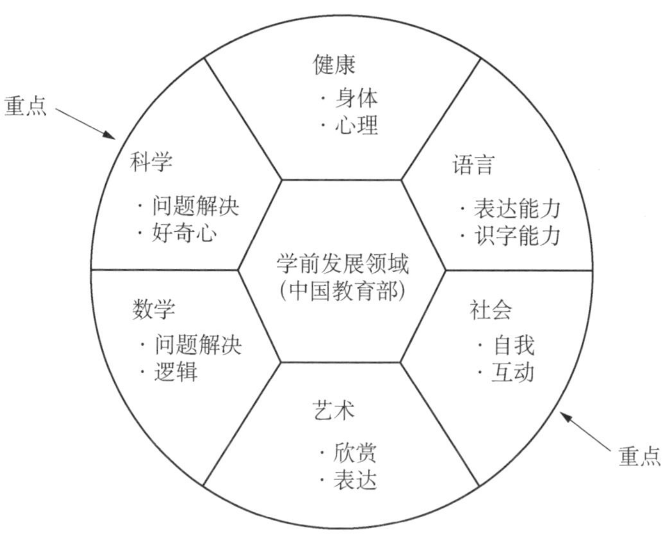

图 1　中国教育部对于学前教育的描述

例如，如下图 2 所示，CL/CD 方法在关注幼儿生活世界的两个方面（比如科学和社会性）的同时，总是包含两种语言（在本例中为中文和英文）。对于任何所选择的故事，其中一个方面是社交世界的语言；另一个方面可能是框架中其他五个领域中的任何一个。(语言既是其中一个目标领域，也是通向其他所有领域的媒介。)

举例来说，我们可以将两个领域：社会性和科学融合在一起（见图 2）。在读一本关于交通的书时，可以提供关于交通工具以及什么使它们移动的知识（自行车和滑板靠人力，车辆和摩托车靠内燃机）。一些幼儿可能会积极参与这个主题，因为他们喜欢装载车和摩托车。另一些儿童则对这个故事主题不太感兴趣。然而，在和幼儿讨论或者解释故事时，将重点同时放在故事的科学知识和社会情感方面，可以使不同的儿童有不同的切入点。那些对于机械世界不那么着迷的儿童可以理解卡车、公交车和其他交通工具的信息，扩展他们自我能动性和自我效能的基本人类需求（四处走动、看事物、见其他人）。

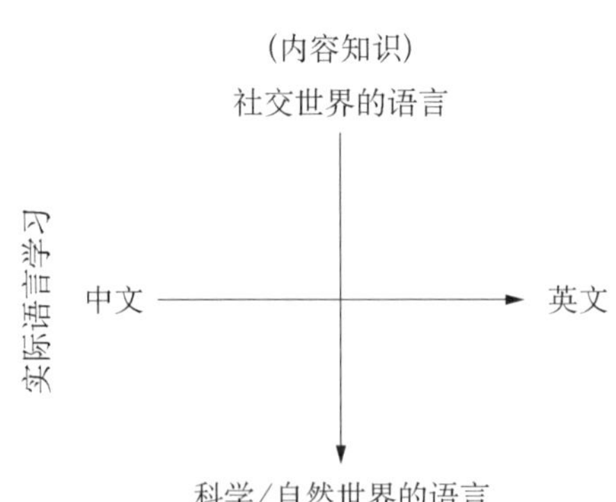

图 2　此概念框架强调语言作为交流工具(中文和英文)和幼儿在社交世界生存的方法

此外，当一个小孩想了解卡车是如何动起来的，不管他们是否有能力发动汽车（自我能动性），他们都需要从故事中推断谁会允许他们这么做，同时谁会确保他们这些正在读或听故事的孩子的安全（安全），并得到其父母的支持（自我认同）。人类心理发展的这些基本社会基础（安全、自我效能和社会认同）可能在不同的文化中以不同的方式表现出来，但对儿童健康、教育和福祉的发展始终相当关键。

在早期儿童教育中，为什么强调社会技能和社会交往中的语言？

幼儿的社会交往能力的发展为未来的道德发展及公民社会的行为奠定了基础。因此，教育者需要确保儿童的社会技能发展与其他五个领域中的每一个领域相结合。完成这一项，不仅需要教育者管理教室里的社交互动，而且需要确保正式课程将社交学习与新内容知识和跨内容的技能相结合。

推动社会性发展的主要媒介，尤其对于幼儿来说，是语言。儿童发展语言最初是为了完成社会交往的目的（与他人建立联系，引导他人的注意力，给予和接受帮助）。随着儿童发展自己的语言技能，他们通过与他人沟通时使用的词语，为自己（和他人）建立了一套更微妙、表达更清晰的社交目标（Ninio & Snow，1996）。随后，儿童也开始使用语言来完成认知的目标——学习新事物，满足他们的好奇心。当儿童与获取知识的成人“专家”建立了牢固、积极、信任的关系时，他们做得最好，也最快乐（Harris P et al.，2018）。

语言为孩子提供了有力的工具，让他们可以与朋友玩耍、讨要玩具或告诉别人自己的感受。因此，儿童的社会性与语言技能、社交语言能力的发展相辅相成。语言学习是社会性发展的必要条件，早期的沟通技能为幼儿早日进入社会性互动和进行社会交往创造了机会。此外，在一个围绕成人-儿童共读图画书设计的课程中，比如我们所推荐的课程，对于任何一个课本所关注的领域，社会关系总是被“写入”课程内容中（Selman，2017；Snow，2002）。

培养孩子双语技能的最好方法是什么?

研究证据表明，第二语言学习最有效的条件，是首先用母语学习内容，然后用第二语言学习相同的故事、信息、主题、词汇。因此，一个可行的方法是以儿童的母语开始内容的教学。当学生熟悉了背景知识并熟练掌握了方法后，他们就可以沉浸在第二语言环境中（Snow，2017）①。然而，很重要的是认识到这个方法是针对特定主题的我们并不赞成在儿童的母语达到一定的熟练水平之前，推迟第二语言的引入。相反，我们建议用母语介绍一个特定的、吸引人的、某范围内的主题（例如，交通工具及其相关的工程挑战，或者游乐场器材及其创造的玩乐机会）；在儿童用母语对于特定的话题有了一定程度的熟悉之后，才可以用第二语言介绍同样的信息。

如何实现这一目标?

我们将以 Jez Alborough 为中国双语幼儿园中 2—5 岁的儿童创作的绘本《抱抱》为案例典型，阐释教学框架中的原则。每一个教案都包含了不同的教学活动，包括热身游戏、发现故事、探索阅读、课堂讨论、拓展延伸和家庭参与。

每一个单元都包含了完成 CDCL 框架的四个基础教学原则的建议：

- 寻找吸引人的故事、活动和素材
- 识别儿童的社交语言世界，并作为“锚”

① 另一方面，中国“国际学校”的标准方法实际上常常相反——从 100%浸入第二语言开始，然后逐渐地将在母语环境中的时间增加至 50%。在双语课堂中，这两种方法各有利弊，并且效果随着社会大环境变化。

- 建立以讨论为导向的活动，以提高口语和批判性思维的能力
- 设计包含父母参与活动的单元

每一个单元选择核心词汇，使学生用每一种语言学习。 以绘本《抱抱》为例，尽管在书中并没有包含词汇，然而以下列表中的词汇可以按照学生的年龄，进行教授和学习：

- forest 森林
- grassland 草原
- giraffe 长颈
- hippo 河马
- chameleon 变色龙

故事《抱抱》的简介，以 Jez Alborough 的绘本为例：

Bobo 是一只年幼的猩猩，他开心地准备去丛林里散步（见下图）。 当他遇见了不同的动物时，他发现遇到的每种动物都在被他们的父母抱着。 久而久之，他看见丛林的伙伴们与父母们的拥抱，Bobo 说“抱抱”。 这是小猩猩第一次说出这个词，这可以理解小猩猩的观察—对一个场景的描述。 但是久而久之，Bobo 看到了更多这样孩子与父母间的拥抱，发现自己却孤身一人，他变得感伤与焦虑。 最后，Bobo 看到了他的妈妈，他们开心地拥抱，之后他还开心地拥抱了别的小动物。

虽然这本受人喜爱的书只包含了三个词，但是它引人入胜地传达了一个关于爱与依恋的故事。 最重要的是，这个故事可以从不同的角度来理解。 孩子们可以使用语言去讨论社会上主要的依恋之情和跨物种的友谊；同时，他们也可以通过学习数学、美术、科学和健康来了解 Bobo 所在的具象的（物质世界）、抽象的（逻辑世界）和美学的世界。

例如，对于一个阅读经验丰富的读者来说，能很清楚地意识到，在故事最开始的时候，Bobo 只是简单地指出他遇到的第一对大象母子在拥抱。但是，当他继续行走，书中对 Bobo 的描述表达了情感上的变化，特别是他的面部表情：在图 1 中，Bobo 感受到了一点伤心与孤单，然后他的难受开始加深，直到他和他的妈妈相遇。他的表情、心情与情绪有了很大改变（如图 2 所示的大字和笑脸）。

这些情绪不止在人类中存在，而且普遍存在哺乳动物世界里。虽然在《抱抱》这本书里没有几个词语，但如果我们想要把 Bobo 的故事讲完，通过不同的角度去理解，最终把它与听众的生活联系在一起，我们需要用到许多词汇。这种将故事留白，为读者、听众保留发挥空间的审美手段，是我们教育者可以参考的。我们可以用它来促进跨语言或跨领域技能与知识的发展。这将帮助孩子提高阅读及讲故事的技能，促进他们的教育、伦理和审美发展。

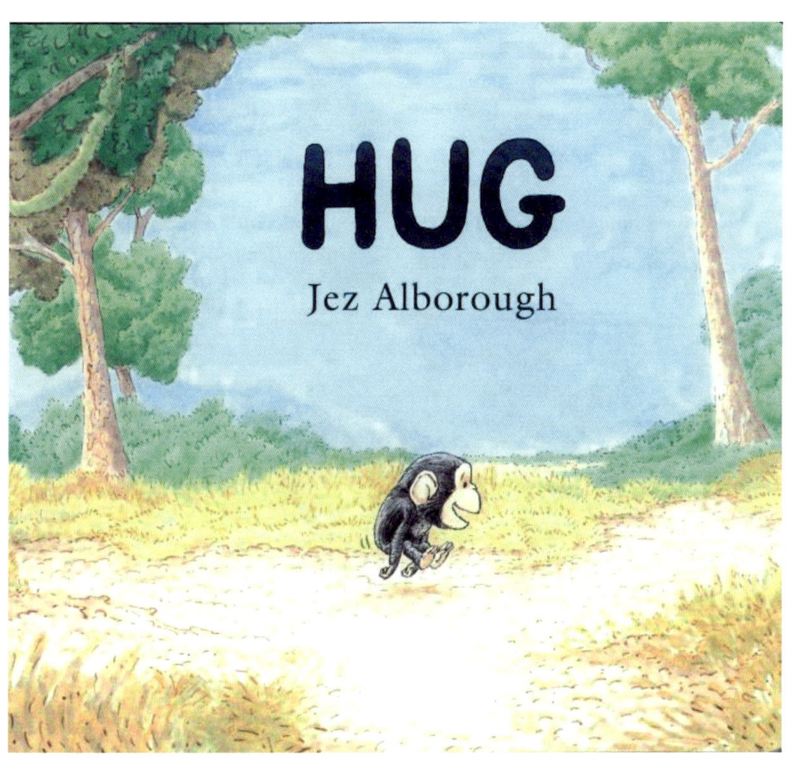

ISBN：10 0－7636－1576－5

图 1

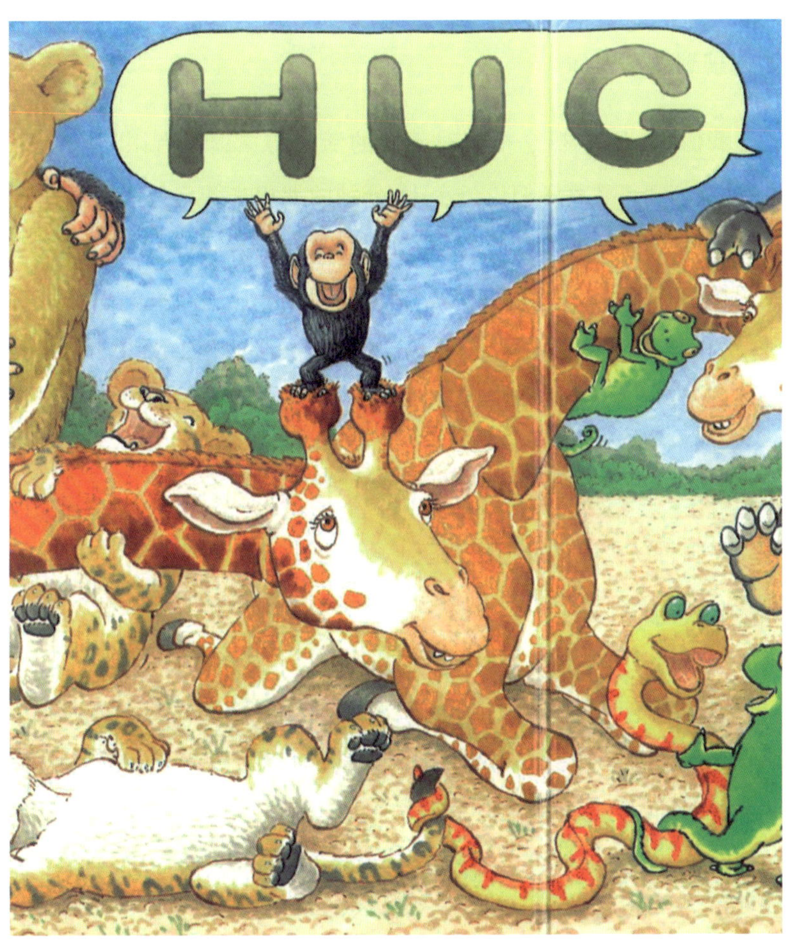

图 2

II. 跨语言/跨学科教学框架：给教育工作者的建议

如何规划教学时间

我们的 CDCL 概念框架对不同的活动与主题没有限制一个时间。我们建议教育者们以一个 15 分钟的课程去开启每个活动，因为 15 分钟大致是两岁到三岁小孩们能集中精力的时间。老师们可以根据不同年龄组的特点去调整活动的时间，比如四岁的小孩比较适合 20 到 25 分钟的课程。对于一些年龄稍小的孩子来说，如其已经适应了课堂的规律，也可以尝试 20 至 25 分钟的上课时间。

如何在学校和家庭营造良好的语言环境

老师可以在值得讨论的话题上多问一些开放式问题，同时也要对孩子的答案保持开放的态度。对于具有争议性的话题来说，答案没有对与错之分，只有更好的答案和相对没有那么好的答案。

家长的参与是帮助孩子们建立一个良好语言或识字环境的重要因素。孩子们在学校和家里讨论的话题都与他们更丰富的社会关系网及更多样的语言形式相联系。如果家长们知道孩子们在学校参加的活动与讨论，他们可以通过家庭里的交谈来帮助孩子们巩固这些知识。

如何展示适合孩子年龄的教学内容

在这个单元有很多为教育者们准备的活动，老师可以根据孩子的发展水平来挑选教学活动、决定活动内容、选择活动工具、安排活动顺序。

如何将中英文课程结合

我们建议在每个单元教师们能用两种语言去传递同样的信息：先用普通话，再用英语。 老师们可以在不同时间使用英语与中文。比如，在讨论 Bobo 的情感时，老师们可以周一使用普通话教学，然后周二使用英文去传递同样信息。 或者，在一周内多次用中文阅读书本，然后在下一周用英文阅读。 我们之所以先使用普通话教学，是因为可以让孩子在学习英文词汇和结构之前，先牢牢掌握相同内容的母语。 同时，为了确保每一种语言的新知识得以巩固，课程安排需要为涉及各主题的普通话课和英文课之间预留出一段时间。 至于究竟预留多久（几个小时？ 一天？ 几天？），我们需要近一步探讨。

虽然用英文和中文教的内容是一样的，但是我们建议老师在不同的语言课程中能选择不同的活动。 比如，如果用中文来讲解书中的内容，老师可以让孩子们手工做出故事中的木偶和做出丛林的模型。 如果使用英文来讲解书中的内容，老师可以让孩子们表演出故事中动物的样子（这比只重新创造这个故事要简单一些），然后，他们可以通过用笔画出或用陶土捏出动物的样子。

使用这一教学框架的老师可以为自己的课堂选择最合适的活动，在保证教学目标不变的前提下，必要时可以对活动内容进行修改。

基本原则的总结

老师是专家：考虑到孩子们的年龄和这本书里少量的词汇，我们建议老师先把故事讲一遍。 但是，我们建议老师直接地让孩子们知道，这是老师自己的见解，然后鼓励孩子们形成自己的想法与理解。

在每个课程结束后，孩子们都会通过自己的方式重述从而受益，他们可以借助于故事书中的图片，教师也可以为其提供必要的鹰架教学支持。 教师应鼓励孩子对故事内容形成自己的理解，并学会尊重和欣赏其他同学对同一本书的不同诠释（Selman，2003）。

在游戏中学习： 把玩融合在学习的过程中是很重要的一点。 我们鼓励老师更多地在学习中融入玩的成分，因为爱玩是孩子们的天性，他们能在玩中学习（Vygotsky，1967）。

家长扮演着重要的作用： 家庭的参与是我们教学框架的四大首要原则之一，而我们也在每个课程中设计了家庭活动（请参考原型实例）。 家庭参与对孩子的成长至关重要。 孩子们在家里得到的语言帮助对于双语教学的时间限制有极大的帮助（Bowlby，1982）。所以，幼儿园的责任之一就是提供相关的活动，提高孩子们学习家庭语言的能力。 比如，可以把原本要在课堂上阅读的书让学生们带回家，让学生用家庭语言学习；为孩子推荐相关主题的书籍，其中则涉及孩子已经学过的一些词汇，让家长和他们共同阅读。

此外，幼儿园也有责任让父母明白“家长”这个角色的重要性：即支持使用家庭语言并使之更为丰富，增加孩子对家庭语言的掌握与理解。 如果家长开始对孩子说第二语言，那这将有可能会破坏本项目潜在的原则。

参考文献

Bowlby, J. (1982). Attachment (2nd ed., Bowlby, John. Attachment and loss; v. 1). New York: BasicBooks.

Harris, P. L., Koenig, M. A., Corriveau, K. H., & Jaswal, V. K. (2018). Cognitive foundations of learning from testimony, Annual Review of

Psychology, 69, 251 – 273. (2018)
Ninio, A. , & Snow, Catherine E. (1996). Pragmatic development (Essays in developmental science).
Selman, R. (2003). The promotion of social awareness : Powerful lessons from the partnership of developmental theory and classroom practice. New York: Russell Sage Foundation.
Selman, R. (2017). Fostering Friendship: Pair Therapy for Treatment and Prevention. Taylor and Francis.
Snow, C. (2002). Reading for Understanding. RAND Corporation.
Snow, C. (2017). Early literacy development and instruction: An overview. Routledge.
Vygotsky, L. (1967). Play and Its Role in the Mental Development of the Child. Journal of Russian and East European Psychology, 5(3),6 – 18.

2. 跨学科跨语言(CDCL)教学框架:基于《跷跷板》一书的参考教案

罗伯特·L·塞尔曼、凯瑟琳·E·斯诺

哈佛大学

《跷跷板》是一本已经在多个国家翻译出版的儿童图画书。我们将用这本书来一起探索传统的大声朗读法,进而引入跨学科跨语言(CDCL)教学框架在学前教育中的应用。CDCL框架可以适用于任何一所双语幼儿园。在此我们主要关注如何在已经采纳了英语作为第二语言的中国幼儿园使用这本教材。

根据中国教育部的规定,学前教育应该关注六大领域(见图1)。我们承认所有这六个领域的重要性,但在本书中我们只强调其中两个领域与儿童发展的相关度,并为教育工作者提供相关指导。因此,在不排除其他领域的基础之上,我们在此主要关注科学和社会技能这两个领域,《跷跷板》一书便是特别为此设计的。

《跷跷板》的故事讲述了一只年幼的长颈鹿想和它的朋友们玩跷跷板,却因为小长颈鹿比其他朋友体重要重、体型要大而遇到了不少麻烦。显然这个故事提供了大量可能会遇到的社会话题供孩子们思考，比如一起玩耍、交朋友、相似和不同；同时提供了大量机会探索科学知识，比如重量、密度、平衡等。下面我们将特别基于中英双语幼儿园的背景展示一系列围绕社会与科学两个方面的教案。

我们使用《跷跷板》一书设计课程的方法可以作为 CDCL 课程设计法的参考样本。具体步骤如下：

- 把社会关系作为故事的重要关注点
- 为了能够有效地引导孩子对书本内容进行讨论（本文侧重于社会及科学内容），教师需要确定最合适的中英语言形式。换句话说就是为每一个故事预备一些关键词，先用中文教授这些词（即孩子所掌握的相对强的语言），再用英语讲授一遍
- 为了让孩子们锻炼如何生成属于自己的想法，教师需要为孩子设计一些集体活动，从而拓展书本的主题内容，比如说让孩子设计一个操场、在天平上测试砝码重量、将书本情节演绎出来等。同时也应为孩子提供机会，让他们去使用新学到的词汇，探索刚接触到的新理念
- 认真观察孩子对于哪些话题或活动更为有兴趣，鼓励他们继续加强母语的学习（此处指的是中文）以及第二语言的学习（此处指的是英文），以助力他们在课堂上不断提高
- 寻找一些其他可以和孩子共同阅读的书籍，由此拓展主题，尽可能让孩子在这个过程中重复练习之前学习到的关键词汇。比如，有一些书会描述不同种类的操场或游戏，有一些书会描绘非常大和非常小的事物，还有一些非虚构类关于长颈鹿的书籍，都可以尝试与孩子一同阅读。

我们的案例

为了更具体地体现如何将 CDCL 教学框架运用在教学当中，在

此我们将向读者展示一个已经经过广泛实践的教案——《跷跷板》的故事。 教师可以以此为原型，开发其他课程内容。

图 1　跷跷板的故事

《跷跷板的故事》—参考案例样本

第一天：社会的语言—中文

❖ **激发灵感**

本单元重点词汇

一起 (together)	合作 (collaboration)	帮助 (help)	开心 (happy)	伤心 (sad)

* 教师需要反复使用和强调这些词汇。

- ➢ 活动一：认识一下我们故事的主角：小动物们。
  - ■ 使用卡片帮助孩子认识故事里提到的小动物们：长颈鹿　猴子　小狗　小老鼠

续　表

- 一起阅读故事书中的图画，让孩子们辨识、命名和描述里面的小动物（比如："刚刚我们学会了几种小动物的名字，那么哪些小动物在我们的故事里呢？ 你能在这张图画里找到它们吗？""长颈鹿是什么样子的呀？ 小老鼠呢？"）
- 聊聊动物：你最喜欢什么动物？ 你最喜欢的动物长什么样？

➢ 活动 2：认识一下故事发生的环境：操场
- 6—7 页：认知操场的物体：跷跷板　滑梯　秋千
- 聊聊操场上的游戏：操场上还有其他东西吗？ 你去操场上的时候一般会做什么？ 你最喜欢在操场上做什么？

❖ **探索故事(大声朗读)**

➢ 给孩子展示图画书的封面，询问他们看到了什么：有哪些主要角色？这些角色在哪？ 你觉得这个故事讲了什么？

➢ 教师大声朗读，加入更多关于灵感、情感和观点的词汇

➢ 阅读对话：检查孩子是否理解，鼓励孩子大声说话、描述图片、提问，并提供图画书的其他解读方法。

➢ 以下是大声朗读的内容的参考样本：

今天我们来讲一个长颈鹿和跷跷板的故事。 我们一起看这幅图，**猜一猜，这是一个什么样的故事呢？** 长颈鹿说："今天我要去公园，到公园的广场上去玩。"

长颈鹿来到了公园里。 **公园里有(指出操场里的几种设备，等待孩子们说出它们的名字)跷跷板、滑梯和秋千**。 长颈鹿看到了公园里有这么多游戏可以玩，**它心里有什么感受呀？(关键词：开心)我们大家一起做一个笑脸好不好？** 长颈鹿看了看四周，说："我现在不想荡秋千，我想去玩跷跷板。"

但是现在长颈鹿遇到了一个难题，**你们说是什么难题呢？ 长颈鹿想，**一个人怎么玩跷跷板呢？ 我需要和别人**一起**玩跷跷板。 **长颈鹿可以和谁一起玩跷跷板呀？** 它看到了小老鼠。 小老鼠或许愿意和长颈鹿一起玩跷跷板。 **现在长颈鹿要怎么做呢？**

"你好，小老鼠！"长颈鹿说，"你愿意和我一起玩跷跷板吗？"长颈鹿邀请小老鼠一起玩跷跷板，**小老鼠要怎么回答呢？** 小老鼠说，"好啊，听起来很有趣呢！"所以呀，小老鼠愿意和长颈鹿一起玩跷跷板。 "嗖"的一下，小老鼠就跳到跷跷板上了。 你们猜，下面会发生什么呢？ 小老鼠和长颈鹿能够**开心**地**一起**玩跷跷板吗？

"哎呀！"小老鼠说，"我们不能一起玩跷跷板，因为你太重了。 看，我只能一直停在上面，不能继续玩。""我没有那么重，"长颈鹿说，"是你太轻了。看，我不能往上，只能坐在下面。"

那么现在它们遇到了一个难题，这个难题是什么呢？ 遇到难题的时候它们要怎么办呢？ 小老鼠小心地从高高的跷跷板上爬下来，然后看到了小猴子。 小老鼠有了一个好主意："或许你可以问问小猴子，小猴子个头比我大，也比我重，

续　表

或许你可以和小猴子一起玩跷跷板。”**小老鼠为什么要提出这个建议呢？**小老鼠知道长颈鹿想玩跷跷板，它这么做是为了**帮助**长颈鹿，让长颈鹿**开心**。**长颈鹿听到这个建议，会怎么做呢？**

…

长颈鹿想和朋友们**一起**玩跷跷板，但是没有成功。它现在很**伤心**，很难过。“没有人可以和我一起玩跷跷板了。”长颈鹿说。**看到长颈鹿伤心的样子他的朋友们要做什么呢？**小老鼠，小猴子和小狗狗想帮助长颈鹿，于是它们想了一个好办法。是什么好办法呢？它们要**一起合作**来解决这个难题。生活中有些事情不是我们一个人可以完成的，要和别人**合作**才可以呢。

小猴子**开心**地说：“我们几个一起坐在跷跷板上就不会太轻了。”小狗狗和小老鼠叫道：“你也不会太重了。”长颈鹿**开心**地说：“这样我们就可以一起玩跷跷板了。”

❖ **课外探索：**

➢ 活动1：学会社会认知和解决问题的能力

再次阅读故事，检查孩子对故事的理解是否正确，并要求孩子去思考不同角色的观点（朗读时嵌入问题），注意结合关键词教学：

- 第12页，老鼠发现它不能和长颈鹿一起玩跷跷板。老鼠说了什么？（“你太重了，我不能和你一起玩。”）你觉得长颈鹿听到后是什么感觉？你觉得对朋友这样做好吗？如果你是老鼠，你会说什么或做什么？
- 第14页，老鼠会说或做什么？（它邀请猴子和长颈鹿一起玩）你认为这是一件好事吗？你会怎样描述老鼠的行为？（美德：帮助他人，善良，关爱他人等）
- 第26页，长颈鹿很伤心。长颈鹿为什么难过？长颈鹿的朋友说了和做了什么？（它们提出了一个好主意）如果一个朋友伤心难过，你会说什么或做什么？

➢ 活动2：绘画和讲述

- 让孩子画一张他和朋友在操场上玩乐的场景（鼓励孩子去回想过去的事情），或者未来在操场上玩乐的场景（提示孩子设想并计划未来）
- 把一起、合作、帮助、开心、伤心五个词组合在一起，向你的同伴描述：你在玩什么？那时候你开心吗？你们对彼此说了什么？

第二天：社会世界的语言——学习英语

❖ **激发灵感**

本单元词汇

Together	collaborate	help	happy	sad

❖ **发现故事**

❖ **课外探索**

续　表

第三天：科学世界的语言——学习中文

❖ **激发灵感**

本单元词汇

大 小	重 轻	高 矮	上 下

➢ 活动：衡量和描述

器械：

将对象之间进行比较：老师的椅子和儿童的椅子；皮革与铅笔；图画书与字典等

测量工具：电子天平、尺子

教学方法：老师以两人一组等形式，教授孩子词汇，为他们展示相应的物件。之后，老师让孩子通过拿着或测量这些物件来“感受这些词”，然后描述他们的感觉。

❖ **发现故事**

➢ 活动：大声朗读课本，把重点放在科学内容上

➢ 大声朗读的参考内容：

P.1：今天我们再来讲一遍长颈鹿和跷跷板的故事，看看大家会不会有新的发现呢？记得我们刚刚学过的词，看看大家能不能在今天的故事里找到它们？

P.4：长颈鹿到公园的广场上玩。在广场上，长颈鹿看到了很多玩具。看！有跷跷板、秋千、滑梯。长颈鹿说：“现在我不想荡秋千，我想玩跷跷板。”

P.5：“但是一个人怎么玩跷跷板呢？我需要和别人一起玩跷跷板。”长颈鹿想。**确实是这样，不是吗？你可以想象一下，当长颈鹿一个人坐到跷跷板上的时候会发生什么吗？（等待孩子的回应并提供反馈，如果有的话。）**幸运的是，它这个时候看到了小老鼠。它或许愿意和长颈鹿一起玩跷跷板。

P.6：于是长颈鹿走过去说：“你愿意和我一起玩跷跷板吗？”“好啊，听起来很有趣呢！”小老鼠说。嗖的一下，小老鼠就跳到了跷跷板上了。**你们猜猜，小老鼠坐上跷跷板之后会发生什么呢？**

P.7：“哎呀！”小老鼠说，“我们不能一起玩跷跷板，因为你**太重了**。看，我只能一直**停在下面**，不能继续玩。”“我们有那么重，是你**太轻了**。看，我不能**往上**，只能坐在**下面**。”

小老鼠小心翼翼地从**高高的**跷跷板上爬下来，然后看到了小猴子。“或许你可以问问小猴子，”小老鼠对长颈鹿说，“小猴子的**个头比我大**，也**比我重**，或许你可以和小猴子一起玩跷跷板？”

P. 8—13：……

P. 14：小伙伴们想帮助长颈鹿，于是他们想了一个好办法。**如果你是长颈鹿的朋友,你会想什么办法来帮助他呢?**

P. 15：看！小伙伴们一起跳到了跷跷板上。小猴子说："这样我们几个就不会**太轻了**。""你也不会**太重了**！"小老鼠和小狗狗说。就这样，跷跷板取得了**平衡**，小伙伴们可以一起开心地玩跷跷板了！

❖ **课外探索**

- 检查基本内容的理解：
  你可以按照它们的重量来排列书中的人物吗？谁是最重的？谁是最轻的？
- 检查深层内容的理解：
  器材：小跷跷板，不同尺寸和重量的手指布偶（例如兔子，狮子，青蛙，恐龙，熊猫）
  教学方法："现在，如果你有机会邀请更多的动物玩跷跷板，你会邀请谁？你认为谁应该和谁一起玩？"
  活动：学生分为四组。每组有一个小的跷跷板和几个手指布偶。孩子们在他们的团队中进行实验（最好是通过探索如何在他们的跷跷板上实现平衡），然后在课堂上分享他们的发现。

针对年龄稍大孩子的拓展内容:除了在跷跷板的一边添加几只动物,还有什么办法可以让他们愉快地玩耍?

第四天：科学世界的语言—英文版

[用英文重复第三天的活动]

❖ **激发灵感**

本单元的词汇

大 小	重 轻	高 矮	上 下

❖ **发现故事**

❖ **课外探索**

第五天：跨语言融合：社会与科学知识

❖ **回顾：**

- 使用中文和英文单词卡片复习关键的社交及科学词汇
- 故事复述，虽然大多数学生可能会使用中文，但是也允许他们使用英文，并鼓励学生们使用这单元学习到的关键词汇

❖ **合作的力量——一个有创意的活动**
- ➢ *小组分配：* 学生们四人为一组。小组内每一位学生都得到一只和其他组员颜色不一样的蜡笔。每个小组分有一张纸。
- ➢ *指导：* “请大家画一画我们学校的操场。和你的组员一起合作创造一幅色彩丰富的画！等大家创作完后，请和课上的其他同学分享一下你们画了什么及你们是怎么分工合作的。”

❖ **语言的魅力**
- ➢ 用中文和英文教学同义词和首字母缩略词

《跷跷板》故事拓展

为响应教育部提出的六大发展领域框架，我们需要更多的书籍，分别在各领域发展相应的主题、话题、词汇（内容）和技能。《跷跷板》故事涵盖了两个领域，分别是社会性和科学，例如物理规则的介绍。在之后的故事选择中，我们将寻找涉及其他四个领域（数学、艺术、健康和语言）的书籍。具体模型如下图所示。

六大领域	去游乐场	去图书馆	去商店	去博物馆	去电脑房	去诊所
社会	XX	XX	XX	XX	XX	XX
语言	X	XX	X	X	X	X
数学			X			
艺术				X		
科技					X	
健康						X

例如，艺术领域的课程可以是一次去剧院或者去听交响乐的故事，这样音乐和戏剧相关的知识都能被覆盖到。而具体的课程活动设置，可以同时关注艺术欣赏（艺术知识）和艺术表达（艺术技能）。一次去医院的经历，也可以变成健康卫生相关的课程，比如介绍一下为什么我们需要在饭前洗手，以及一些相关的小技巧（例

如如何刷牙）。此外，健康类课程也可以涉及到心理健康，比如说我们如何保持快乐、积极、敏锐的心态，以及一些具体的小技巧（例如和父母倾诉烦恼）。

随着儿童年龄增长，他们的表达和理解能力逐渐提高，并且开始参与到家庭外的社会活动，因此相较于之前的广泛覆盖六大领域，我们建议在教学中可以加入“特定发展领域方法”。例如，当五岁孩子的班级里出现互相取笑以及不愿分享的情况时，老师可以有意地让孩子读一些相关话题的双语图书。文字对于矛盾的解决是非常重要的，因此一个优秀的双语教学项目应当鼓励孩子多参与到这些话题的双语讨论中来。

当然，我们也可以重温读过的故事，随着儿童逐渐长大，他们对故事会有新的解读。以《跷跷板》为例，早期我们借助这个故事帮助儿童学习社会、科学相关的基本词汇；到四至五岁时，我们可以重读这个故事，并与儿童现实生活中的经历相联系：如故事中长颈鹿比其他的伙伴都要高，儿童在生活中也可能感觉被冷落、感觉与旁人不同。

参考文献

Bowlby, J. (2005). A secure base: Clinical applications of attachment theory (Vol. 393). Taylor & Francis.

Children's wall art-wooden animal letters. Retrieved August 1, 2017, from Alphabet Gifts: http://www.alphabetgifts.co.uk/Childrens-Wall-Art/Sevi-Animal-Letters.

Jalongo, Mary Renck (2000). Early Childhood Language Arts: Meeting Diverse Literacy Needs through Collaboration with Families and Professionals [M]. Second Edition.

Numbers song let's count 1 - 10 new version. (2012, May 16). Retrieved August 1, 2017, from You-tube: https://www.youtube.com/watch? v=85M1yxIcHpw

Primary colors song for kids/Secondary colors song for kids. (2015, April 27). Retrieved August 1, 2017, from You-tube: https://www.youtube.com/watch?v=bmquqAP2w_8.

Selman, R. (1971). Taking Another's Perspective: Role-Taking Development in Early Childhood. Child Development, 42(6), 1721 - 1734. doi: 10.2307/1127580.

Selman, R. (2007) The Promotion of Social Awareness. Russell Sage Foundation, N. Y. C.

Snow, C. (2002). Reading for Understanding: Toward an R&D Program In Reading Comprehension. Santa Monica, CA: RAND.

Wood, D., Bruner, J. S., & Ross, G. (1976). The role of tutoring in problem solving. Journal of child psychology and psychiatry, 17(2), 89 - 100.

Zhao Minghui, Kou Aili. (2016). Analysis of Color Words Age Suitableness and Writing Strategies of Preschoolers Literature [J]. Journal of Pingxiang University. Vol. 33. No. 2.

泥娃娃. (2009, July 12). Retrieved August 1, 2017, from Youtube: https://www.youtube.com/watch?v=DPIDWnfz.

附录：图 4

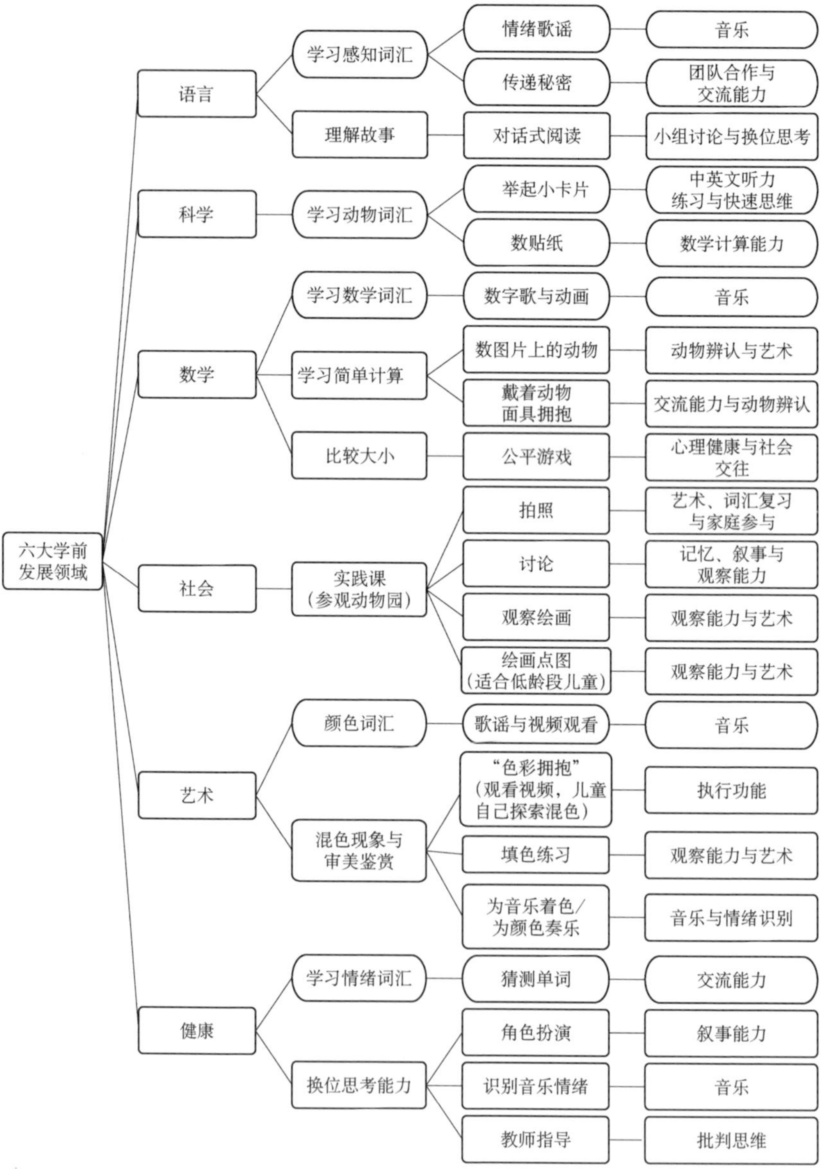

- 六大学前发展领域
  - 语言
    - 学习感知词汇
      - 情绪歌谣 — 音乐
      - 传递秘密 — 团队合作与交流能力
    - 理解故事
      - 对话式阅读 — 小组讨论与换位思考
  - 科学
    - 学习动物词汇
      - 举起小卡片 — 中英文听力练习与快速思维
      - 数贴纸 — 数学计算能力
  - 数学
    - 学习数学词汇
      - 数字歌与动画 — 音乐
    - 学习简单计算
      - 数图片上的动物 — 动物辨认与艺术
      - 戴着动物面具拥抱 — 交流能力与动物辨认
    - 比较大小
      - 公平游戏 — 心理健康与社会交往
  - 社会
    - 实践课（参观动物园）
      - 拍照 — 艺术、词汇复习与家庭参与
      - 讨论 — 记忆、叙事与观察能力
      - 观察绘画 — 观察能力与艺术
      - 绘画点图（适合低龄段儿童） — 观察能力与艺术
  - 艺术
    - 颜色词汇
      - 歌谣与视频观看 — 音乐
    - 混色现象与审美鉴赏
      - “色彩拥抱”（观看视频，儿童自己探索混色） — 执行功能
      - 填色练习 — 观察能力与艺术
      - 为音乐着色/为颜色奏乐 — 音乐与情绪识别
  - 健康
    - 学习情绪词汇
      - 猜测单词 — 交流能力
    - 换位思考能力
      - 角色扮演 — 叙事能力
      - 识别音乐情绪 — 音乐
      - 教师指导 — 批判思维

图 4　教育部学前发展领域—实际课程设计—实际教学活动（知识领域与技能）的分层模型

3. 幼儿社交意识发展：为什么要促进孩子的换位思考能力？

罗伯特·L·塞尔曼[①]

哈佛大学

无论是在哪个国家或文化中，所有极力呵护并关爱孩子们的父母都希望自己的孩子健康成长，并在未来拥有幸福的家庭与成功的事业。这些父母们都会希望自己的孩子学会结交好朋友，懂得和他人保持亲近又互相尊重的社会关系，并且理解建立和保持这种紧密的社会关系的重要性。同时，他们也希望孩子们能够在尊重他人的前提下解决家庭内部以及在外所遇到的冲突，并且能够在激烈的社会竞争中脱颖而出，最终有所成就。那么，孩子们是怎么理解这些来自父母对其社交以及未来社会生活的期待呢？在成长过程中，他们会不断意识到牢固的社会关系对人类发展的重要性。我们把这个

① **罗伯特·L·塞尔曼**，是哈佛大学教育学院 Roy E. Larsen 教育与人类发展教授，也是哈佛大学医学院精神病学部心理学教授。当前，他的主要研究方向是从发展心理学和文化的角度探讨儿童和青少年构建和维持积极社会关系的能力，以及预防教育，社交和健康对人的负面影响的方法。

过程称为社交意识发展。

当今，许多人都意识到儿童看待社交的方式与成人不同。幼儿的父母以及为幼童服务的教育者都在努力让孩子们适应并遵循家庭文化、同龄人文化、校园文化、民族文化及其背后的规则。在这个过程中，父母和教育者根据自身对孩子和国家的理解，可以通过许多不同的途径来培养与促进孩子们的社交意识。

当我们在观察父母对自家孩子在社交场合的言行期待时，文化价值观在其中的作用和影响力是显而易见的，与之相比，并不那么明显的是隐藏在孩子们某些社交言行背后的原因。当孩子不遵循某些成人习以为常的社会文化的规则时，这些孩子并不仅仅是没有意识到某些事实，或是没有理解一些在他们长大后会接受并遵循的成人社交价值观。事实上，即便这些孩子年龄还小，他们自己也有一套对社交生活的理解和理论，具体来说，是孩子们对社交世界里，大众的偏好、情感、社交参与度、冲突以及分歧的看法和应对方式。

如果我们对比来自世界各地学前到小学一年级的孩子们对社交关系的理解，我们会发现对于处在这个年龄段的孩子们来说，即便他们身处不同的文化和地域环境，他们自己对社交世界所构建的理解和理论是十分相似的，但是，与日后他们从自己的父母、老师及生活中其他重要社会成员那里学到的却有所不同。对学前到小学一年级的幼儿来说，他们对社交关系有限的理解源于这个年龄段的语言和脑神经的有限发展，这就是我们平日里所说的生理因素或所谓的发育因素，比如说幼儿在这个年龄段对社会的认知发展有限。然而，即便孩子们的社交认知能力会随着年龄的增长而自然增进，这并不表明所有孩子社交认知能力发展的程度、速度以及复杂程度都一模一样。

换位思考能力（Social Perspective Taking skills，SPT）是一系列非常重要的社交认知能力，这些能力会随着年龄的增长而“自然”发展。这些社交技能可以帮助孩子们理解在社交生活中别人的想法、感受，以及自己和他人的社交言行和互动。换位思考能力会随年龄的增长而累积增进，并会影响孩子在青少年阶段许多与之相关的社交认知技能的发展程度。在孩子年龄还小的时候，我们很难分辨这些相关的社交技能。但是从本质上来说，它们会随着孩子年龄的增长而慢慢发展并凸显。同时，这些社交能力具有很强的可塑性，对周围人和环境的健康与不良影响十分敏感。对于孩子来说，在其所有的社交意识和社会化过程中，换位思考能力是十分关键的一部分，同时这项技能也是孩子日后在构建和维系社交关系的社交认知（发展）核心和基础。

如前文所述，这些重要的换位思考能力是人类自然发展过程中重要的一部分，但这并不意味着这些技能是可以在任何条件下自然习得，人们仍需要在健康的社交环境中通过努力来获取并且增进这些换位思考技能。比如说，要努力尝试包容并清晰表达他人的观点，理解别人与自身在看待事物的角度及观点间所存在的差异及其原因，能够尊重对方的过去及当下的个人生活经历和处境，并在此基础上换位思考，尝试去理解对方与其他人的差异，及这些差异对双方的影响。当然，以上所有的这些，也是目前社交认知领域所面临的挑战。

在儿童成长的早期，换位思考能力与语言发展密切相关，因为在这个年龄段，随着孩子语言能力的发展，幼儿可以更好地表达自己的观点。当孩子上小学和初高中时，这些换位思考社交技能则在孩子们的学习能力和表现上承担着非常重要的角色。比如说，这些社交认知能力可以帮助学生更好地做深度阅读理解，例如在查阅与社会发展或历史相关的学术资料时，通过运用换位思考能力将自己代入到文本中，从而可以更深入地分析和理解材料。不仅如此，随着孩子年龄的增长，换位思考社交技能对其未来发展的助益将拓展到其他更广阔的范畴和领域，而不仅仅局限于阅读和写作能力。目前，随着现代科技的普及，当代青少年会遇到的问题远远比那些传统的典型的青春期困境更多，其背后的原因也更复杂。即便如此，在当下，这些换位思考能力仍可以切实帮助学生更好地理解他们在青少年阶段会遇到的问题和挑战。

在换位思考能力发展的初期，即从学前到幼儿园这个年龄段，幼儿换位思考能力深受其脑部发育、认知能力以及语言能力的制约；即便如此，发展心理学家们已经明确了那些可以辨识普遍孩子换位思考能力发展的一些重要变化。在这个年龄阶段，孩子每一次换位思考能力的进步都可以看作是他们社交意识的增长。而孩子每一次社交意识的增长都是值得令人兴奋的，因为这也意味着孩子们对自我、人性、人们的社交动机及互动有了更进一步的了解和发现，并就此发展出自己新的一套社交理论。对于每个孩子来说，他们新构建的社交“理论”都将对其在社交情境中的判断力、成熟度以及社交技能有着重大影响。

在这一章节，我将为家长和老师们介绍相关的理论背景知识。同时，我也将讨论如何在幼儿日常课堂教学中应用这些理论知识，并且将深入探讨教育者们——特别是老师们，如何最大化利用在这个年龄段孩子换位思考能力的可塑性，利用日常课堂讨论活动帮助幼儿发展换位思考技能并强化其社交认知能力。

理论背景

孩子换位思考能力方向的科学探索植根于 1934 年乔治 · 赫伯

特·米德（George Herbert Mead）的研究，并在1947年，让·皮亚杰(Jean Piaget）等人的探索中得到了进一步的发展。皮亚杰通过分析儿童对宇宙世界的构想（例如，孩子们对空间和时间的认知）描述了儿童的心理发展阶段，并表明这些构想是随着年龄增长成系统发展的。同时，这些对物理宇宙的构想与大部分孩子们的认知发展——换句话说也就是推断能力的发展——密切相关。由此表明，换位思考能力取决于孩子的逻辑或认知发展，并且是其中重要的组成部分。很多时候，孩子在成长过程中会习得许多基本的社交认知技能，从而对世界及社交生活有更多的了解。但是，这并不能保证孩子将在未来成长过程中会自然地掌握那些更复杂的社会认知技能。皮亚杰认为，社交认知能力及其在诸如道德推理等场景中的实践能力需要在一个健康、开放的社交讨论环境中发展；同时，这些讨论并不仅局限于孩子与父母或其他有权威的成人之间，更应该发生在孩子以及他们的同龄人间。①

那些探讨孩子从婴儿时期到青年阶段换位思考能力的研究表明，社会个体在成长过程中对存在于自己和他人的观点间联系的理解水平会呈阶段式发展。个体的换位思考能力在一定程度上基于过往的水平，同时也为其下一个阶段的能力发展作铺垫。孩子们在经历这些发展阶段时的速度可能会有所差异，但在大多数情况下总是

---

① 长久以来，我们的团队关注孩子的社交发展，尤其是他们换位思考能力发展。到目前为止，我们已经在这个细分领域研究了快50年，而我们的研究工作也已在许多书刊和实证研究论文中被引用。在我2007年的著作中，The Promotion of Social Awareness: Powerful Lessons from the Partnership of Developmental Theory and Classroom Practice. New York: Russell Sage (Outstanding Book Award, American Educational Research Association Section on Moral Development and Education)，您可以找到一个与之相关的详尽总结。如您对我们科研工作背后的实践根源以及一些应用在教育实践和研究方向的小故事感兴趣，请参阅Selman, R. L. and Byrne, D. (1974) First Things: Social Development. Guidance Associates, Harcourt, Brace, Jovanovich, Inc., New York, (primary grades.)

按照相同的顺序经历各个发展阶段。再者，身处不同文化中的孩子对人际关系的理解还有他们应对社交挑战时的策略也会在许多重要的层面有所差别。总的来说，我们认为，孩童在换位思考能力上的变化以及增进与他们的生理年龄紧密相关。如上文所述，这些水平在很大程度上深受成长发育因素尤其是语言和认知发展的影响。

我们将每个发展阶段都看作是孩子习得新的换位思考能力并借此发展其他社交能力的机会。在我们重点关注的早期幼儿阶段，我们常常可以在孩子换位思考能力发展的过程中辨识并区分出三个重要的阶段或技能——第一人称技能，第二人称技能和第三人称技能、但是同时也要谨记，影响孩子对社交生活整体认知的因素众多，而上述这些社交认知技能仅仅是其中的一部分。

接下来，我们将借助一个孩子们很可能会在生活中遇到的典型的社交困境，并且通过孩子们对这个社交难题的回答来更深入地阐述上文所提及的理论。（在面对这个社交困境时，孩子们的换位思考能力将在很大程度上决定他们的应对方式或建议。）

> 两个小男孩 Tom 和 Greg 正在为他们的朋友 Mike 准备生日礼物。此时，Greg 已经为 Mike 买好了跳棋，但是 Tom 仍无法决定该给 Mike 送一个足球还是一辆小玩具卡车。在这个时候，他们看到 Mike 正在街对面，于是决定尝试去问问 Mike 他想要的生日礼物是什么。
>
> Greg 和 Tom 问 Mike 他喜欢玩具小卡车还是足球，但似乎他对这两个选项都不太感兴趣，并且 Mike 说，他现在非常难过，因为他的宠物小狗 Pepper 在两个星期前走失了。Mike 的家人已经在报纸上刊登了寻找 Pepper 的小广告，但就目前的情况来看，似乎很难找回 Pepper 了。听了 Mike 的想法后，Greg 建议 Mike 养

一只新的小狗,Mike说这与养Pepper不一样,他现在不想看到其他狗,因为它们会让他非常想念Pepper。说到这里,Mike难过得快哭了,说完之后,他告别了Greg和Tom,往回家的方向走去。

然而,Tom仍然不知道该给Mike买什么作为生日礼物。在Tom和Greg前往玩具店的途中,他们经过了一家商店,商店的橱窗上贴着标语"小狗待售",他们进店一看,发现店里还有两只小狗,而且它们都很可爱。Tom应该给Mike送一只小狗当生日礼物吗?Greg记得Mike说过,现在他不想看到其他小狗,因此他认为送Mike一只小狗会让他在生日那天很难过。但是Tom却认为Mike会喜欢这只可爱的小狗,因为那会在他生日的时候成为他的宠物。这个小故事最终以Tom的一句话结束,他说:"我知道该怎么做。"

在给孩子们讲完这个故事之后,我们以一对一或小组讨论的形式,向孩子们提出以下问题:你觉得Tom会怎么做?为什么?对于这些年幼的孩子们来说,他们对这个故事的理解,尤其是对Tom的想法的理解,在某种程度上与他们生活环境中的文化规条密切相关。但在文化之外,孩子们对故事的理解也取决于他们在社交情境中的换位思考能力。尽管孩子们的回答都很不一样,但我们却发现,在以下四个年龄段,孩子们在表达其社交意识时的一些规律。

(以下将展示当年孩子们的一些回答,我们希望用这些回答来展示各年龄段孩子在社交场合中换位思考能力的层次,尤其是他们的社交推断能力,而不是讨论孩子们的回答是否正确。)

婴儿到学龄前幼儿。这个年龄段的孩子有一定的换位思考能力,但是却很难能通过口头表达呈现,因此他们也很难去回顾并思考自己与他人的社交关系以及这些社会技能。这个年龄段的孩子们常常很难通过语言告诉我们他们是如何区分自己和他人的观点。因此，当他们在进行社交推断时，我们常会感觉他们把自己的观点看作是唯一的事实。这并不是因为他们认为别人的看法是错误的，而是因为他们无法或不知道如何从他人的角度理解并表达别人的观点。比如说，在这个故事情境中，婴儿与学前幼儿常常会这样回答我们的问题，他们会说："Tom 应该送 Mike 一只小狗。我喜欢小狗。它们很有趣。"他们没有从 Mike 的角度思考，他可能不希望新来的小狗代替 Pepper 的这个可能性。同时，这个年龄段的孩子们也有可能会这样回答："我不喜欢狗，所以我不会送 Mike 一只小狗。"

当然，对于这个年龄段的孩子们来说，无论是他们在讨论中提出的假设或是现实生活中做的决定，都只是他们世界观中的一部分。孩子的个性、他们身边有可能发生的事情、父母对孩子的社会化行为，以及在大环境中那些对人影响深远的文化规则都影响着孩子的实际言行，但同时，他们的世界观，以及换位思考能力，也将在各个年龄段作用于孩子的实际言行。

学龄前晚期到幼儿园前期。在这个年龄段，孩子们开始更清晰地意识到自己和他人可能对同一个社交情景有不同的理解。当前，影响孩子在这个年龄段社交认知的因素越来越多。这些影响因素可能是每个人所掌握的客观信息不同、家庭成员间价值观的差异，以及家人选择告知的信息，等等。

我们可以将这种意识看作是儿童早期发展中的第一项换位思考能力。即便如此，这个年龄段的孩子们仍然很难把自己完全放在他人的角度去思考，因为他们没有意识到别人也有可能在揣测他们的想法。回到这个故事的情境以及我们在当时给孩子们提出的问题，学龄前晚期以及幼儿园早期孩子典型的回答会是这样："Mike 说他不想要小狗。Tom 喜欢小狗，但他不应该给 Mike 送小狗。"

幼儿园晚期到小学前期。孩子开始意识到人们彼此之间的想法或感受会有所不同，并开始了解到其背后的原因不仅是人们所掌握的信息不一样，还因为人们各自拥有不同的世界观。这一意识是孩子在童年时代发展的第二种换位思考技能。在这一阶段，孩子能够将自己放在他人的处境思考，从而可以开始从别人的角度看待自己的言行，意识并理解到一个人是可以在思考的同时顾及他人的看法。对于以上这个故事情境，幼儿园晚期到小学前期的孩子可能会这样回答："如果我是 Mike，我会想要一只小狗。可能 Mike 也不知道如果他养了一只新狗，他会有什么样的感受吧。"

小学及初中阶段。这个年龄段的孩子能够意识到自己和其他人有可能正同时考虑彼此的观点。孩子可以像旁观者一样，观察自己与他人的互动。这是一项非常重要的换位思考能力，也是一个很大的进步。因此，处在这个年龄段并掌握了这项技能的孩子可能会这样回答我们的问题："如果 Tom 给 Mike 送了一只小狗，而 Mike 不喜欢它，Tom 仍然知道 Mike 会明白自己只是想让他开心。"

在每个年龄段孩子发展的换位思考技能并不会替代前一个阶段所发展的能力，后期发展的换位思考能力会融合较早发展的换位思考技能，从而使孩子能够更好地理解自己、人性以及复杂的人际关系。而随着孩子换位思考能力的不断增进，他们的社交意识也会逐步增长。

随着换位思考能力发展所增进的社交意识竞争力

前文中，我们曾讨论，对于那些十分明显、可以观察到的社交技能和意识来说，换位思考能力是其发展的重要的基础。在此我将展开讨论四项重要的社交技能和意识。

- **解决社交问题**。过去，当手机还没有普及的时候，如果两个人在一家繁忙的商店中分开而又没有计划在哪里见面，双方必须考虑对方的想法，才有可能在商店中成功会面；如果两人计划在公园见面，但又忘记具体在哪个公园，则双方都必须站在对方的角度换位思考一下，才能到达同一个公园见面；许多决策游戏都需要玩家判断对手下一步可能采取的行动，才能获得胜利。要在协作和竞争的社交关系中获得成功，从他人的角度出发思考问题是其中的关键和基础。

• ***案例分享：通过换位思考解决社交难题***

Alex："Billy 等等我。我答应了 Timmy 要帮他把彩笔带回家，这样在他生病的时候也可以有事可做。"

Billy："好啊，彩笔在哪儿？"

Alex："啊，我忘了问他。可能在他桌子底下。不不不，不在这儿。我不可能把整个房间找遍吧？我可能要跟他说我找不到他的彩笔了。欸，他肯定会失望的。"

Billy："等等，让我想一想。唔，如果我是 Timmy 的话，我会把笔放哪儿呢？我想我知道了，他平时喜欢在那个艺术角工作，他估计是把笔放那儿了。"

案例分析：在很多情况下，合理利用个人的换位思考能力是解决问题的关键。在这个案例中，当故事主人公们找不到彩笔的时候，Alex 只是考虑到了 Timmy 对画画的热忱，但 Billy 更进一步把自己放在 Timmy 的角度来思考，并最终因此解决了问题。在这个案例中，Billy 展示了他在思考的同时揣摩对方看法的推断能力，并最终找到了 Timmy 的彩笔。

• ***理解他人的感受***。*如果一个孩子在妈妈生日的时候，给妈妈送口香糖作为礼物，这并不意味着这个孩子很淡漠或自私。他可能只是认为别人也会像他一样喜欢口香糖。要在做出实际行动前理解*

和考虑他人的感受和兴趣，孩子必须要知道，即便身处同一个社交场合，他人也有可能拥有与自己不一样的感受。

- ***案例分享：通过换位思考理解他人的感受***

老师："好啦孩子们，现在你们有二十分钟的自由活动时间，之后我们会继续上数学课。"

Helen："Jane，我们一起来拼完这个拼图吧！ 我们快拼好啦。"

Jane："好吧，好像还有时间。 说不定我们能拼完。"

Helen："哦，Brenda 来了。 我猜她应该也想一起玩儿。 但是她人可真不怎么样！"

Jane："呃，她也没那么差劲。"

Brenda："哈喽，我可以跟你们一起拼拼图吗？"

Helen："别了吧。 你别来。"

Jane："Brenda，Helen 的意思只是说因为之前都是我们两个人一直在拼这个拼图，所以我们想两个人从头到尾地把它拼完。 我们可以下次一起玩呀！"

Brenda："好呀，好呀。"

Helen："为什么你这样和她说呀？"

Jane："你想想如果别人和你说，我不想和你一起玩儿，你会有什么感受？ 你也不会希望别人伤害你的感受呀。 再说了，如果你试着和她接触，说不定你会发现她没有这么糟糕。"

案例分析：在这个案例中，换位思考在理解对方感受的过程中扮演着非常重要的角色。 Jane 之所以能够在自己和 Brenda 以及 Helen 的社交关系中取得平衡并且表达自己的观点，是因为她能够使用站在对方的角度考虑。 从发展心理学的角度来看，和 Jane 处在同一学龄段的 Helen 可能也拥有相同的社交技能，但是她的言行表明，至少在这个场景中，她并没有使用这些社交技能。 在这个故事里，Jane

使用的换位思考能力通常在孩子的小学阶段便开始发展。

- ***做出公义的论断**。如果你去问一个孩子："当别人打你时，你觉得什么样的应对方式是公义的？"那么你很可能得到一个这样的回答，"打回去"，和原因，"因为我想打他"，"因为他只比我大一点儿"，或者"因为他应该要接受惩罚"。然而，如果要深究什么样的回应与决断才是"公义"的，这些年轻的孩子们可能暂时还无法从他人的角度去思考以上冲突的根源。然而，如果他真的认真去思考这个问题的话，那么，他给出的回答可能是这样的："我会去思考他的感受以及为什么他会这样做。可能他没有恶意。"*

- ***案例分享：通过换位思考做出公义的决断***

Bob："看着点儿，Tom！别推，小心我揍你。"

Tom："放松哥们儿，我只是不小心碰到而已，我不是故意的。"

Bob："算了，你下次小心点。"

Jerry："老哥，他脾气也太暴了吧，你怎么都没反应？要我早开揍了！"

Tom："呃，他生气只是因为他以为我故意撞他。要这样两人还打一架，无不无聊。"

案例分析：这是一个关于做出"公义决断"的案例，在这个故事里，Bob 没有思考 Tom 行为背后的意图就指责并意图打他。无法分辨他人行为背后的意图是幼儿早期换位思考能力发展的特征。然而，Tom 却意识到 Bob 误解了他的动机。这个故事涉及到了解对方能够识别自己的想法及其背后原因的社交意识。在这个案例中，Tom 的社交推断比 Bob 更高级，而他也因为使用了这项社交能力从而化解了一场同伴间的打斗。

- ***游说与沟通**。对很多家长来说，理解在电话那头孩子所说的*

“这个”和“那个”所指代的事物已经是他们生活中习以为常的小事一桩了。然而，对于在电话另一端的孩子来说，他们却很少考虑对方是否知道他们口中所说的“这个”和“那个”的意思。与对方沟通自己的观点是一项非常重要的社交技能，尤其是当孩子在社交场合中想要说服他人接受自己的观点时，清晰的表达至关重要。要有效地沟通或说服对方，孩子们必须要尝试思考并考虑听者的需要和愿望。在这个阶段，能否正确理解他人的需要并不重要，最重要的是去鼓励孩子多去尝试理解对方，从而锻炼孩子的这个能力。

案例分享：通过理解听众的需求理解对方的观点

Art：“哈喽，Gloria。让我用一下这个螺丝刀呗。我看你都用完了。”

Andrew：“欸，等等，我得用一下。”

Gloria：“怎么办？所以接下来谁用?”

Art：“啊，我做这个项目从头到尾都需要这个螺丝刀。”

Andrew：“Gloria，或许你可以想想谁最需要这把螺丝刀？Art要用很久，而且他很多活都需要它。但是我现在只需要借用螺丝刀一下，就可以开始做我的项目。你应该不会希望我等大半个小时，等到Art用这个螺丝刀把他的项目做完了，我才能短暂地用它一下吧？

案例分析：当你想要说服他人时，使用换位思考社交能力是至关重要的。在这个故事中，Art和Andrew都试图游说Gloria先把螺丝刀借给自己。然而Art仅仅从自我需求的角度去陈述自己的观点，但Andrew却结合了双方的需求和处境去争取自己的诉求，这是一项非常复杂的换位思考能力，这一能力在大多数情况下会在儿童早期发展的晚期开始成型。

总结：关于换位思考能力的理论思考

1. 幼童的换位思考能力会经过一系列发展阶段，而该能力的习得是有条件的。

作为老师或家长，您可能对这个社交认知的发展过程感到疑惑。社交认知的发展当前并不是基础教育的重心，但目前却是学龄前和幼儿园教育的关注重点。如果所有孩子在发展其社交认知时都会经历一样的过程，那么老师可以教什么呢？为什么要去教授孩子们一定会发展的一些技能？而且，从实际考虑，人真的可以通过教育给孩子传授换位思考能力吗？这些都是十分重要的问题，若读者们对这个问题感兴趣，我建议各位可以去查阅讨论换位思考能力发展本质的相关资料，相信这方面的理论会对回答这个问题有所帮助。

2. 当孩子在完全掌握了一个阶段的换位思考能力之后，他/她才能进阶到下一个发展阶段

对于那些孩子们在课堂上习得的学业技能，如阅读、语言能力和算数技巧，等等，他们需要日常练习才能熟练并准确运用。而对于在本章节中我们所讨论的社交和逻辑思维能力来说，这些软技能也需要日常练习，这样孩子们才会开始意识到，在他们的日常社交生活中，社交推断能力对于解决社交难题的助益和重要性。

3. 尽管换位思考能力不会自然而然地在我们需要的时候自发出现，但是如果我们能够充分地练习使用这些技能，这些复杂的能力是有可能在我们需要的时候，“自动”显现并发挥作用的。

孩子们是可以把自己放在他人的角度去思考的，但却可能无法理解为什么要这样做。甚至当他们在与他人沟通遇到难题时，也不会意识到换位思考能够帮助他们解决问题。对于那些促进孩子社交技能的项目或课程，它们的其中一个目的就是希望能够鼓励孩子在合适的场合下使用他们所掌握的各种技能。从这个目的出发，在项目设计时，可以设置一些需要使用换位思考能力的讨论活动来帮助提高孩子沟通、共情、道德推断，以及解决社交问题的能力。

4. 不要用社交能力的各个发展阶段来定义孩子的成长。当他们在某一个发展阶段停滞不前时，需要成人的介入来帮助孩子进入到下一个发展阶段。

有时候，我们可以在孩子的一些换位思考行为中，看到发展阶段理论在现实生活中的体现。但同时，我们需要谨记，发展阶段理论仅仅是在描述孩子在某个年龄段的典型行为和特征。

孩子换位思考能力的发展除了受到正常或典型的大脑和生理发育影响之外，学界认为当孩子在经历社交理念冲突或身处一个需要他/她运用略高于其自身推断能力的社交场景时，他们的换位思考能力有可能会有进阶式的发展。在这里，社交理念冲突指的是，当孩子通过自己推理并意识到其身处的社交冲突的结果时，他们的换位思考能力有可能会在此机制的刺激下进阶到下一阶段。在这个过程中，老师可以根据每个孩子自身的推理能力，设置有挑战的实践情景，让孩子的推理能力更好地发展，其中最自然且有效的实践教学活动组织是学生与其同龄人进行小组讨论。

5. 孩子换位思考能力从当前阶段到下一个阶段的发展是一个长期的过程。

研究表明，换位思考能力的进阶耗时几年之久，老师们不应寄希望于能够在短短几个月内就看到孩子们的换位思考能力从其原有的阶段跨越到下一个水平阶段。同时，就本章节所关注的年龄群体来说，我们的关注在于大部分孩子在特定年龄段的思考和语言表达，而不在他们的行为。 即便在本章节中，我们就这一系列的发展阶段进行了详细的描述并且强调大部分孩子们换位思考能力的发展都会遵循这这一发展顺序；但是在实际的案例中，有的孩子有可能会在更小的年龄就习得一些高阶的换位思考能力，有些孩子的社交能力甚至会在两个发展阶段间切换。 因此，虽然我们提出的建议还有理论观点可以帮助大部分家长和老师们在他们的孩子或学生的换位思考发展中扮演一个更好的辅助角色，但是在此我们仍建议读者们尊重每个孩子的成长步伐和道路。

最后，成长中的孩子们以及他们的社交世界

纵观世界各国的教育现状，老师们大多都理解并认可换位思考能力对孩子未来成长和发展的重要性，然而，当他们在试图帮助孩子发展这些技能的时候，都不可避免地会陷入各种矛盾中。 例如，家长们似乎总是迫切地希望在短时间内看到自己孩子在学业上取得显著进步，以至于老师们常常感到自己的专业知识或经验无法满足家长对孩子的期待。 同时，家长对孩子学业表现的重视在无形中也给老师们施加了许多压力，以至于常常使得其他十分重要的，但是与学业发展关联不大的教学活动被排除在孩子们的校园生活之外。实际上，孩子们是需要发展社交意识的，他们需要提高对他人想法和感受的理解能力。 那么，对于老师们来说，有没有可能在学校里，能够像日常教授阅读和写作一样，帮助孩子们习得这些重要的社交技能呢?

在当前的世界范围内，人们越来越关注儿童的社交和情感发展，以及老师在促进这些社交技能时所扮演的角色。 因此，大家都在寻找一种可以平衡学生学业和社交能力发展的教育模式。 然而，在这个时候，发展心理学家发现，孩子们理解他人观点以及与他人看法建立联系的这一社交能力不仅是孩子社交意识成熟发展的基础，同时也在孩子的学习进程中扮演着重要的作用。

在这一章节的最后，我也想说明，我写这篇文章的主要目的不在于推广社交认知和换位思考社交能力，而是希望能够从实践的角度与读者们一起来思考和讨论社交困境（小故事）对孩子成长和发展的意义。 在本章节中，我们通过以上的探讨，看到了在教育实践中，鼓励孩子们就社交困境进行讨论和思考可以帮助他们移除那些他们社交意识发展过程中的障碍，这样做也可以让孩子在一个安全的环境中运用和练习他们新发展的社交技能，并帮助他们学会在各种社交关系、问题以及场合中合理运用他们日渐增强的社交推断能力。 如果我们坚持这样做，那么在不久的将来，当这些孩子长大成人后，他们的这些社交技能不仅能够帮助他们在事业上取得更进一步的成功，同时也将造福社会，推动社会的进步。

参考文献

Mead, George Herbert. *Mind*, *Self*, *and Society*. Chicago： University of Chicago Press, 1934.

Piaget, Jean. *The Moral Judgment of the Child*. New York： The Free Press, 1965 (reprint of 1932 edition).

Selman, R. L. *The Promotion of Social Awareness*： *Powerful Lessons from the Partnership ofDevelopmental Theoryand Classroom Practice*. New York： Russell Sage, 2007.

Selman, R. L. and Byrne, D. (1974) First Things： Social Development. Guidance Associates, Harcourt, Brace, Jovanovich, Inc. , New York, (primarygrades.)

4. 如何通过引导讨论人文故事中的社交困境提高儿童的社交意识

罗伯特·L·赛尔曼

哈佛大学

每一位父母、祖父母、小学教师、儿童医生或是咨询师，无论他们是否有所意识，在教育的过程中他们都无时不在对孩子进行社交技能和品德的培养。他们可能因为孩子坚持公平、信守承诺，或者遵从某项社会规则去称赞孩子，以此强化期望行为；他们也会因为孩子说谎、夺取他人东西，或者违反规则去责骂或者惩罚孩子，希望对孩子的行为产生积极的改变。赞扬或者批评都会管用，尤其在行为发生时。但是，当没有权威人士在场（进行当面赞美或指责）时，孩子会如何表现？老师或父母可以采取哪些做法来增强孩子的内在道德信念，并使之坚定不移？

儿童公平推理规则的自然发展

文化心理学家倾向于描述和理解不同成长环境中的儿童如何在步入社会的过程中内化不同的道德准则与社会规则。与文化心理学家不同的是，发展心理学家则注重研究某个年龄段儿童社会化发展过程中的共性特征，即便每个儿童身处的社会文化环境不尽相同。这是我在本文中使用“自然”一词的缘故及其内涵。发展心理学研究清楚地表明，孩子的公平推理能力（fairness reasoning ability）越强，他越有可能做出社会性或符合道德标准的行为举动，即便这并非必然发生。当没有大人在身边时，一个知道为他人福祉而分享或表达同情的儿童比只想着以此举来逃避惩罚的儿童更有可能持续性地做“对”的事情。可以肯定地说，文化心理学者关注家庭、社区、社会文化环境中对儿童有特殊意义的社会规范，而发展心理学研究者则试图寻找具有普遍性的社会规范，尽管他们承认社会文化价值观随着时代变迁在多元人类社会中已发生重大变化。

从发展的角度来讲，在一开始，幼儿并不了解，或仅模糊地意识到他们身处的社会中的公平规则，无论这些规则是普遍的还是特殊的。例如，所有学龄前儿童都开始“自然”地学习或者关注成人世界的公平规则。他们遵守这些规则主要为了逃避大人的惩罚，尤其在他们做了大人不允许的事情，或者做了大人们认为对他人（主要指与儿童进行日常互动的人，比如家人或者同辈）“不公平”的事情的时候。

随着他们的年龄增长到我们一般所说的小学阶段，大多数孩子会在一项新且关键的公平规则基础上建立公平观，这项规则即“己所不欲，勿施于人”。在生活中观察了人们之间的交流互动后，儿童不再只是听从成人权威，而是开始自己建立公平规则。在小学的中高学段，大多数（并非全部）儿童开始真正关心他人福祉，学会换位思考，这很大程度上是因为他们慢慢开始懂得这其中的重要性。他们懂得，要结交朋友和保持友谊，避免被孤立，需要按照自己希望被对待的方式对待他人。他们明白这是一项好的社交规则，即使一直遵守这项规则不是一件容易的事情。

因此，不足为奇的是，过去50多年的发展心理学研究指出，如果我们去深入洞察儿童外显的社会行为，我们会发现其背后有一条“自然”的发展路径。这就像一条河流，河中流淌着所有儿童在公平推理发展过程中都需要的知识、技能与价值观。尽管这个深层的社会化发展过程对于世界各地的孩子来说都非常相似，但这并不意味着每个孩子的发展过程或发展速度是相同的。尽管人类的生物和认知因素很大程度上决定了这些深层社会知识、技能的增长和价值观形成，它们在不同的地方以不同的形式呈现，其发展的速度和一致性也是可干预的。换言之，教育和社会化实践对儿童社会化发展尤为重要。

讲故事的重要性：如何选择和使用故事有益促进儿童自然的社会化发展

本文建议道德教育应该利用故事去教给孩子适用于所有人类社会的基本公平规则。在21世纪，这可以通过任何孩子能够接受的媒介完成（电影、书籍、课堂讨论、戏剧等，或者把故事读给孩子听——这一点在现代仍十分重要）。只要被很好地讲述出来，这些故事便能助力世界上任何一个地方儿童的成长。这是因为故事传递着共通的社会经验，而儿童在听故事的过程中理解了公平规则的最佳适用情境。

在发展的早期阶段，让儿童接触到有趣且有个人意义的故事，让他们了解什么是满足自己需求的同时照顾到其他人需求的公平做法，是儿童人际道德发展的核心。具体而言，儿童理解了公平推理（fairness reasoning）对于建立友谊中互助关系的重要性。我需再次强调，在世界上不同地区的不同历史发展时期，人们对培养友谊的重视程度相较于知识学习可能有所差异。但是，无论如何，正如存在规范儿童行为的文化规则一样，存在公平发展规则帮助提高儿童维持和谐社会关系的能力。

那么，哪些是对学龄前和小学低年级儿童最重要的公平话题呢？这当中必然包括信守诺言、讲真话、尊重所有权、分享、轮流做事以及理解规则建立的原因。研究表明，运用故事讲述（story-telling）、故事讨论（story discussion）以及故事演绎（story-acting）能有效帮助幼儿发展公平推理能力，帮助他们结交朋友，并与朋友友善相处。这类活动可以在学校、家庭以及任何能提供幼儿与同伴互动机会的社区中展开。有些时候，这些故事由一个孩子讲给另一个孩子听。但本文的重点会放在大人给孩子讲故事的情况。

虽然讲故事在家庭和学校都很普遍，但我们不禁要问，要如何甄选故事，并利用特定故事促进儿童对基础性人际公平规则的理解？学界认为，选择有*开放性结局*和有*指向公平的道德困境*的故事对实现这些教育目标非常有益。特别地，如果这个故事中道德困境的结局所体现的价值观与儿童所处的社会文化环境相悖，那么这样的故事会更具价值。因为这类故事为儿童提供了与他人（父母，老师或者同伴）讨论的机会，促使他们在虚构情境中探索可能的公平解决方案，而这类问题通常是没有明显绝对的，或者根植于文化传统的“正确答案”的。因此，这对促进儿童发展不同形式的社交推理能力非常有效，并帮助他们应对自己在与同伴游戏过程中不可避免出现的冲突与困境。

能触发开放式讨论，发展儿童道德推理能力的故事通常有如下特点：

- 讨论话题涉及“什么是公正的”，这些话题对这一年龄段的儿童非常重要

- 鼓励儿童针对该公平问题找寻自己的答案，这个问题可以由家长和老师加以引导和阐释，从而支持孩子的社会化发展
- 促进儿童讨论本源性问题，比如“什么是好，什么是真”
- 借故事中的人物对白展现更为成熟的道德推理过程，从而帮助作为听众或读者的儿童发展自身的道德推理能力。 我们称这些故事的建构是*符合发展规律的建构*

这种方法并不意味着孩子将成为或应该成为权威，或者拥有完全的“决定权”。 相反，我们认为这些*符合发展规律*的故事本身呈现了故事人物解决自身问题的过程。 这些讨论对故事中的人物来说是真实的。 尽管故事人物的对话或独白对于读者来说是虚构的，但这些话展现了每个人物的行动和思想，以及行动背后的原因。 这样一来，故事中具有普遍性的社交场景就可以作为教学开展的基础。 儿童通过阅读故事，思考故事人物的道德推理过程，并就人际交往方面的话题与同伴展开沟通与协商。

无论是在教室还是在家中进行，我们认为这些关于虚构困境的讨论对于孩子未来发展良好的人际关系有重要作用。 这些故事能促使儿童思考和讨论公平话题，帮助他们联系自身处境，也让他们理解尊重和倾听前人智慧的重要性。 这些故事也需要大人去读给孩子听，或者与孩子一起读。 这会帮助父母或老师了解孩子关于公平困境的社交推理或者道德推理的“自然”发展水平，从而成人能支持孩子去挑战社会化层面更为复杂的思考。 在教室或者家庭进行研究去评估此类教育方法的有效性也是相当重要的。

两个例子：

许多年前，在我刚完成关于儿童社会观点采择能力与道德推理关系的博士论文答辩后，我与著名发展心理学家劳伦斯 · 科尔伯格

（Lawrence Kohlberg）开始共事，他那时正在从事青少年发展方面的研究与实践工作[①]。科尔伯格让我照着他给青少年设计的开放性问题，为儿童撰写一些有开放式结局的道德两难故事。在我和我同事创作的这些故事中，人物对话不仅呈现了不同的观点，也呈现了故事人物在论证自己观点时采纳别人观点的程度。下面是两个我最喜欢的适用于幼儿园和学前班儿童的故事[②]。我将介绍故事梗概，并讨论上文所述的思路是如何运用在“讲故事（story-telling）”活动中的。之后我会讨论这些“符合发展规律”的故事所蕴含的故事演绎（story-acting）的教育机会，让儿童可以利用故事对白和同伴一起在课堂上进行表演。

这是一个发生在魔法世界（fantasyland）的故事。在魔法世界，所有生日赠礼的社会（至少在西方社会）传统被完全颠覆。有两个四五岁左右的小男孩（他们的英文名叫 Eddie 和 Andy）在地上发现了一枚戒指。当他们把戒指捡起来时，发现自己瞬间来到了魔法森林，这里有着奇怪的植物和会说话的动物（故事的人物设定可以根据具体情境变化，可以是两个小女孩，人物也可以有中文名）。一只小熊和一只小鹿走近他们，告诉他们所有的动物都在去魔法师生日会的路上。然而小熊在路上被一根长木绊倒伤了腿，于是小鹿决定一个人去排队拿礼物。

小熊说，魔法师会在他自己生日这天给森林里每一个小动物派发礼物（而非等别人给他送礼物）。所有的小动物都会在魔法师家

---

① Kohlberg, L., & Selman, R. L. (1972) Preparing School Personnel Relative to Values: A Look at Moral Education in the School. ERIC: Clearing-house on Teacher Education. Washington, D. C. See also, Selman, R. L. and Kohlberg, L. (1972) First things: Values. Guidance Associates, Harcourt, Brace, Jovanovich, Inc., New York, (primary grades.)

② 这些故事随后被我的同事和作家 Thomas Glynn 改变成剧本，便于通过多种形式的媒体以较低的成本传播（这些故事能改编成真人电影或者动画，或者利用现代数字媒体呈现）。

门前排队拿礼物。小熊担心如果等它到一瘸一拐走到时，礼物已经发完了。于是 Eddie 和 Andy 主动帮助小熊，三人一起向魔法师家走去。

当他们到达时，他们发现只剩下三个礼物尚未分发，而他们前面还排了两个小动物。小熊坚持让 Eddie 排在它前面，Andy 在小熊后面。这样至少能确保 Eddie 拿到一份礼物。

但果真如此吗？实际上小鹿早早地来排队了，但在排队等待的时候它的帽子被风吹掉了。就在它离开队伍去找自己的帽子时，Eddie 站到了小鹿原本站的位置。Eddie 会让小鹿站回他前面吗？还是他代替小鹿为自己拿到最后一个礼物呢？怎样做才是公平的？

老师和家长如何利用这类故事引导开放式讨论？

像“魔法师的生日会”这样精心设计的故事似乎能自然地能引发孩子们的持续性讨论，但这并不意味着讨论不应该受任何控制或引导。我们需要拥有丰富经验的成人引导儿童对这类开放式人际或道德两难故事进行讨论，从而支持儿童沿上文所提到的公平推理发展路径不断提升。

教师对于赋予这样的故事以清晰的教育目标有至关重要的作用。若没有教师的辅助，这些故事便流于娱乐，而不具有发展层面或者文化层面的教育意义。从发展的角度看，教师能引导富有成果的讨论，从而帮助儿童进行更好的道德推理实践。最热烈的讨论发生在对什么是“公正”的道德选择存在强烈分歧时。如果班上孩子对某一故事人物的行动选择“一边倒”，那么老师可以站在反方提问挑起冲突。

例如，在“魔法师的生日会”这一故事中，如果多数孩子都认为 Eddie 应该让小鹿站回他前面，教师可以这样问：

- 为什么小鹿不能等到拿到礼物之后再离开队伍去找它的帽子？
- 谁会出现在魔法师*下次*的生日会上，Eddie 还是小鹿？

为促进孩子进行换位思考，老师可以继续问：

- 当小鹿要离开它站的队时，它理应做些什么去保留自己在队伍中的位置？
- 当有人插队到你前面时，你是什么感受？

另一方面，假设多数孩子认为 Eddie 不应该让小鹿站回他前面，教师可以通过以下问题制造冲突：

- 帽子被吹掉是小鹿自己的错吗？ 是它故意离开队伍的吗？
- 如果你发现自己的位置被别人占了，且不是你自己主动想离开位置的，你会是什么感受？

同样，下列是发展换位思考能力的问题：

- 当你自己的位置被别人占了的时候你是什么感受？
- 小鹿非常希望从魔法师那里得到滑雪板。 如果 Eddie 不让它站回队伍，小鹿会是什么感受？

有时，儿童会尝试通过逃避来解决这类困境。 例如，在这个故事中，一些孩子会说：“魔法师是有魔法的。 他可以再变出一个礼物，这样 Eddie 和小鹿就都有礼物了。”在这个时候，教师必须坚持“道德两难原则”，指出孩子忽略的故事情节：“记住，小熊提到它很担心魔法师的礼物送完了。 所以这种（没有多余礼物的）情况在之前是发生过的，对不对？”或者老师自行确定条件：“魔法师没有变礼物的魔法。”这样一来，教师便能鼓励所有孩子去直面困境。所有这些方法都是为了制造“社会认知”冲突，这不仅存在于作为听众的孩子之间，也存在于每个孩子的脑海里。

例二：魔法师丢了眼镜

这是第一个故事的续篇，也同样发生在有魔法师和会说话动物的魔法世界。故事的开头讲到魔法师在找他的眼镜。没有戴眼镜的魔法师看不清东西，他把他邀请到生日会上的两个男孩，Eddie 和 Andy，看成了一个叫 Meeddiemeandy 的“生物”。

尽管如此，Eddie 和 Andy 还是提出要帮助魔法师找眼镜，魔法师也答应如果找到眼镜就给他们奖励。Eddie 和 Andy 骑着飞牛看遍了很多地方寻找眼镜。飞牛说，魔法师可能把眼镜落在了薄荷池里，他经常在那里泡澡放松。果不其然，Andy 在薄荷池水底中发现了眼镜。Eddie 让 Andy 抱住他的后腿，自己潜入水下捡回了眼镜。

找回眼镜的魔法师非常高兴。但他现在清楚地“看”到了自己犯下的错误—Eddie 和 Andy 不是一个“Meeddiemeandy”，而是两个男孩。魔法师手里只有一个奖品——真正的魔力手表。谁应该得到奖品呢？Andy 发现了眼镜，但 Eddie 潜到水下拿回了眼镜。魔法师应该把奖品给谁？怎么做才是公平的？

通常，孩子会提出一些无关痛痒的处理办法。比如，在“魔法师丢眼镜”的故事中，一些孩子会说魔法师不应该把手表给 Eddie 和 Andy 中的任何一个人。然而，当孩子自己面临这个情况时，他会很难接受这样的解决方案。教师可以通过强调“道德两难”的特点，帮助孩子用更现实的角度看问题，他可以这样问：

- 假设我是魔法师，你是 Andy——那个最先发现魔法师眼镜的男孩。你要怎么说服我给你手表？
- 现在假设你是 Eddie——那个潜到水下捡回手表的男孩。你会给我怎样的理由去说明你应该拥有这块手表？

● 假设你是魔法师，并且听到了两方的理由。对你来说，怎么做才公平？

在第二个故事中，同时帮助魔法师找到眼镜的两个孩子要分一个奖品。这不仅是选择某一方的问题，其背后是一个更具挑战性的问题：如何分配奖赏才是公平的？比判定手表归谁更重要的，是面面俱到地讨论奖赏分配的不同策略。

比如：

1. 手表一天归 Eddie，一天归 Andy。

2. 一个人得（能让他们来到魔法世界的）魔戒，另一个得魔力手表。

3. 猜硬币决定谁得这块表。

比起日常的数学、科学甚至语言教学（通常注重词汇理解），教师在这里扮演的角色将更难定义。毕竟，要成为一个优秀的读者或者演讲者，一个学生要意识并记住一个词的不同含义。但是公平推理教学——探讨在帮助魔法师找眼镜的过程中同时出了力的 Eddie 和 Andy 关于奖赏的分享与妥协——对孩子来说极为有趣。他们不再只单纯从词典上背诵词义，而是在表达、倾听和分享中理解词汇在具体语境下的不同含义。

儿童在讨论中偏离大人划定的边界是很正常的事情。教师需要判断这些“偏题”讨论是否是有益的。比如，听完魔法师丢眼镜的故事，孩子们可能会开始讨论奖品本身的性质。只要这些推论与公平主题相关（比如魔法师应该找出另一份礼物让两个男孩都有奖励）就可以继续讨论。但如果是完全不相关的话题（比如魔法师应该给男孩们新的手表而不是旧的），教师便应该自然地把讨论拉回到情境内。

孩子们也会寻找折衷方案解决两难问题。有效的折衷方案应被视为重要的公平抉择。教师应强调折衷之所以是好的方案的原因。例如，在丢眼镜故事中，孩子们可能会提出这样的折衷方案：手表一天归 Andy，一天归 Eddie。

如果讨论小组中的孩子们对某一做法达成了共识，教师接下来便要敦促他们挑选出支持他们观点的最佳理由。老师需要强调，在解决道德问题的过程中，原因和观点同样重要。

教师可以把自己看作是一个公平向导。他/她的主要任务是帮助孩子：

1. 关注冲突；
2. 思考他/她解决冲突的推理过程；
3. 考虑可能被忽略的道德问题；
4. 在所讨论的推理过程中寻找矛盾的地方；
5. 寻找解决此类矛盾的方法。

如此一来，教师便可以在悬置自身立场的情况下鼓励和引导学生进行人际和道德问题的思考和讨论。实际上，班上的孩子可能想知道老师眼中的“正确”观点。在使用我们设计的故事时，老师开始可以说：“我不想过多影响你，你应该自己做决定。”等到合适的时候，老师便可以放心地分享自己的观点，但需要强调他/她的答案不是唯一解，且有自己的看法很重要。教师还应准备好阐述他/她观点背后的理由。当然，让班里的不同成员尽可能多地想出正当理由总是好的。教师还可以建议学生在课下继续思考这个故事，和家人或者朋友讨论，或许能一起想出更好的理由（在这里，“好的理由”指的是考虑到各方观点和感受的，更为复杂的理由）。

对日常生活中人际关系故事进行引导式同伴讨论（guided peer-discussion），其主要目的之一是促进每个孩子的社交推理和道德推理实践；同时，分享各方观点的讨论通常能提升整个小组的推理质量。 这两个故事关注人际交往情境，故事中无论是解决意见分歧的方法还是公平分配奖赏的问题，都对儿童结交朋友、维持友谊、发展和谐良好的人际关系有所裨益。 讲完故事后立即进行讨论是最有效的。 以下步骤将有助于讨论更富成果：

A. 与全班同学一起回顾故事

在进行公平主题的讨论之前，孩子们需要确切地知道他们即将讨论的是什么。 教师可通过提问来确保孩子对故事有完整的理解，并且意识到故事中的道德两难问题。 注意回顾故事人物的名称，以及人物相关的情节。

B. 向全班示范讨论过程

讲完故事后，教师可向全班演示讨论过程，便于接下来活动的开展。 示范讨论至少需要三人，他们可以是大一点的学生，其他老师或助手。 三人面对面围坐。 以生日会故事讨论为例，一人需持让小鹿回到原位的观点，另一人需持不让小鹿回到原位的观点，第三个人则持不确定态度，随着讨论的深入两边倒。

C. 全班分小组讨论

尽管教师可能希望由全班来共同讨论这一两难问题，但通常情况下 4—6 人一组的小组讨论会更有效。 小组的成员组成应该尽可能多样。 不同的小组分散到教室不同角落围坐，或是围在桌边，或者坐在地上，总之要确保在每个人讨论时能看到其他人的脸。 孩子们要求模仿讨论示例，提出问题，给出理由，*倾听*并把观点讲给*其他组员听*，而不是只给老师听。 老师可以自由走动，倾听小组讨论，保证讨论不要偏离主题，及时澄清问题，并在适当时机插入新问题。

D. 运用提问让讨论面面俱到

创造性地运用提问是让小组讨论成功转化为道德推理实践工具

的关键。通过提问引导学生充分讨论道德困境中每一方的观点，在不断的冲突中，学生的道德水平走向更高阶段。

我们理解父母、老师或者咨询师可能会反对同伴讨论的形式，因为这样的讨论偶尔会让儿童选择说谎而非诚实，选择欺凌而非合作，选择违背承诺而非信守承诺。在现实生活中，每个孩子的确都会面临无法履行承诺或者不说真话的情况，然而出现这些情况（例如我们在这里讨论的）的原因是发展未成熟，或者是该行为表现不符合文化传统。但是，无论在哪种社会文化情境下去讨论这些故事，发展心理学的方法都强调了**公正行动需要充分理由支撑**的重要性。这种方法鼓励孩子*深度思考*，不要盲目接受道德陈词滥调。这种方法强调思维的推理和碰撞，并需要一个深谙开放式讨论所蕴含价值的教育者领导。这个教育者明白，运用这样的方式能帮助学生对“公正、公平和关怀”有更深刻、更个体化的认识。

从故事讲述到故事演绎——下一个延续传统的有价值行动

到目前为止，我们主要阐述了讨论和反思在促进道德推理和社交推理方面的作用。具体而言，我们讨论了由故事衍生的推理。这些故事适用于世界上几乎任何地方的儿童，它们既有理解难度，又对儿童非常具有吸引力，因为故事中的情景都是每个孩子日常生活中很可能会遇到的。由于这里的讨论对象主要是学龄前儿童，我们并没有涉及故事讲述对阅读和写作能力的重要性。针对这一点，我会在未来讨论年长一些儿童的情况时再做详述。

然而，我想说说此类方法下另一种能促进幼儿发展的手段，即故事演绎（story-acting）。到目前为止，我们大概可以想见一个大人向一群孩子朗读一个故事，或者让孩子们观看由演员表演的故事。那么，如果这些可听可讲的故事被设计成能让孩子们自己参与表演的形式会怎样?

实际上，当我们在很多年前在设计这些社交和道德困境时，我们是用有人物对白的剧本形式呈现的。我们请同事 Tom Glynn 按照电影或话剧剧本的标准进行故事创作。我在这里节选了第一个故事中的结尾片段，可以看到，这由 Thomas Glynn 以真实剧本的格式撰写的不同故事人物之间的对话。这样一来，虚构的公平困境对于正在经历类似困境的儿童来说便显得更为真实了。

让我们进入故事片段。这时，(因腿受伤而)一瘸一拐的小熊，魔法文化的新人 Eddie 和 Andy 终于到达了生日礼物分发点。小动物们都在耐心地排队等待魔法师分发礼物。Eddie 说:“我没有看到你的朋友小鹿，我在想他去哪了。”

小熊

“我不知道,可能他走丢了。我们快排队,免得其他人又来了。你可以在排我前面。”

Eddie

“不对,我认为你应该在我前面。如果不是你,我们不会知道有这个礼物派发点哩。”

小熊

“不对不对,你们排在我前面才是公平的。是你们帮扶我走到了这里。”

Andy

“好吧,那我们一个人在你前面,一个人在你后面。这样公平吗?”

小熊

“完美! 哦天呐,快看——只剩下三个礼物了! 哦,我担心的事情还是发生了。

Eddie,你很幸运,你排到了第三个,你能拿到最后一个礼物。”

小鹿

“让我进去,我之前站在这里的。”

Eddie

“不,你没有。是我们站在队尾的,你之前不在这儿。”

小鹿

“我在你之前就来了。我刚离开队去找我的帽子了。它被风吹走了,我哪也找不到它。”

小浣熊

“对,小鹿之前在我后面。我还记得他说他希望今年能拿到一个新的滑雪板。”

Andy

“那他在离开队的时候就已经失去他的位置了。你应该要一直站在你的位置上。如果你离开了,你就必须重新去队尾排队。这才公平。”

小浣熊

“我不觉得那很公平。这个小鹿之前就站在这里,他比你朋友等得更久。谁等得最久,谁才应该拿到最后一个礼物,这才公平。”

小熊

“等得久不算数。当小鹿离开队伍的时候,他就已经放弃自己的位置了。”

小鹿

“不,我没有。我打算立马回来的。那仍然是我的位置。他应该让我回来。”

猫头鹰

“先生们,先生们！容我说两句。不要那么草率做决定,试着从别人的角度考虑考虑吧。”

小浣熊

“确实,想想小鹿是什么感受吧。丢帽子不是他的错,为什么他要重新从队尾开始排,放弃本应该是归他的礼物呢？我不认为这很公平。小鹿在队里有他的位置,他比你朋友等得更久。谁等得最久,谁就应该拿最后一个礼物,这才是公平的。”

Andy

“没错,但是想想 Eddie 的感受吧。他不知道你之前在那,也不是他让小鹿离开队伍的。况且,Eddie 之后可能再也不会来魔法师的生日会了,所以要 Eddie 让你重新进来肯定是不公平的。”

小鹿

“你现在打算怎么办？你让我进还是不进?”

猫头鹰

“是啊,Eddie,你要怎么办?”

Eddie

“我不知道。要知道什么是公平真的太难了。小鹿之前站在这,而且他可能比我等得更久。但是我现在在这。我应该放弃我的位置,仅仅因为他现在决定回来吗？怎样才是最公平的做法?”

请注意我们是如何创作脚本的。 在片段中，故事里的每个角色都参与了讨论。 他们提出的观点基于他们觉得重要的他人视角（比如浣熊为小鹿考虑，Andy 为 Eddie 考虑），同时给予理由进行支撑（猫头鹰不持个人观点，但鼓励所有讨论者运用他们社交推理和公平推理）。

例如，让我们回到 Andy 和小浣熊的对话：

Andy

“那他在离开队的时候就已经失去他的位置了。你理应一直站在你的位置上。如果你离开了，你就必须重新去队尾排队。这才公平。”

小浣熊

“我不觉得那很公平。这个小鹿之前就站在这里，他比你朋友等得更久。谁等得最久，谁才应该拿到最后一个礼物，这才公平。”

在上述对话中，Andy 认为最后一个礼物应该给 Eddie，小浣熊则认为礼物应该给小鹿。 当年，我们把这些指向公平的社交和道德两难问题对美国 4 至 8 岁儿童进行了测试。 通过比较不同年龄段学生对问题的回答，我们能从发展的视角纵向审视儿童在不同年龄阶段所持的不同观点、判断和行为。 我们发现，对于礼物归谁（Eddie 还是小鹿）的问题，孩子们的看法一半一半。 大约一半的孩子认为小鹿应该得到礼物，而另一半则认为 Eddie 应该得到礼物。

我们把儿童在回答问题中表述的观点和态度统称为他们推理的“内容”（注：支撑观点的原因称作“结构”）。 我们设计的两难问题要尽可能多地触发孩子们富有想法的态度和观点。 除此之外，通过对比年龄较小和年龄较大儿童的不同回答，我们能提炼公平推理发展的阶段性差异。 我们利用这些源自儿童的真实回答去编写不同角色在故事中所表达的观点。 对于第二个故事中的两难问题我们也进行了类似的研究。 在我们的研究群体中，针对谁应该得到魔法师手表的问题，一半的孩子认为应该给 Eddie，另一半认为应该给 Andy。 有时，孩子们也会想出非常聪明的折衷方案。

现在，想象一群三年级学生组成的表演团。 他们在自己的教室里排演了剧本，每个人都参与担任一个角色。 这个表演团来到学前班，表演故事“魔法师的生日会”。 他们可以读出或者背诵他们的台词。 无论哪种方式，学前班里年幼的孩子都会有机会向演员提问，而这些演员在几年前的年纪和观众一样大。 我们认为这样的教育体验会让虚构的社交情景更贴近现实生活。 我们也认为这样的方法值得推广应用，或者进行严谨的研究和评估，类似于我们之前提到的对于*符合发展规律故事*展开讨论的实效性研究。

某一文化或跨文化情境下促进公平推理发展的一些思考

文章的最后，我有必要回顾发展视角和文化视角对于解释儿童理解、思考和讨论这些故事的关系。 当前我们主要讨论了从发展视角去理解幼儿道德、公平和社交推理，但我们尚未充分讨论文化分析(cultural analysis)视角，即学生的观点差异与学生的居住地、相处的人及不同情境之间的关系。 通常，文化价值观对一个良好社会秩序的建立十分关键。 如果关于公平的社会规范在同一文化内部，或者不同文化间存在差异，那么我们需了解这些观点态度的背后是怎样的价值观在发挥作用。 这里的文化比较不仅指宏观的文化（如东西方文化），也指宏观文化下的微观文化，比如幅员辽阔、有着多元文化的国家里来自不同社会阶层的学生之间的比较。 不同文化视角（比如性别、地区、学校、不同家庭收入背景）下儿童对同一问题的看法存在怎样的差异?

假设有这样一个小孩，他总是默许别人在他前面插队。 这个小孩的妈妈说，无论是拍照还是拿圣诞礼物，他总是一群孩子们中的最后一个。他妈妈说：“他认为没有必要冲到前面。他相信总会轮到他，并且他不太关心最后自己能否拿到（礼物）。”在体育课上，他的朋友总插队站这个男孩前面，即便他朋友比他来得晚。当他妈妈问儿子对他朋友的做法怎么看时，儿子说：“这是他的问题，不是我的问题。”

那么，我们如何理解这个孩子的社会行为？什么理论框架能帮助我们理解？实际上，我们可以从任何一个理论视角去理解“这是他的问题，而不是我的问题”这句话。例如，进化论会告诉我们，抢占先机的雄性生物能繁殖最多的后代（这解释了男孩朋友的插队行为）；人格理论会讨论诸如抑制或非抑制的个人特质，而这和生物遗传相关；更有甚者，社会心理学会探讨两人友谊存在的具体情境（谁更强壮，谁更富有，谁更有攻击性，谁更有同理心，等等）。但是，当我们从青少年儿童社会化发展的角度出发，我们的公民，通常是那些有权威的成年人会思考我们需要传递给年轻一代怎样的文化价值观，考量个人发展和社会政治上层建筑的关系。文化理论会关注权力结构在维持秩序和促进和谐的重要性。如果一个社会的文化价值观是“不允许插队”，那么这就是教育者希望儿童能学到的东西。

我们看到，发展视角和文化视角是研究人类社会行为的不同层面，就像生物学研究“进食行为”一样。我们可以看到另一个人进食，但没有好的研究工具，我们无法清楚胃的构造和运作方式。理解消化过程需要深入器官层面（胃）理解，甚至要深入生化层面（消化酶）去理解。对胃的观察就好比不同文化动态博弈的分析。换言之，分析文化就好比理解胃的结构和功能。对胃里细胞和化学物质的观察则是更深层次的研究。分析发展就好比研究胃里细胞的功能及化学物质。我们需要同时从器官层面和生化层面去解释进食行为，这就是我们所谓的有机体研究。

文化和发展的分析也都是有机的。社会行为中的文化因素和发展因素并非一开始显而易见。然而，文化视角仍比发展视角更容易被理解，就像器官比细胞更好观察一样。这也就解释了当文化视角和发展视角有冲突时，发展视角往往退居二线，容易被家长或者老师所忽略。

例如，在我们的第一个生日会故事中，用于支持小鹿站回原来位置的原因可能不是发展层面更成熟的观点采择能力的表达（为小鹿设身处地着想），而可能是小鹿的身型看上去比男孩要大得多，因此要听小鹿的。有时在一些特定的文化中，音量最大的声音会压倒最公平的声音。在某些情况下，有权威在场时小鹿和两个男孩两方的抉择可能完全不同于朋辈文化规则下两方的抉择。

但是，发展分析能让我们去理解每个孩子当前的社会理解、社交技能和价值观。无论在哪种文化下，这些知识和技能都很重要。我们能在不同的道德发展水平上去分析一个儿童对小鹿观点利弊的论证。这就是为什么我认为让孩子在有经验的教育者指导下通过我们设计的道德两难故事进行同伴间讨论是极有意义的，因为这样可以让孩子在虚构情境下实践他在该发展阶段的道德推理技能，并能倾听其他孩子的想法。这样一来（可能有些矛盾地说），幼儿能在安全环境下理解他们文化中或隐性或显性的社会规则，同时建立个人对公平正义的理解。他们能在具体情境下考虑自身处境，也会对自身所处的社会文化传统更为敏感。他们需要同时能够实现这两方面（文化层面和发展层面）的发展。

我们的研究团队认为，一个促使读者、听众或者观众产生意见和论证分歧的道德两难故事不仅对促进公平推理发展有所裨益，对于提升讨论技能也极其重要（毕竟，讨论是促进道德发展的动力和源泉）。当文化没有给出明确规则时，年轻人会提出自己的想法。例如，当我们将社交经验里的发展和文化因素融入到故事中时，我们有意地呈现了问题的不同视角。在每个视角上，故事角色也都表达了不同发展水平的推理过程。回到故事，小浣熊在提出初步看法后继续说道：

> “确实！想想小鹿是什么感受吧。丢帽子不是他的错，为什么他要重新从队尾开始排，错过拿到礼物的机会呢？我不认为这很公平。小鹿在队里有他的位置，**他比你朋友等得更久**。谁等得最久，谁就应该拿最后一个礼物，这才是公平的。”

无论你是否赞同小浣熊的观点，我想你会同意小浣熊第二次的论证比第一次要好，这并不是因为第二次它说得更长，而是该论证呈现了社交层面更复杂的理由，并在论证过程中采纳了更多他人视角。这样的故事之所以能促进任何文化下的儿童的公平推理发展，是因为其能促使儿童在这一过程中考虑和调和不同观点，只是教学活动的设计需要考虑到讨论发生的具体文化环境。这意味着这些开放式结局故事必须在“本地”撰写，撰写人应该是行业专家，他/她深刻地理解参与讨论的儿童、教师和家长所处的文化。然而，我们也不能忽视或遗忘社会认知的普遍性（如果这样的论断是正确的），即我前文所提到的，那些符合发展规律的社会认知结构。这是我们建立不同文化群体间联系的科学与实践的基础，无论是自下而上还是自上而下。你怎么看？我们认为，进一步深入研究这些问题任重道远。

5. 适合学前教育课堂的课程主题

凯瑟琳·E·斯诺

哈佛大学

儿童早期教育工作者发现了一些关于幼儿的秘密，而他们却鲜少与人提及。其中一个就是：实际上，孩子们的思维复杂得惊人。我们经常会低估 2 至 5 岁的孩子，认为教育者只需确保他们学习许多基础的技能——背诵字母表、写出几十个汉字、读写自己的名字、认识不同的颜色和形状、数到 50 等等，这样孩子就能顺利完成学前教育并为日后的学习做好准备。但是，最优秀的幼儿教师不仅仅关注我们能教给孩子什么，他们同时也很看重成年人能够从幼儿身上学到什么。我们到底可以教给孩子些什么——这是我们能从孩子身上所学到的第一件事，也是本章的主题。

向孩子学习

向孩子学习始于学会聆听孩子的话。当孩子与自己所信任的成年人自在地相处时，他们往往会说很多话，以及问大量的问题。有研究者对四个在美国长大的、18至65个月的儿童进行了追踪研究，发现他们每小时会提出75至150个问题（Chouinard，2007）。尽管有些时候他们提问是为了提出某种要求（如："我能看电视吗？你能帮我系鞋带吗？"），但是大部分的问题是为了从大人那里寻求信息。显然，孩子们对这些问题的答案是真正感兴趣的，因为如果大人没能回答出来或是回答的结果不令人满意，他们就会不断追问下去。

的确，孩子们会问许多问题，而我们又能从这个事实中得出什么结论呢？首先，很肯定的是，这意味着他们有着强烈的好奇心。其次，他们清楚哪些是他们所不知道的事情。第三，他们认为成年人愿意并且能够帮助他们找到答案。对我们教育工作者来说，我们从哪儿还能找到这么理想的学生啊！让我们来计算一下孩子们为自己所创造的学习机会：

每小时100个问题
×每天互动3小时
×每年365天
×4年
=390000个在上幼儿园前学习的机会

当然，并不是所有的孩子都有上述如此多的学习机会。有时候，大人并不会鼓励孩子提问。有时候，大人不能或不愿回答孩子的问题，可能是因为他们认为话多的孩子有些无礼或不受管控；也可能是比起好奇的孩子，他们更欣赏安静的孩子；又或者是因为他们相信他们想教给孩子的比孩子想学的更为重要。这种态度可能适用于年龄较大的学生——想要通过大学入学考试的高中生——通常愿意学习他们内心不感兴趣的内容。但是，2 至 5 岁的孩子没有那么愿意服从。当孩子所学既能满足他们的好奇心又能帮他们解答问题时，他们的学习效率将会更高、效果亦更加明显。

关于儿童早教课程的争论

那么，这是否意味着一个优质的幼儿课程只需要及与孩子们聊聊天，谈谈他们的兴趣爱好？事实上，在儿童早期教育的范畴里长期存在着这么一个争论——早教课程应该以“教师引导”为主，还是以“幼儿回应”为主。根据前美国幼教协会（NAEYC）的标准，“幼儿回应”模式是一种十分恰当，甚至是非常理想的教学方法。该标准注重儿童发展的适宜性并将其视作判断早教的主要目的——教学质量及社会学习能力是否达标的重要依据。在“回应式课程”模式中，最著名、最具有代表性的例子是“瑞吉欧模式”。事实上，在运用瑞吉欧模式时，人们往往会辅以层次丰富的教学课程，只不过这些课程不是预先设立好的，而是根据课堂上一些突发奇想或是不在意料之中的情况当场应运而生的[①]。其他例子还包括 20 世纪 60 年代由美国密歇根州伊普西兰蒂的高瞻研究所开发的“高瞻课程”（Frede & Barnett，1992），随后有美国许多早教中心使用了这个课程，包括 Head Start，在欧洲也是如此（如 Kaleidoscope，荷兰语版本）。

不过，这套以“幼儿回应”作为主导的“高瞻课程”受到了一些批评。有人指责其不太严谨缜密，无法确保所有儿童享有平等的学习机会。同时，尽管瑞吉欧模式具有丰富的“回应式课程”，如要达到良好的效果，还需依托理想的外部条件——如，师生比保持

① http：//www. aneverydaystory. com/beginners-guide-to-reggio-emilia/main-principles/

在较高的水平，需具备适应不同孩子兴趣爱好的多种教学资源，教师需有较高的专业素养。有人还提出要为老师和学生提供一个与瑞吉欧模式所倡导的行为相符合的、更为宽广的文化语境。所以不难得出，虽然有许多美国早教课程声称自己是受到了“瑞吉欧模式”的启发，但实际上，没有人能真正践行这种教学模式。

在“幼儿回应”课程模式的运用缺乏新意，并面临很多批评争议的情况下，教育工作者往往会转向另一个选择——这也是许多人的做法——撰写紧凑的早教课程方案，制定详细的学习目标与标准，并且确保协助幼儿顺利毕业，为日后进入小学教育做好准备。例如，荷兰各大城市的早教课堂上曾充斥着许多以荷兰语为第二语言的移民家庭的孩子。为了加快他们的学习速度，荷兰引入了“金字塔教学法”，即课堂上主要采取直接教学，并辅以详细的教案，引导孩子将所学对话内容加以记忆并重复练习，对简单的词汇进行读写操练。“直接教学法（DI）”在美国的盛行归功于齐格飞·恩格曼。他提出的这种方法能够为每个孩子设计可以学会的学习任务，从而促进教育公平[①]。在早教的范畴中，如此教学模式几乎很少用到，尤其是当人们发现，相较于“高瞻体系”以及中规中矩的幼儿园教学模式，“直接教学法”的每一项指标都相对落后（Schweinhart & Weikart，1998）。

一方是贯彻“直接教学法”的课程项目，其指令性强、缺乏发展适宜性；另一方是开放式的、回应式的课程项目，对教师的经验知识、教学技巧，对教学材料及教学资源的丰富性、多样性都提出了相当高的要求——那么，我们该如何在两者间找到平衡呢？预先设置的课堂活动与课堂上根据孩子的好奇心进行互动引导，这两者

---

① https://www.nifdi.org/15/index.php?option=com_content&view=article&id=52&Itemid=27

的比例应该如何调节？ 我们有没有办法可以使“直接教学法”更具吸引力，抑或是把“幼儿回应式”课程项目变得更加容易操作，使课程即使是在不同的地方实施，都能够确保同等的教学质量？ 我们可不可以将孩子们林林总总的问题融入到那些具有详细教案、以教师本身为主导的课程项目中去，或者是在开放式的课程项目中将更多丰富的答案加以呈现？ 如果我们可以将以上这些矛盾点稍加解决，早教课堂的质量也许会更高，可复制性也会更强。

我认为如果我们认真地去思考孩子们所提出的问题，或许我们会更加清楚该怎么做，更加明白他们知道什么、需要知道什么。 因为事实上，许多儿童都有他们想要去了解的话题，而我们可以将这些话题变成更深、更广的学习机遇。 因此，早教老师需要针对这些问题搜集充分的教学资源，这样问题来临时，他们就可以轻松应对了。

我将通过一个例子来说明这个观点。 在一个回应式的课堂中，学生是 3 至 4 岁的儿童，老师每天安排的第一个活动通常是晨读。学生往往会在此环节大声朗读一本或是多本书籍。 这种晨读互动（如果老师或多或少受过一定专业的培训），一般来说会为孩子们提供提问的机会。 有些问题可能只局限于本书里的内容，有些可能更为广泛，涉及与本书相关的各类主题。 例如，让我们来设想一下，读完《抱抱》这本书之后，孩子们会有怎样的反应。 他们可能会围绕与此书相关的多个话题进行发问： 如生物学类的问题（生活在丛林中的动物、不同小动物的名字、不同动物所发出的声音、动物们吃什么、它们如何睡觉）；与地理和生物群系相关的问题（丛林到底是什么？ 它们与沙漠、山脉、草原和动物园有什么不同？ 在不同的地方都居住着怎样的动植物？）；情感类问题（书中的猩猩先是好奇，再是难过、苦恼，最后竟是狂喜）；社会关系类问题（敌友关系、手足之情、亲子关系）。

当然通常情况下，老师们不太可能在课堂上穷尽所有与本书相关的话题，而穷尽所有话题本身也不一定就是一个好主意。但是，如果老师愿意仔细聆听，并基于学生所提出的问题清楚地认识到他们对某一个或某几个话题兴趣盎然，这样老师就可以引导全班进行讨论，看看他们是否愿意围绕一个方面进行更为深度的学习。在一间设备齐全的教室里，老师可以调动起所有的课程资源，围绕不同的主题进行教学。例如，教室里可能有一个箱子，里面装着关于丛林的书籍，记载着群居或独居动物（参见附录），以及一些相关课堂活动的策划。这些活动可以分几天举行：让学生分成不同小组，用卡纸做出不同的动物形状或动物面具、研究并搭建出丛林动物的栖息地、研究不同的动物喜欢吃什么食物，把这些食物画下来或是把它们的照片贴在海报上等等[①]。这个箱子可能还含有与课堂主题相关的诗歌或歌曲，或是一些 YouTube 视频，向学生们展现动物在生活在大自然中的场景。丰富多彩的教学资源可以帮助孩子深入了解动物及它们的生活，也可以将数学、音乐、美术及科学知识融入课堂活动中去。接下来几日大声晨读的活动可以继续集中在相关的话题上。倘若有一天孩子们满足了他们的好奇心，对这个话题不再有兴趣了，那时他们也已经掌握了许多有用的知识。

如果在大声朗读了《抱抱》这本书后，孩子们并没有对动物表示出好奇心该怎么办？这时应该还有第二个箱子，里面装着情感学习类的书籍、推荐活动和课程计划。第三个箱子可以关乎友谊，第四个箱子可以关乎母亲和小宝宝等等……因此，通过有策略地调动教学资源，课程本身可以有针对性地对儿童的兴趣点作出回应。课

---

① 请参阅为期 7 周的《Let's Know preK》动物课程单元中的资源和材料 http：//static. ehe. osu. edu/downloads//projects/larrc/1_Animals_PreK_Teacher%20Manual_cohort%202_digital_r. pdf 。

程设计者可以充分发挥积极性，将课程设计得丰富多彩，并且清楚地意识到当儿童对某个话题表现出强烈兴趣时，他们将学得更快、更好。

结论

儿童早期教育现如今已经开发了几十门不同的课程，有商业性的，也有非营利性的。其中许多课程都会以研究作为基础，大部分的课程都为孩子推荐了相当不错的书目清单，指导老师该如何巧妙地开展小组活动并且充分利用教学资源。不过，广义上来说，并没有研究表明这些教学资源可以大大地提升儿童的学习成果。我认为我们应当思考，研究结果之所以令人失望，之所以没有对孩子的表现产生更为显著的影响，原因或许并不在于课程设计薄弱或是执行有误，而是在于没有将儿童兴趣的点纳入考量。我在本章简述了如何设计丛林动物课程的一些想法，我非常确信丛林动物、它们的栖息地、习性可以是一个相当不错的早教课程主题。但是不管书本内容有多么迷人，歌曲、儿歌多么好听，课件活动安排得多么妥当，如果孩子们不感兴趣，他们什么也学不到。我们目前所挑战是如何将优秀的课程设计与孩子参与度结合起来，做到这一点的最佳办法就是去倾听孩子的问题。他们会告诉我们他们对哪些主题感兴趣，想要去学哪些知识。

事实上，我写本章的目的是为了呼吁儿童早教领域开发出更多设计优良的课程，让教师可以去充分观察孩子想要学些什么，并确保他们可以找到合适的教学资源来回应学生所提出的问题。与其把自己局限于预先设计的课程或是开放式的教学探索，我们完全可以把早教课堂当作是一个自然历史博物馆，孩子们可以自由地去参观恐龙展览、观察花草或海洋动物，以便他们能够在自己兴趣盎然的时候学习他们眼里最有趣的东西。 不过，自然历史或科学博物馆这样的比喻有点过于狭隘，因为孩子的好奇心可能会促使他们对历史、艺术、人际关系或其他任何未呈现在自然历史或科学博物馆中的事物进行提问。 相较而言，一个更好的比喻可能是维基百科——它可以根据读者和编辑对某个主题的好奇心收集信息，并将其对外公布。 不过，维基百科是一种相对被动的知识存储设备，而对于优质的早教课程来说，人们既可以浏览、收听、使用、与之互动，还可以不断将其加以扩展。 如果我们把我们的设计资源全部组合一起，那么我们就可以为孩子们提供属于他们个人的维基百科——一个可以帮助他们解答疑问的地方。

附录：丛林动物课程单元的资源

以下为部分书目推荐，可供孩子大声朗读。

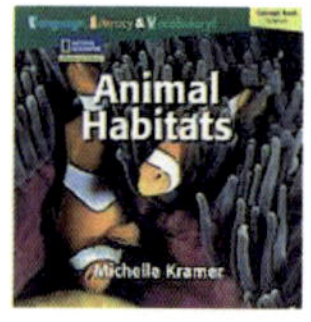

Michelle Kramer 所著《动物栖息地》

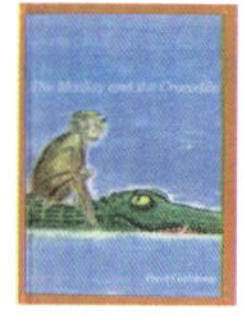

Paul Galdone 所著《猴子和鳄鱼的故事》

Bobbie Kalman 所著《生物系列》

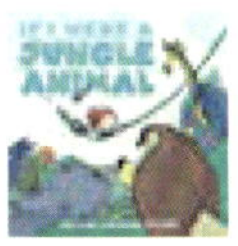
Amanda Ellery 所著《如果我是丛林动物》（精装本）

James Warhola 所编的《如果你高并且知道：丛林版》（精装本）

Giles Andreae 所著《想爱的狮子》（果园图画书）

Mwenye Hadithi 所著《热河马》（平装本）

识字活动的想法：

从一首已有的诗/歌开始，然后与全班一起为编写其他动物的版本，例如来自 https://www.pinterest.com/pin/277956608224083593 的斑马之歌。

工艺品和艺术活动的创意来源（并非所有这些都同样好，但它们为不同年龄的儿童提供了一系列的创意）：

https://www.kidssoup.com/craft-and-resource/deep-in-the-jungle-preschool-lesson-plans-and-activities

http://www.preschoolexpress.com/theme-station12/jungle.shtml

https://www.educatall.com/page/447/Jungle.html

歌曲和旋律：

https：//www. youtube. com/watch？ v=NNELmTbw9yM

运动活动：

https：//www. youtube. com/watch？ v=GoSq-yZcJ-4

参考文献

Chouinard, M. (2007). Children's questions: A mechanism for cognitive development. Monographs of the Society for Research in Child Development, Serial No. 286, Vol. 72, No. 1.

Frede, E. & Barnett, S. (1992). Developmentally appropriate public school preschool: A study of implementation of the high/scope curriculum and its effects on disadvantaged children's skills at first grade. Early Childhood Research Quarterly, 7, 483-499.

https://www. researchgate. net/profile/Lawrence _ Schweinhart/publication/234577267_Why_Curriculum_Matters_in_Early_Childhood_Education/links/00b7d539f27f8d25cf000000. pdf.

Schweinhart, L. & Weikart, D. (1998). Why curriculum matters in early childhood education. Educational Leadership, 57-60.

6. 幼儿读物选择：不同形式、不同互动方式

凯瑟琳·E·斯诺

哈佛大学

每个家长及早教工作者都会反复听到的一个建议是：应该多花点时间与孩子一起读书。人们之所以如此推崇亲子共读，是因为有大量研究证明，这种方法能够促进儿童多方面的发展（参见 Mol, Bus, de Jong & Smeets, 2006），并且还能让孩子接触到与文化相关的故事，从而让他们开始思考有关道德困境和人际冲突的话题（Dowdall，Melendez-Torres，Murray，Gardner，Hartford & Cooper，2019）。当然，亲子共读还能鼓励孩子分享及讨论书中有趣的描述，从而使这项活动具有一定的社会价值和认知价值。

与幼儿共读绘本这样的建议虽然相当普遍，但尚未充分引发人们对很多问题的深度思考：1）大人与孩子共读绘本时，应当扮演什么角色？2）共读绘本的积极作用是否对于各种类型的书本都是一样的？3）大人的角色应该如何随着绘本类型的不同而转变？

大人的角色

首先，我们必须明确一点：在不同的文化及社会阶层中，大人应该如何与孩子一起读书或玩耍的定义是截然不同的。例如：在日本，人们往往建议家长不要采取任何行动，而是让孩子自己去享受读书的过程。这是因为人们认为与孩子一起读书，或是在读书时与孩子讨论书本内容会限制他们的想象力。当然，这种观点并非是基于确凿的证据，而是源于一种对当地人十分重要的文化理念，即给予孩子充分的自由，并重视他们的创造力与想象力。

不过，显而易见的是，如果想要通过阅读来提升孩子的语言、认知及社会能力，大人则需要扮演更加积极的角色，并加强与孩子的互动(Wasik, Bond & Hindman, 2006)。美国儿童早期教育所推崇的一种阅读方法叫作“对话式阅读”，这个观点是由 Russ Whitehurst 第一个提出的(Whitehurst, 2002; Lonigan & Whitehurst, 1998)。据研究，家长、图书管理员以及儿童早期教育者都可以十分轻松地掌握这套阅读技巧，同时“对话式阅读”能够有效提高儿童的语言能力。“对话式阅读”指的是在第一次为孩子讲故事或是读故事的时候，先看着图片通读全书，但在之后的阅读过程中，逐渐地让孩子参与进来——让他们去描述书中的插图，独立地把故事复述出来，以及鼓励他们对问题进行推理和评价（为什么大灰狼要把小猪的房子给吹倒呢？如果是你的话，面对大灰狼，你会做什么来保护自己呢？）这是大多数美国儿童早期教育工作者会运用到的方法，因此我们可以把它默认作一项“不错的做法”。

不同种类的书

然而，“对话式阅读”方法并不适用于所有的书籍。设想一下我们和年龄最小的孩子会一起阅读哪些书籍——字母书和数字书。诚然，我们的目标是教会孩子认识字母、学会数数，但如果让他们围绕这些书做推理、做评价，这就讲不通了。“为什么 A 代表苹果？”可不是一个 3 岁孩子能回答得了的问题！

同样地，那些以押韵或是无厘头为主的书籍也不适合让孩子去推理或评价。例如，Seuss 博士所写的 *Hop on Pop* 以及 *Green eggs and ham*，虽然读起来很有趣，但既没有太多的故事性可以探索，也没有人物动机可以深究。阅读这类书籍的标准方法是让孩子不断地去熟悉韵律。最终，许多孩子的确能把整篇文章都背下来，但这并不能算作是“对话式阅读”的技巧起了作用，因为标准的“对话式阅读”所塑造的是理解的过程而不是认字的过程。

在为儿童挑选读物的时候，我们通常都会默认选择故事书。尽管大多数适合幼儿阅读的书籍都是叙事性的，一些研究学者表示，还需要为孩子提供一系列科学知识类、纪实的、非叙事性的书籍（如 Duke，2004），因为这种书籍可以更有效地帮助儿童掌握背景知识，而且有些儿童可能相比叙事类的也更喜欢这类书籍。显然，科学知识类书籍的阅读方式与故事书的阅读方式不尽相同。对于故事书来说，人们可以去解读书中人物的行为、情感。而“对话式阅读”的有些理念是与之相关的，比如说，最重要的一个就是儿童应该积极参与信息处理的过程。不过，有些其他理念可能一点都不适用。

选择可供讨论的书籍

简单来说，“对话式阅读”的核心思想是：在与孩子们共读绘本的时候，应该更多地让他们去表达自己的想法，而不只是聆听。儿童是通过不断地交流来学习如何说话的——这个观点相当关键，而

“对话式阅读”便是最好的例证。在某些场合下，大人们认为孩子只需要听就行了，而“对话式阅读”的技巧确保了孩子能够拥有表达的机会。

如果提高孩子们的语言能力是阅读的主要目的，那么自然地，成人会考虑挑选能够供孩子们（至少 3 岁及以上）讨论的书籍。有一些书让孩子听大人讲就已经很不错了，但还有一些书需要分成很多小片段，并且详细地进行讨论。儿童早期教育的课堂正需要这种可以让孩子们聚在一起讨论很久的书籍，而课堂里的小组讨论能够为所有参与者拓宽视野，增长见识，无论大人还是小孩。

Todd Parr 所著的《和平小书》就是一本典型的可以引发儿童丰富讨论的绘本。这本书的插画对小孩子来讲也很容易画——他们可以去临摹或是在此基础上自由发挥。《和平小书》的每一页都会展现一个关于“和平”的例子供读者讨论，并且整本书在通过不同的维度对“和平”进行解读。“和平”可以是关心自己（和平就是小憩一会儿，或是想着你爱的人）。“和平”的定义或来源也可以是与他人的关联（“和平”是结交一个新朋友，“和平”是帮助你的邻居，“和平”是学习一门新语言）。“和平”还可以是对大自然的关心（“和平”让鱼儿在清澈的水中畅游，“和平”是种下一颗树）。“和平”还可以是接纳各种形式的多样性（“和平”是欣赏不同种类的音乐，“和平”是阅读所有不同类别的书籍，“和平”是穿不同风格的服饰）。本书中最有力的一个观点可能是，“和平”等同于社会正义（“和平”就是每个人都有披萨吃，“和平”就是每个人都有一个家）。以上只是一部分 Parr 在书中所提出的关于“和平”的定义。

这本书的精妙之处在于，其中关于“和平”的每一种说法都给读者留了讨论的余地（为什么给别人一个拥抱就算是“和平”？听一听别人的音乐与“和平”有什么关系呢？）。书中所提及的许多观点不仅可以给三四岁的孩子讨论，还可以给大人讨论。例如，作者还提出了一个出乎众人意料的观点——“‘和平’就是保持街道干净”。这个观点引发了许多不同的见解：肮脏的街道会导致混乱与争端吗？肮脏的街道是否表示社会中的个体并不重视与他人和平共处？肮脏的街道是否证明了这个社会无法维持和平的秩序？如果我们认同承担公民责任能够推动和平事业的发展，那么这无论是对于学校教育、法律法规抑或是社会政策的制定都有着深远的意义。这类话题既适用于幼儿园的孩子，也适用于政治学专业的研究生。在这两种语境当中，如果我们可以不断地去探索什么是“和平”，对我们所有人来说都将意义非凡。

结论

想要挑选一本非常适合与幼儿共同阅读的书籍取决于许多因素——儿童的年龄、儿童的兴趣，但同时还有活动的短期及长期目标。字母书可以帮助儿童达到初级的识字水平，童谣书可以帮助孩子培养语感并让他们觉得语言很有意思，故事书则能够帮他们去考虑他人的想法及感受，而科学知识类书籍能够为孩子们所感兴趣的话题提供背景资料。有些书以独到的眼光来点出人生中重要的话题，有些书则会涉及到社会中的争议性话题——通过阅读这些书籍，孩子们可以学会如何处理生活中的重大事件，以及如何深层次地去思考问题。

当然，如果要达成所有这些目标，那么大人在与孩子共读绘本的过程中必须确保他们能够积极地参与、充分地思考、踊跃地表达，而不仅仅是被动地听着。因此，我们在选择和孩子一起朗读的书籍时，要重点考虑该书是否具有讨论的空间。与孩子共读书籍可以为他们提供一个培养语言能力（其中包括叙述能力）（Lever & Senechal，2011）、建立理解能力（Dowdall 等，2019 年），及拓展词汇量及知识面的机会（Smith & Dickinson，1994；Snow，2017）。在共同阅读的过程中，孩子们的积极性、全情投入对于产生上述积极效果至关重要（Kang，Kim & Pan，2004），与此同时，书本对于促进成人表述的质量及语言的多样性，也有着十分关键的作用（Massey，Pence，Justice & Bowles，2008）。与孩子们共读绘本的潜在积极影响可以说是巨大的，不过只有当孩子本身的状态、读书的方式、书本的质量，及大人与孩子之间的互动都达到最佳水准，才可以达到这种积极效果。

参考文献

Dickinson，D.，& Smith，M.（1994）. Long-term effects of preschool teachers' book readings on low-income children's vocabulary and story comprehension. Reading Research Quarterly，29，104 - 122. doi：10.2307/747807.

Dowdall，N.，Melendez-Torres，G. J.，Murray，L.，Gardner，F.，Hartford，L. & Cooper，P. J.（2019）. Shared picture book reading interventions for child language development：A systematic review and meta-analysis. Child Development，xxx 2019，Volume 00，pages 1 - 17. https：//doi. org/10.1111/cdev. 13225.

Duke，N. K.（2004）. The case for informational text. Educational Leadership，61，40 - 44.

Kang，J.，Kim，Y. -S.，& Pan，B.（2009）. Five-year-olds' book talk and story telling：contributions of mother-child joint bookreading. First Language，29，243 - 265. https：//doi. org/10. 1177/0142723708101680.

Lever，R. & Senechal，M.（2011）. Discussing stories：On how a dialogic reading intervention improve kindergartners' oral narrative construction. Journal of Experimental Psychology，108，1 - 24. https：//doi-org. ezproxy-test. uio. no/10. 1016/j. jecp. 2010. 07. 002.

Lonigan，C. & Whitehurst，G.（1998）. Relative efficacy of parent and teacher involvement in a shared-reading intervention for preschool children from low-income backgrounds. Early Childhood Research Quarterly, 2, 263 - 290. https://doi-org.ezproxy-test.uio.no/10.1016/S0885-2006(99)80038-6.

Massey, S., Pence, K., Justice, L. & Bowles, R. (2008). Educators' Use of Cognitively Challenging Questions in Economically Disadvantaged Preschool Classroom Contexts. Early Education and Development, 19. https://doi.org/10.1080/10409280801964119.

Mol, S. E., Bus, A., De Jong, M., & Smeets, D. (2008). Added value of dialogic parent-child book readings: A meta-analysis. Early Education and Development, 19, 7 – 26.

Parr, T. The Peace Book.

Snow, C. (2017). The role of vocabulary in children's language learning: A fifty-year perspective. Infancia y Aprendizaje. http://dx.doi.org/10.1080/02103702.2016.1263449.

Wasik, B., Bond, M., & Hindman, A. (2006). The effects of a language and literacy intervention on Head Start children and teachers. Journal of Educational Psychology, 98, 63 – 74. doi: 10.1037/0022 – 0663.98.1.63.

Whitehurst, G. R. (2002). Dialogic reading: An effective way to read aloud with young children. https://www.readingrockets.org/article/dialogic-reading-effective-way-read-aloud-young-Mol, S. E., Bus, A., De Jong, M., & Smeets, D. (2008). Added value of dialogic parent-child book readings: A meta-analysis. Early Education and Development, 19, 7 – 26.

赵旭

赵旭博士，加拿大卡尔加里大学副教授及中国青少年心理健康研究主任。毕业于哈佛大学教育学院发展心理学专业。她长期关注的问题是在学业压力繁重的情况下，家长和学校如何保护儿童和青少年的心理健康。她的主要研究方向为：（1）儿童及青少年社会性及道德发展；（2）如何增强儿童和青少年跨文化沟通和社会交往能力。她的学术研究集中发表在《中国教育中的竞争力与同理心》。该书在2015年由纽约Palgrave Macmillan出版。

7. 双语教育的双文化问题

赵　旭

卡尔加里大学

中国的教育工作者及城市中产阶层的家长大多认同儿童早期双语教育（英汉）的意义(Feng, 2005)。人们期望双语教育能够结合中国悠久的文化传统及现代西方儿童发展和教育科学的精华，培养出有国际视野和跨文化能力的下一代。但是，正如同双语教育（通常为英西双语）在美国是一个很有争议的话题，中国双语教育的研究和实践也没有定论。双语教育有哪些好处？成本多大？什么是适合的教学理论及方法？对中国社会的政治和文化发展有哪些长期影响？这些都是学者不断地探讨与争论的问题(Gao & Wang, 2017; Gao & Ren, 2019)。然而，在这些探讨中，专家学者关注了一些必要又重要的问题，却忽略了其他同样必要和重要的问题。最受关注的热点问题包括最新大脑研究如何为在儿童发展关键时期引入第二语言提供科学证据，如何引用西方的几种双语教育模式，哪些教材和学习活动最能促进幼儿学习英语的兴趣等等。在这些讨论中，双语教育被当作一个类似于自然科学的领域来研究，似乎儿童是在一个无文化、无阶级、无性别的科学实验室中长大。 在这里，他们学习如何使用语言代码，身心发展均遵循西方科学找到的适用全人类的自然规律。 事实上，这种关于早教的观点早就受到了来自西方学术界内部的批评。 尤其是西方人类学家及文化心理学家，多年来一直在针对教育理论和实践不考虑儿童发展的社会文化背景和学习中的个体差异的问题提出批评（例如，Mallory & New，1994；Rogoff，2003）。

目前，东西方关于双语教育研究的一个共同的问题是：一个关键的事实经常被忽略。 那就是双语教育不仅涉及两种语言体系，它还将两个甚至多个文化世界聚合在一起。 这些文化世界可能有着不同甚至是截然相反的教育传统、交流方式、人际交往准则、社会价值及关于儿童如何学习的理念。 在教学实践中，东方的双语早教项目往往以西方的早教理论及课程模式作为范例，却忽视了理论与实践之间的差距，很少考虑西方的课程安排与中国家长的教育目标之间存在的文化脱节。 经常等到冲突发生了，教育工作者才会察觉到问题的存在。 其他亚洲社会同样存在这样不加判断地采用西方早教理论及模式的现象（Lee & Tseng，2010）。 但是除了及少数的文献（例如，Cheng，2012；Johnston & Wong，2002；Lee & Tseng，2008），很少有实证研究关注双语教育中的跨文化的问题。

双语教育本质上就是一个跨文化交流的过程。 目前被西方学术界广为接受的一个观点即是从社会文化的角度讨论语言学习的目的。 这一学派的学者，以哈佛大学教授凯瑟琳·斯诺为代表，认为对一门语言的学习过程和结果的评估都不应该以学习者对语言本身的掌握程度作为衡量标准，而应该考虑学习者在应用该语言和他人沟通时，是否能够有效地达到沟通目的，同时表达方式是否符合该语言的社会规范(Snow, 1992)。对于英语学习者来说，我们不应该把重点放在孩子们是否在学“标准的”英语，而是要关注他们在与以英语为母语的人交流时，是否可以有效地、恰当地表达自己，来实现沟通的目的。这意味着，为了培养儿童在跨语言、跨文化的背景下进行有效沟通的能力，好的双语教育一定为孩子提供与英语为母语者各种场景下的交流互动的机会。同时，双语教育需要引导孩子去理解和领悟不同文化的深层差异，包括不同社会背景的人如何与他人互动和沟通。只有这样，双语学习的孩子才会掌握一个最重要的能力，那就是在与人沟通时，根据对方的文化背景和对话的具体的情况，变换自己的沟通方式，达到有效沟通的目的。

以中国的双语学校为例，孩子们需要分别和母语为中文的老师以及母语为英文的老师沟通。在这些过程中，他们需要适应不同的文化环境，包括适应学校和家庭环境的不同。因此，中国和其他亚洲国家的双语教育实践需要建立在对东西方相遇问题的系统了解上，尤其是双语教育中东方文化和西方文化碰撞融合的问题。这其中包括学校和家庭之间的关系，以及学校和家庭所处的社会环境、经济及政治因素对学校和家庭的巨大影响。但是目前，还没有文章系统地讨论双语教育中的跨文化问题。由于漫长的历史原因，西方英语国家与中国社会存在着巨大的文化鸿沟。在今天的中国社会，也同时并存着不同甚至是互相矛盾的教育理念及做法，家长和教师迫切地需要相关的信息及指导。因此梳理和解决这些双文化的问题对于中国的双语教育十分重要和迫切。这不仅需要哲学和社会学层面的探讨来明确中国社会和中国教育的未来方向，同时也需要更多的实证研究来支持不同的论点。

在这篇文章中，我会根据有限的文献提出跨文化研究的几个关键的领域，同时结合我自己对中国儿童跨文化发展的观察和研究，来分析几个主要的跨文化问题如何影响早期儿童双语教育，希望对中国和其他亚洲国家的双语早教实践有所启发。

由于双语教育领域本身没有很多关于跨文化问题的实证研究，我也会借鉴相关领域的研究成果，包括关于母语学习的理论、跨文化儿童心理学，以及中国及其他国家的家长观念研究。其中，跨文化儿童发展领域最基本的观点是，不同文化对于儿童发展有着不同的观念，包括教育的最终目的、儿童在社会中的地位，以及成年人与儿童互动和沟通的方式方面都存在巨大差异（Ochs & Schieffelin, 1984; van Kleeck, 1994）。研究早期儿童语言发展的学者 Van Kleeck（1994）和 Crago 和 Cole（1991）等指出，在儿童通过与成年人互动来学习语言的过程中，不同的文化传统之间存在着以下五个方面的文化差异。第一，参与和儿童互动的人以及话题不同；第二，对语言表达赋予的价值不同；第三，互动双方的相对地位不同；第四，关于儿童的主观意愿的假定不同；第五，关于如何促进儿童语言发展的观念不同。因此，在不同的文化中使用不同的沟通技巧、不同的教学方法是非常重要的（Crago, 1992; Schiffelin 以及 Ochs 1986）。这些文化差异不仅影响双语教育的过程，也会对儿童长期的发展有深远影响，尤其是在自我认同及社会认同方面的健康成长。因此，学者认为语言教学必须针对一个社会的文化和价值观、成年人和儿童互动方式，以及儿童发展的目的做相应调整（Ball, 2010; van Kleek, 1994）。

受以上文献启发，同时结合文化心理学的文献，在这里我会集中分析与中国双语教育直接相关的四个方面的文化差异。（1）自我观念的文化差异以及成年人儿童间互动的方式；（2）对语言表达的文化观念；（3）关于学习的文化观念；（4）关于个人意愿和情感表达以及相关的道德观念。用通俗的话说，这四个方面涉及到东西方文化在孩子应该成为什么样的人，孩子说话多好不好，孩子怎么样才能学好语言，以及孩子表达自我意愿是否应该鼓励等方面存在巨大文化差异。 尽管中国的社会经济发展带来了巨大的文化变迁，但是一方面，中国传统文化价值和观念对家庭关系和学校教育的影响仍然存在；另外一方面，中国的教育工作者和家长也需要反思哪些有别于西方文化的中国传统需要保存和发扬。 因此，这些跨文化差异值得认真探讨。

我在分析中会介绍相关的跨文化研究，举例指出在中国的双语教育的情况下，会出现哪些跨文化的具体问题。 我的讨论主要围绕三至六岁的儿童，在读或者申请读双语学校，既有以中文为母语的老师，也有以英文为母语的老师。 由于讨论中涉及儿童长期发展的问题，我也会加入对青少年的研究成果的介绍。 接下来，我首先介绍和分析以上提出的四个方面的跨文化问题。 之后，我会探讨为什么双语教育中需要加入文化教育，以及如何解决家庭和双语学校之间可能存在的沟通理解问题。

孩子应该成为什么样的人？成年人怎么对孩子讲话？

文化差异中十分关键的一点在于自我或自我观念构建的差异。其具体指的是个人在进行自我定义时所使用的方式——或独立自主，或与他人互为依存。 跨文化心理学家通常将西方文化与个人独立与自治联系在一起；而东方文化强调将个人的自我意识嵌入到社会关系当中(Markus & Kitayama，1991)。 因此，在成年人与孩子的互动中，东亚文化中的儿童的理想品质是听话、尊重和顺从，而西方文化则鼓励孩子从小就展现自我意识、主动性以及自信的特征(Chao，1994，2001；Johnston & Wong，2002)。

自我观念构成的文化差异对于人与人之间交流互动的方式有着

深远的影响。对双语孩子来说，讲中文的老师和家长和以英语为母语的老师会用非常不同的方式照顾他们，包括给他们指令的方式。比如，研究发现中国的家长在和两三岁的孩子互动的时候，往往使用更多带有指令性质的表达方式，直接告诉孩子要做什么或不要做什么。在中国的语境之中，父母的这种表达方式并不会被当作是不好的育儿方法，也不会与“专制”或是“支配欲强”这样的概念挂钩。但是在北美情况却相反(Helle & Mariner, 2001)。北美主流文化中，尽管孩子也要尊重成年人，但成年人在引导或管教孩子的时候，所用的语言听起来会是让孩子自己做出选择(Hoffman, 2001)。

不难理解，孩子学习如何与成年人和其他孩子沟通的过程会受到以上所说的文化差异的影响。当一个中国孩子习惯了成年人带有“指令性”的直接沟通方式，听到一个西方老师以提问题的方式给他的指令时，他会不明所以。讲英语的老师可能会以征求孩子个人意愿的方式问，“你想把你的鞋子放在鞋架上吗?”孩子的内心反应可能是:“我不知道。你想让我怎么做?”同样，当一个孩子适应了西方老师的教导及互动方式，但还没有理解沟通方式中所存在的文化差异的时候，他可能会认为中国老师及家长说话凶，不尊重他做为人的独立和自主。

孩子如何解读成年人的沟通方式取决于他们如何看待汉语和英语在中国社会的权力关系和相对的社会地位。尽管近些年中国已成为世界上的经济大国，但在中国社会还有一个普遍看法，即认为西方的家庭及学校教育比中国传统更“科学”。学习西方的教育理念和模式，会促进中国社会“现代化”的进程。这种观念会潜移默化影响孩子对于成年人沟通方式的理解判断，甚至影响他们与讲汉语的老师及家长之间的和谐关系。这些成年人和孩子之间的文化差异的不断累积，会扩大中国社会由于快速变革在家庭和社会中已经形成的文化隔阂。如何帮助双语儿童理解这些文化差异的产生，对中国儿童长期社会心理的健康发展以及中国家庭关系的和谐和社会的稳定都至关重要。

安静的孩子和话多的孩子

不同文化的社会在儿童教育以及日常生活中对语言表达有不同的重视程度。这些不同表现在至少三个方面：（a）对说话数量的认可；（b）说话在培养儿童技能方面起到的作用；（c）口头表达能力在儿童表现知识方面起到的作用（Van Kleeck，1994）。在北美主流文化中，儿童从出生到上学，成年人会一直鼓励他们通过发出声音或说话来表达自己的需求和想法。安静和害羞的孩子通常不被大人看好（Chen et. al. 2009）。在北美占主导地位的文化中，成年人会引导儿童自由频繁地和大人互动，随时展示他们与人沟通的技巧。但在中国和日本等东亚社会或在北美非主流文化群体中，情况并非如此。比如北美地区原住民的孩子往往被告知“要倾听不要表达”（Crago，1990）。同样，日本裔的移民父母常常认为安静的孩子才是好孩子（Coles，2003）。

传统的中国家庭也认为孩子不应该参与成年人的谈话（Johnston & Wong，2002）。大人说话的时候往往不许孩子发表意见。如果小孩在大人说话的时候插嘴，通常会被大人或温和或严厉地告知“小孩子别插话”。尽管西方教育观念已经影响了城市父母的想法和做法，许多中国父母仍然认为孩子不该养成在大人谈话时插话的习惯。为了帮助孩子改掉插话的习惯，很多家长会在网上的教育论坛寻求帮助。近年来，网上对这一问题的讨论明显受到了西方儿童发展和教育观念的影响。比如一些参与讨论的人强调儿童应被视为独立的个体，他们的自尊应该受到保护（如：Zhihu，2015）。中国的家长开始认为孩子话多并不是无礼的行为，而是好奇心的表达，孩子希望得到大人的关注，希望表达他们的想法。 因此家长应该鼓励孩子参与成年人的谈话，密切关注他们所说的话，并且认可他们想法的价值。 但是也有参与讨论的人认为，孩子随便打断大人谈话是不合适的行为。 除非需要成年人紧急处理的情况（如，孩子吐了或流鼻血了），否则孩子应该控制自己的冲动，培养自己的耐心，不去打断成年人的谈话。 他们为父母所提供的建议包括举手示意正在靠近的孩子，让他知道不应该打断大人的对话，或是先跟其他的人道歉，然后快速地与孩子沟通，提醒他/她不可打断大人的谈话。 尽管这些观点不同，却都越来越接近西方育儿书籍的常见的建议。

不喜欢孩子插嘴也不是中国或者东方社会的特有文化。 无论东方还是在西方，家长都希望孩子不要打断成年人的谈话。 正如那句英语谚语所说，“小孩儿可以出现，但不要出声”。 即使今天，一些传统西方家庭仍然这样教育孩子。 中国双语教育面临的挑战是：老师和家长是应该采纳西方的教育观念，重视儿童的语言表达，鼓励他们和在成年人互动中自由表达自己的想法；还是应该尊重中国传统的教育观念，教导孩子只听不说?

在过去20—30年中，中国城市家长的价值观和教育理念发生了很大的变化。 研究发现，之前中国家长普遍更喜欢害羞安静的孩子，现在却更希望自己的孩子性格外向和善于表达（Chen et al.，2009）。 我们2008年在上海做的研究也发现，中产阶级父母一致认为害羞是孩子的一个弱点，家长需要帮助孩子克服羞怯，使他们更善于和不同的人打交道（Zhao & Gao，2014）。 我们近年来还观察到，很多国内中产阶层3—6岁的孩子在成年人面前不再胆怯，反而会抓住机会，积极地展示自己的语言能力，与西方中产阶级家庭的孩子如出一辙。 这一现象说明了中国中产阶级的家长和私立幼儿园的老师鼓励甚至要求孩子积极地表达自己的观点，与同龄人竞争来展现他们的语言能力和知识水平。这个变化是在中国引入市场经济并且在教育领域鼓励竞争机制和培养学生竞争意识的大环境下产生的(Zhao, 2015; Zhao, Selman & Luke, 2018)。但是我们的研究也发现，中国家长关于培养孩子的观点常常自相矛盾，游走在中国传统价值观和市场经济价值观之间(Zhao & Gao, 2014)。因此，双语学校的孩子会面对如何处理不同价值观和社会规范的挑战，比如关于什么情况下孩子可以讲话，什么情况下应该安静和倾听，如何加入与成年人或者其他孩子的对话等等，都是双语教育中的双文化问题。

孩子怎样才能学好语言？是否应该用同样的方式学习中英文？

不同文化有不同的教育理念，包括儿童如何学习、如何为他们创造好的学习环境等等(如：Li, 2013)。现代西方教育强调儿童主要是通过玩儿和游戏学习。教学尽量以儿童的兴趣为中心。与此不同的是东方的传统大多以老师的教学目的为主导，通过反复练习来训练儿童的读写能力(Zhang & Pelletier, 2012)。西方的课程设计强调运动、玩耍、与人交往，并且为孩子创造充满关爱的学习环境(Epstein & Hohmann, 2012)。而东方的课程设计则是强调培养孩子勤劳自律的习惯以及对学习的尊重。在儿童语言学习的方面，北美中产阶层父母会有意识地让孩子参与“孩子主导的谈话”(van Kleech & Garpenter, 1980; Snow, 1977)。在这样的谈话中，成年人会把他们的语言调整到适合孩子的水平，以简单明了的方式对孩子说话，讨论孩子们能理解的具体事物。在日常生活的互动中，家长都会抓住机会和孩子进行以他们为主导的谈话，向他们解释正在发生的事情，并引导他们描述自己要做的事情(Health, 1989)。在这个过程中，教育者（老师与家长）的任务是鼓励孩子尽可能多地与他人沟通交流，鼓励孩子以平等的身份参与对话，了解孩子的语言发展水平，在和孩子交谈时简化自己的语言，向孩子提问以鼓励他们分享自己知道的事情，帮助孩子解释正在进行的活动，并对孩子的行为作出回应(Van Kleech, 1994)。直接教孩子怎么做的内容仅限于告诉他们如何使用像“请”和“谢谢”这样的礼貌用语。

这种西方的教育理念显然已经影响了北京上海等城市双语早教课程的设置，也影响了一些曾在海外学习或工作过的家长的育儿方式(Zhao, Selman & Luke, 2018)。但是在中国的家庭或是生活在西方国家的中国移民家庭中，传统教育观念仍然盛行。同样在加拿大，比较本地出生的欧洲裔妈妈，更多的华裔妈妈会认为孩子要学好语言必须有老师直接教，而不是通过玩耍学习知识。更多的华裔妈妈会利用图画书或闪视卡片来直接教孩子学习生词(Johnston & Wong, 2002)。重要的问题是：在双语教育中，如何将西方以儿童为中心、以游戏为基础的学习理念与中国传统以教为主的教育方法相结合，尤其是中国教育中通过直接授课和背诵经典的方法教孩子学习汉字的传统？更具体的问题是，由于儿童学习英语和汉语需要掌握不同的能力（比如学习用中文进行阅读和书写，首先需要对汉字进行记忆），如果放弃中国传统的教学方法，完全采用西方开发语言能力的方法，双语早教课程如何能帮助双语儿童从能够说汉语过渡到能够写汉语？另外一方面，如果继续采用传统的中文教学方法，如何在理论上及实践上协调这两种不同的教学方法？是否需要以及如何保证双语儿童今后在中文方面可以和只学中文的孩子一样达到小学入学水平？

回答上述问题需要更多的实证研究，来了解目前中国双语早教学校的具体情况。在北美的汉语语言教学，什么年龄开始教孩子拼音和汉字书写（比如幼儿园阶段还是一年级）以及如何教这些内容一直是有争议的问题（Everson，Chang，& Ross，2016）。但是学者一致认为，中国传统教育中要求孩子背诵、大声朗读课文、反复书写汉字的做法不仅仅是一种文化传统，还有着重要的教学意义。反复的背诵与书写可以帮助孩子开发识字能力，培养对汉语语言的感觉，帮助他们日后理解能力的发展（Leung & Ruan，2012）。通过书写训练，孩子们学会如何将汉字解构成独特的笔画及偏旁部首，然后将这些字符重新组合成为真正的汉字。这个能力不仅有助于提高孩子对汉字内部结构的认识，帮助他们理解汉字书写体系中的字形、字义和字音之间的联系，而且可能有助于他们对句子组合的长期记忆（Flores d'Arcais，1994；Guan，Liu，Chan，Ye，& Perfetti，2011）。因此，研究人员认为文本记忆以及手写汉字的练习，应该是汉语课程的重要部分，但是这些练习需要在有实际意义的沟通活动中进行（Everson，Chang，& Ross，2016）。

孩子的需求和选择

另外一个非常重要但常常被忽视的跨文化问题是：不同文化对于个人愿望和情感表达以及相关的道德观如何影响儿童语言和心理发展。在北美中产阶层文化中，成年人经常有意识地帮助儿童用语言表达他们的意愿和情感，借此扩大孩子的词汇量（Van Kleeck，1994；Snow，1977）。这样做的理论根据是，儿童从出生起就已经具有愿望和目标，因此成年人需要帮助他们了解自己内心的状态。因此，在北美社会的主导文化中，成年人对儿童的"社会化"教育过程通常包括鼓励儿童清楚地表达自己的需求，并根据自己的需求和愿望做出决定。早教课程的设计也以儿童作为中心，遵循儿童的兴趣，培养他们的独立性、创造力以及自我管理的能力。

在中国，传统上成年人不太会像西方人那样关注儿童的愿望和他们对愿望的语言表达。和日本早期的研究发现相同的是(Caudill & Weinstein, 1969)，中国大人在照料孩子的时候，经常会估计孩子有哪些需要（比如需要食物或水），直接满足他们的需要。这一过程中通常不需要和孩子有语言交流。关于新一代中国的老师和家长是否有意识引导以及如何引导孩子表达他们的愿望和情感，目前仍然没有实证研究系统地调查。关于这一代的中国父母和老师多大程度上为孩子提供在各个生活领域自己做决定的机会（比如选择食物、衣服，以及和教育有关的选择等），也同样缺乏广泛的实证研究。同样，实证研究也没有关注中国父母和老师在与儿童交谈时使用了哪些有关个人内在思维和情感状态的表达方式。但是可以肯定的是，不同于生活在单一文化世界的孩子直接接受他们周围的成人的说法和做法，生活在两种文化世界中的儿童将观察两种文化中成年人的言语和行为方式，并作出好与不好的判断。

社会心理学和道德观方面的文化差异也会影响语言的学习。传统上中国儿童社会化教育的首要任务是帮助他们学会控制自己欲望和情绪(Desjarlais, Eisenberg, Good, & Kleinman, 1995)。当一个孩子的愿望与他人的愿望发生冲突时，大人往往会鼓励他学会谦让。一个著名的例子是东汉时期（公元25—220年）的成语故事《孔融让梨》：孔融的父亲带了几个梨回家，四岁的孩子孔融把大的梨留给了自己的哥哥和弟弟，把最小的梨留给了自己。孔融谦让的美德成为两千年来儿童道德教育的典范。这个故事反映了儒家思想对于塑造品德的重视，特别是在儿童早期教育阶段，引导孩子发展人文主义精神，帮助他们学会与他人相处之道。这个传统和现代西方鼓励孩子表达自己的需要和坚持自己的利益受到保护的观念有着巨大的差异。如何处理两个文化的差异是双语儿童的父母和老师需要面对的一个很重要的问题。

儿童学习两种语言有时意味着他们要往返于两个不同的情感世界，甚至是在两者之间不知何去何从（Matsumoto，1994；Ozanska-Ponikwia，2019；Wierzbicka，1999；2004；2009）。一个人如何看待自己与周围的世界取决于他的母语或其他语言给他提供的词汇（Wierzbicka，2009）。对于中国父母来说，甚至很多城市里年轻一代的父母，用中文告诉孩子“我爱你”都会感觉不舒服。对于祖父母一代就更难。另外一个例子是个人对自我的情感。跨文化研究观察到日本人常常做自我批评，而与之相反的是美国人会尽量保持自我肯定的态度（Kitayama，Markus，Matsumoto，& Norasakkunkit，1997）。中国和日本的成年人同样都认为自我反省才能进步。反映在儿童教育方面，中国父母常常会把自己孩子的短处与同龄人的长处相比，以此激励孩子努力提高自己（Zhao，Selman & Luke，2018）。尽管这些教育理念及实践在中国已经发生了不同程度的改变，但仍然影响着中国家长对孩子的期望以及他们和孩子相处的方式。这些观念和做法与西方早教理论及课程设计之间存在着很大的矛盾，也需要引起双语学校的关注和重视。

这里需要强调的是，一定不能从本质化的角度去看待以上所谈到文化差异，即不能认为每一个中国人或西方人在任何历史时期和地理位置都符合我们谈到的东方西方的特点。文化差异需要放在历史背景下去考虑，通过实证研究进行确认。比如，从表面上看，儒家传统对自律和谦让的强调似乎与建立在强调个人成就、潜力和兴趣的西方早教理论相反；在现实生活中，这些价值观在两种文化体系中共存。培养儿童的社会意识，特别是他们从他人角度考虑问题的能力，是西方发展心理学的一个主要研究领域（如，Selman，2007），也是北美和欧洲国家学校课程的重要组成部分。事实上，与被家长和老师督促最大程度专注学习成绩的中国孩子相比，北美的孩子更加关心他们是否可以交到朋友以及如何维护友情。西方的父母和老师可能不会告诉孩子要像孔融一样谦让，但是他们会鼓励孩子对人友善、乐于助人、与其他孩子合作、在必要时控制自己的欲望、在朋友之间发生冲突时做出让步。培养这些价值观与社交能力是北美早教最重要的目的。

而在中国，过去40年来随着社会和经济体制的变化，学校和家庭也在提倡一些个人主义价值观（Zhao，2016）。某种程度上，尤其在城市的学校和家庭，鼓励孩子竞争、展现自我、表现个性已经取代了上文提到的谦虚、礼让、为他人牺牲自己的传统道德教育内容（Zhao，2015）。在城市，受过良好教育的中产阶层或中上阶层阶级的父母都很尊重孩子自己做决定的权利，也重视孩子的自尊心及情感的健康发展（例如，Zhao & Gao，2014；Zhao，Selman & Luke，2018）。但是，父母的教育观念和他们实际的行为仍然存在着差距和矛盾，尤其当孩子的学习成绩不符合父母的预期时，父母的处理方式经常和他们的教育观念背道而驰。

事实上，父母观念和行为之间的距离和冲突在所有社会中都存在，只是表现为不同的方式。比如，尽管美国教育强调自我表达、个人选择和个人自主性等价值，跨文化研究学者却认为，美国老师在课堂上对孩子言行的控制比日本学校程度要高（Hoffman，2000）。他们甚至认为美国学校和社会对自我表达的强调实际上无异于一种强制。孩子们没有选择不表达的自由，并且必须学会辨别在“自由”表达自我想法的时候哪些话是不能说的（Tobin et. al.，1989）。所以，如果中国双语早教课程采用西方早教理论和课程设计，老师应该在多大程度上控制孩子言行？他们是否可以像在传统中国学校一样，设计以老师为主导的教学活动，贯彻“直接教学法”，告诉孩子要自律和勤奋？ 这些问题即不是科学问题，也没有现成的答案。它们是文化和教育理念问题。 解决这些问题需要中国教育工作者和家长一起长期的讨论，也需要更加深入的实证研究来关注理论和实践之间的差距到底在哪里。

如何培养双语和双文化的孩子？

关于中国的双语教育，我的观点是早教项目应该将文化教育纳入其中，鼓励家长和老师就重要的文化议题展开讨论。 中国双语教育的目标不应局限于汉英语言及识字能力的教学，而是应该引导儿童去理解并欣赏两种文化的差异，培养他们从不同文化的角度考虑问题并且知道如何整合不同价值观的能力。 只有这样，他们才能学会如何面对文化间的冲突，从而形成一种连贯的双文化身份。 事实上，在西欧国家，文化教育或是文化遗产教育已成为一门重要的学校课程。 在这些国家，无论是领导人还是普通人都越来越对文化遗产的保护及推动表示关切，唯恐其被全球化的浪潮所吞噬（DICHE，2016）。 尽管中文是世界上最多人讲的语言，但是中国的文化遗产也同样面临全球化的威胁。 年轻一代的中国人倾向于崇尚西方文化，远离他们认为是过时的传统文化（Wong，2002）。

什么是文化教育？ 荷兰格罗宁根大学的 Barend van Heusden 认为，文化教育主要是指反思能力。 通过文化教育，孩子们学会反思自己和他人的文化，以及人类整体文化。 van Heusden 的观点是，这种自我反思的能力首先需要对不同的文化传统有一定的了解；其次，需要清楚地知道一个文化的独特之处，而且需要了解一个文化的独特之处和人类共同面对问题有什么样的关联，对全人类的进步有哪些贡献。 文化教育可以在不同科目中进行，比如：在时事、历史、艺术、哲学、科学和公民课程中都可以包括文化教育。 其目的是帮助儿童发展自我意识及文化自我意识，这些是儿童生活在一个多元文化世界所必备的能力。 对于早教阶段年龄小的孩子，可以通过各种艺术形式和讲故事的方式来激发孩子的想象力，培养他们自我反思的能力。

就以上观点，我还希望补充一点，即文化教育应该旨在减少文化、种族和性别方面的偏见，培养儿童对不同文化价值的兴趣、尊重与欣赏，无论是本国的不同文化，还是西方国家的不同传统。 最重要的是，对于不同文化传统和价值的尊重与欣赏一定要体现在双语早教课程的具体内容中，包括选择中国及西方社会的故事、艺术，以及文化习俗等。 其次，需要认真挑选教材，以消除有文化偏见的内容。 第三，早教工作人员也需要审视自己对中国和西方文化的看法，避免从本质化的角度看待文化差异，而是从历史的角度来看待中国和西方社会。 在与孩子或是彼此之间谈话的时候，老师要注意反省自己在潜移默化中给孩子们的影响是否反映了对不同文化、性别及种族的理解、尊重与欣赏。

最后，我想强调的是文化教育，尤其是有关中国文化和其他文化的共同的方面，对于帮助中国双语儿童成为有担当、有才干的全球公民是至关重要的。 我们的研究其中一项是了解在加拿大高中读书的中国学生面临哪些社会交往的障碍。 通过访谈，我们发现他们所面临的一个巨大的挑战就是他们对中国以外的社会，缺乏道德及政治价值观的了解(Zhao & Arthur, 2017)。 比如，一个 10 年级的女孩，虽然已经在加拿大生活了一年。 可仍然不敢和当地的学生交谈，总是紧张焦虑。 我们发现真正的原因不是她没有足够的英语单词或语法来表达自己，而是因为她不知道该对加拿大的同龄人说些什么。 她不知道加拿大学生看重什么，也不知道自己对事物的想法、判断和感受与她的加拿大同学有哪些相同和不同。 她总是担心自己说的话会让加拿大的同学感到无聊或受到冒犯。焦虑和自我怀疑让这个孩子不能正常发挥她的英语能力。我们的其他研究也发现，对于在北美的中学和大学的中国学生，文化冲击经常是因为他们不了解中国的道德及政治观念和其他社会到底有哪些相同和不同(Zhao, Yu & Zhang, 2019)。

海外中国学生的心理挣扎，尤其是他们的焦虑和自我怀疑，可能与前文所提到的亚洲文化中的自我批评倾向有关。然而，我们的研究也发现，来自其他国家的年轻人，如日本、中东和拉丁美洲国家的留学生，尽管他们的英语知识同样有限，却比中国学生更擅长与加拿大的同龄人打交道。我们发现，这些年轻人的信心建立在他们所持一个观念上，即“人都是这样的”。他们知道无论来自那个国家，尊重、友善和互相帮助是人类共同的价值(Zhao & Arthur, 2018)。相比之下，尽管儒家人文传统几千年来强调同样的价值，中国的学生并没有对他们在国内的人生经验和所学到的人生道理的普世性表现出同样的自信。这其中的问题是，中国孩子从小所接受到的教育缺失了什么？尤其是他们是否有机会讨论什么是中国文化所坚持的价值，这些价值和人类社会的历史和今天的发展有哪些联系，以及他们在中国和海外如何用这些价值观指导自己的言行。

减少家庭和学校之间的文化隔阂

除了以适合其年龄的方式向儿童进行文化教育外，让老师和家长参与有关文化的讨论也同样重要。西方的早教学者主张家长积极参与早教项目以及家庭识字活动，以促进早期学习与发展(Arnold, Zeljo, Doctoroff, & Ortiff, 2008; Powell, Son, File, & San Juan, 2010)。家长积极参与孩子的学习可以提高孩子的学业水平，改善孩子的行为表现，提升孩子的社交能力(Marcon, 1999; Senechal,

2006）。然而，正如上文所提及的双文化问题，双语早教项目与中国家庭之间存在着一些重要的文化隔阂，这对建立互相信任的合作关系造成了很大挑战。比如家长会担心在以游戏为基础、以儿童为中心的西方早教体系当中，学校是否给孩子提供足够的语言、数学、钢琴、绘画方面的训练。根据我们在北京的调研，双语学校家长最多的抱怨是“孩子在学校总是在玩儿，什么也学不到”。事实上，在西方国家的中国移民家长对孩子入读的本地学校有同样的抱怨（Guo，2012）。而另外一方面，双语早教的老师，尤其是来自西方国家的老师和管理人员，抱怨的恰恰是来自家长的压力，“中国家长给孩子太大压力，也给我们老师太大的压力”。这样的问题如何避免和解决？

中国父母对孩子教育的焦虑有着深刻的社会、文化、经济及历史渊源（Zhao，Selman & Luke，2018）。双语学校没有能力从根本上改变家长的理念和做法。然而，教育工作者可以通过让家长参与课程决策，与他们一同探讨影响双语教育进程及结果的重要文化差异，来改善这种情况。家长的积极参与有助于发展家庭与早教项目之间的合作关系，这对解决两者之间潜在的文化隔阂有着重要的意义。理想情况下，老师和家长通力合作，一同对儿童发展教育的理念与实践、中国教育传统与西方早教理论的异同、中西社会语言及文化的差异进行讨论和反思。家长和教育工作者之间的这种合作将为课程开发和实施提供文化及语言方面的帮助。家长的直接参与也将扩大在家庭环境中进行早期学习的机会。

早教项目该如何吸引家长参与和配合学校教育？在这里，我提出一些关于如何增强学校与家庭的联系的建议。这些建议来自于北美双语早教项目的相关推荐（Baker，2019）。而且是由研究证明至少在北美社会行之有效的方法。中国的教育工作者可以根据当地早教项目的情况，探索新的办法增强和家长的沟通。

1）为家长提供课程设计信息

建议在学年年初，老师就向家长发送大量关于早教项目及老师背景的信息。这会帮助家长建立对于学校的信心。此外，经家长同意，老师可以通过建立微信群，将所制作的班级联络单发送给每个家长，上面包括各家庭的姓名、照片以及联络方式。这有助于加强学生家庭之间的联系，在家长中间建立社区意识。

2）邀请家长给学校提供有助于文化及语言学习的材料

老师可以鼓励家长为学校提供教学素材，包括：孩子经常在家里使用的中文单词列表；孩子最喜欢读的书；戏剧排练中可以使用到的一些家用物品，比如空的食物盒、用来打扮的衣服、洋娃娃等。

3）定期组织家长会，鼓励自由交流想法

早教工作人员（老师和管理人员）可以定期邀请家长单独或分组和老师见面，来讨论课程和孩子的情况。双方还可以交流和深入探讨上文提到的跨文化问题。此外，早教工作人员可以欢迎家长随时来访，进行非正式的谈话。在谈话的过程中，早教工作人员努力地塑造一个轻松的环境，让家长可以自由地表达他们的观点。

4）给家长发学校新闻汇总

老师定期（如每周）撰写学校新闻汇总，与家庭分享有关课程和活动情况。这些学校新闻可以包括孩子参与课堂活动或玩耍时的照片。家长和老师可以在微信上交流问题或是对某事的看法。另外，也建议老师在课程开始几周后尝试和每个家长联系，看看他们是否有任何问题或顾虑。

5）把书和故事带回家

在北美的早教项目中，老师通常让孩子每天带回家一本孩子自己在学校图书馆选的书，供家长和孩子在家里一起读。老师还可以建议家长如何与孩子大声朗读书籍及如何与孩子一起讨论书本内容。就双语课程而言，书籍可以是英文或中文。为了让家长能够更多参与，老师也可以让学生把自己制作的图画或书带回家。另外鼓励家长与孩子一起阅读中文书籍（如果家长会说英文的话，可以读英文书籍）。

总结

双语儿童早期教育在中国还是刚刚起步。在这一阶段，从西方儿童心理学和教育学当中寻求指引与帮助似乎是一个捷径。但是中国教育工作者需要思考如何将东西方的教育理念、价值观和智慧加以结合。中国的双语教育一定要对东西方文化语言、价值观和教育实践的异同具备充分的了解。最好的做法是，中国教育工作者及家长通过长期不断的学习、讨论与实践共同做出双语课程的决定。同时，这个过程也需要国内外的教育学者及实证研究人员进行协助、记录及评估。在这个过程当中，教育者和家长需要反思一些似乎永恒存在，但每个时代必须重新回答的问题：中国社会建立在哪些基本价值之上？教育的终极目标是什么？教育要培养什么样的下一代？这些问题的背后是中国教育及社会所面临的一个至少可以追溯到 19 世纪末的问题——如何做中国人？

参考文献

Arnold, D. H., Zeljo, A., Doctoroff, G. L., & Ortiz, C. (2008). Parent involvement in preschool: Predictors and the relation of involvement to pre-literacy development. The School Psychology Review, 37(1), 74 - 90.

Ball, J. (2010). Enhancing learning of children from diverse language backgrounds: Mother tongue-based bilingual or multilingual education in early childhood and early primary school years. UNESCO: http://www.ecdip.org/docs/pdf/UNESCO%20Mother-tongue%20based%20EY%202010.pdf.

Caudill, W., & Weinstein, H. (1969). Maternal care and infant behavior in Japan and America. Psychiatry, 32, 12-43.

Chao, R. K. (1994). Beyond parental control and authoritarian parenting style: Understanding Chinese parenting through the cultural notion of training. ChildDevelopment, 65, 1111-1119.

Chao, R. K. (2001). Extending the research on the consequences of parenting style for Chinese Americans and European Americans. Child Development, 72, 1832-1843.

Chen, X., Wang, L., & Wang, Z. (2009). Shyness-sensitivity and social, school, and psychological adjustment in rural migrant and urban children in China. Child Development, 80, 1499-1513.

Cheng, L. (2012). English immersion schools in China: Evidence from students and teachers. Journal of Multilingual and Multicultural Development, 33(4), 379-391.

Coles, R. (2003). Children of crisis: Eskimos, Chicanos, Indians. New York: Hachette Book Group.

Crago, M. (1990a). Development of communicative competence in Inuit children: Implications for speech-language pathology. Journal of Childhood Communication Disorders, 13, 73-83.

Crago, M., & Cole, E. (1991). Using ethnography to bring children's communicative and cultural worlds into focus. In T. Gallagher (Ed.), Pragmatics of language: Clinical practice issues (pp. 99-131). San Diego: Singular.

Crago, M. (1992). Ethnography and language socialization: A cross-cultural perspective. Topics in Language Disorders, 12(3), 28-39.

DICHE (2016). Research agenda. http://www.diche-project.eu/documents/DICHE_research-agenda_v2016-03.05.pdf.

Epstein, A. S., & Hohmann, M. (2012). The High scope preschool curriculum. Ypsilanti, MI: High Scope Press.

Everson, M. E., Chang, K., & Ross, C. (2016). Developing initial literacy in Chinese. In S. C. Wang & J. K. Peyton (Eds.), CELIN Briefs Series. New York, NY: Asia Society.

Feng, A. (2005). Bilingualism for the minor or the major? An evaluative analysis of parallel conceptions in China. International Journal of Bilingual Education and Bilingualism 8(6), 529-551. doi: 10.1080/13670050508669067.

Flores d'Arcais, G. B. (1994). Order of strokes writing as a cue for retrieval in reading Chinese characters. European Journal of Cognitive Psychology, 6(4), 337 - 355.

Gao, X. & Wang, X. (2017). Bilingual education in the People's Republic of China. In O. García, A. M. Y. Lin & S. May (Eds.), Bilingual and multilingual education (pp. 219 - 231). New York: Springer.

Gao, X. & Ren, W. (2019) Controversies of bilingual education in China. International Journal of Bilingual Education and Bilingualism, 22(3), 267 - 273, DOI: 10.1080/13670050.2018.1550049.

Guan C. Q., Liu Y., Chan D. H. L., Ye F., & Perfetti, C. A. (2011). Writing strengthens orthography and alphabetic-coding strengthens phonology in learning to read Chinese. Journal of Educational Psychology, 103, 509 - 522.

Guo, Karen. (2012). Chinese immigrants in New Zealand early childhood settings: Perspectives and experiences. Early Childhood Folio, 16(1), 5 - 9.

Halle, T., & Mariner, C. (2001, April). Examining survey measures of the mother-child relationship across three racial/ethnic groups. Paper presented to the Society for Research in Child Development, Minneapolis, MN.

Heath, S. B. (1989). The learner as cultural member. In M. Rice & R. Schiefelbusch (Eds.), The teachability of language (pp. 333 - 350). Baltimore: Paul Brookes.

Johnston, J. R., & Wong, M. A. (2002). Cultural differences in beliefs and practices concerning talk to children. Journal of Speech, Language, and Hearing Research, 45(5), 916 - 26.

Lee, I. F. & Tseng, C. L. (2008) Cultural conflicts of the child centered approach to early childhood education in Taiwan. Early Years, 28(2), 183 - 196, DOI: 10.1080/09575140802163600.

Li, J. (2013). Cultural foundations of learning: East and West. New York: Cambridge University Press.

Mallory, B. L. & New, R. S. (Eds.) (1994). Diversity and Developmentally Appropriate Practices: Challenges for Early Childhood Education. New York, NY: Teachers College Press.

Marcon, R. A. (1999). Positive relationships between parent school involvement and public school inner-city preschoolers' development and academic performance. School Psychology Review, 28, 395 - 412.

Markus, H. R. & Kitayama, S. (1991). Culture and the self: Implications for cognition, emotion, and motivation. Psychological Review, 98(2), 224 - 253.

Matsumoto, D. (1994). Culture and Emotion. In L. Adler & U. Gielen (Eds.), Current perspectives in cross-cultural psychology, New York: Praeger.

Kitayama, S., Markus, H. R., Matsumoto, H., & Norasakkunkit, V. (1997).

Individual and collective processes in the construction of the self: Self-enhancement in the United States and self-criticism in Japan. Journal of Personality and Social Psychology, 72(6),1245 - 1267. http://dx.doi.org/10.1037/0022-3514.72.6.1245.

Katarzyna Ożańska-Ponikwia (2019). Expression and perception of emotions by Polish — English bilinguals I love you vs. Kocham Cię. International Journal of Bilingual Education and Bilingualism, 22(4),493 - 504. https://doi.org/10.1080/13670050.2016.1270893.

Ochs, E. & Schieffelin, B. (1984). Language acquisition and socialization: Three developmental stories and their implications. In R. Shweder & R. LeVine (Eds.), Culture theory: Essays on mind, self, and emotion (pp. 276 - 320). Cambridge: Cambridge University Press.

Powell, D. R., Son, S., File, N., & San Juan, R. R. (2010). Parent-school relationships and children's academic and social outcomes in public school pre-kindergarten. Journal of School Psychology, 48(4),269 - 292.

Rogoff, B. (2003). The cultural nation of human development. New York: Oxford University Press.

Ruan, J. & Leung, C. B. (Eds.) (2012). Perspectives on teaching and learning English Literacy in China. New York: Springer.

Schieffelin, B., & Ochs, E. (1986). Language socialization. Annual Review of Anthropology, 15, 163 - 191.

Selman, R. L. (2007). The promotion of social awareness: Powerful lessons from the partnership of developmental theory and classroom practice. New York: Russell Sage.

Senechal, M. (2006). The effect of family literacy interventions on children's acquisition of reading. From kindergarten to grade 3. A meta-analytic review. Washington DC National Institute for Literacy.

Snow, C. (1977). The development of conversation between mothers and babies. Journal of Child Language, 4, 1 - 22.

Snow, C. (1992). Perspectives on second-language development: Implications for bilingual education. Educational Researcher, 21(2),16 - 19.

Tobin, J. J., Wu, D. Y. H. & Davidson, D. H. (1989). Preschool in Three Cultures: Japan, China and the United States. New Haven, Conn.: Yale University Press.

van Kleeck, A., & Carpenter, R. (1980). Effects of children's language comprehension level on adults' child directed talk. Journal of Speech and Hearing Research, 23, 546 - 569.

van Kleeck, A. (1994). Potential cultural bias in training parents as conversational partners with their children who have delays in language development. American Journal of Speech-Language Pathology, 3, 67 – 78.

Wierzbicka, A. (1999). Emotions across languages and cultures: Diversity and universals. Cambridge: Cambridge University Press.

Wierzbicka, A. (2004). Bilingual lives, bilingual experience. Journal of Multilingual and Multicultural Development 25(2&3),94 – 104.

Wierzbicka, A. (2009). Language and metalanguage: Key issues in emotion research. Emotion Review 1(1),3 – 14.

Wong, Q. E. (2002). China's search for a national history. In Q. Edward Wong & George G. Iggers (Eds.), Turning points in historiography: Cross-cultural perspective. Rochester, NY: The University of Rochester Press.

Zhao, X., & Gao, M. (2014). "No time for friendship": Shanghai mothers' views of adult and adolescent friendships. Journal of Adolescent Research, 29 (5),587 – 615. DOI: 10.1177/0743558413520225.

Zhao, X. (2015). Competition and compassion in Chinese secondary education. New York: Palgrave MacMillan.

Zhao, X. (2016). Educating competitive students for a competitive nation: How and why the Chinese discourse of competition in education has rapidly changed within three decades? Berkeley Review of Education, 6(1),5 – 28.

Zhao, X. & Arthur, N. (March, 2017). Social anxiety in adolescent newcomers in Canadian schools: A research-based intercultural relationship intervention. Poster presentation at the 49th Banff International Conference on Behavioural Science, Banff, AB.

Zhao, X. & Arthur, N. (2018, October). Intercultural Relationships between Adolescent International Students and Local Students in High Schools. Paper presentation at the International Metropolis Conference, Sydney, Australia.

Zhao, X., Selman, R. L., & Luke, A. (2018). Academic competition and parental practice: Habitus and change. In M. Mu, K. Dooley, & A. Luke (Eds.), Bourdieu and Chinese Education (pp. 144 – 174). NY: Routledge.

Zhao, X., Yu, E., & Zhang, S. (2019). Intercultural competence in higher education: A normative anchor, a developmental perspective, and a discursive approach. Journal of Educational Thought, 51(3). 261 – 280.

Zhang, J., & Pelletier, J. (2012). Cultural differences: An international perspective on early childhood education. Frontiers of Education in China,7(1),1 – 4.

Zhihu (2015). Is it correct to say, "Adults are talking. Kids should not jump in"? https://www.zhihu.com/question/31384603.

8. 如何培养正直、快乐和成功的孩子?

赵　旭

卡尔加里大学

几千年来，在传统儒家文化的熏陶之下，教孩子做人一直是华人社会教育的目标。 学习做人意味着学会与人打交道、了解和遵守行为的道德原则，以及培养高尚的艺术修养。 当代中国教育提出要培养孩子竞争意识，同时进行素质教育，希望中国的孩子能德智体全面发展，又能成功应对全球范围的日益激烈的考试和职业竞争(Zhao, Selman & Luke, 2018)。 可是“素质”的含义是什么? 哪些品质会帮助孩子成功? 哪些成功能保证孩子今后成为一个健康和快乐的人? 这些问题对于双语（中英）教育的学生家长和老师来说尤为复杂。 双语学校的孩子除了学习语言，家长和老师还往往希望培养他们具有跨国生活和工作的能力，即成为见多识广的“国际人”。语言塑造人的思维方式。 双语教育不仅意味着孩子接触两种不同的语言体系，更意味着他们要学习用不同的方式去做事和做人。 很显然，双语教育不能单靠传统教育理念作为指导，同时中国家长和老师面临的挑战也不是可以通过研究来获得正确答案的自然科学问题。更多情况下，他们面对的问题产生于当今中国社会复杂的社会和文化环境。这些问题往往前所未有，而且具有“中国特色”。答案需要由中国的学者、老师和家长在不断学习探索中寻找。这一过程既需要尊重中国传统教育的经验，也需要从西方儿童发展和教育理论中获得启发，同时在理论和实践中需要反复尝试和跟踪研究。如果说教育本身就是学习的过程，中国当前的教育，尤其是双语教育的发展，有赖于学者、老师和家长做“贯通古今”、“东西结合”、同时跨越多学科的探索和学习。

在这篇文章中，我希望能够为这一探索过程做一点有限的贡献。我将从儿童发展和文化心理学的角度，探讨中国儿童早期教育需要加强的几个方面。我主要讨论中国的学校和家庭教育需要强调哪些品质和技能的培养，来帮助孩子在社会交往、道德和职业发展方面全面成长，以便今后在国内和国外都可以成功地适应和生活。在下结论之前，我首先简短介绍20世纪70年代末以来，中国儿童和青少年在西方媒体报道中的不同形象，通过这个例子来讨论为什么儒家所强调的道德教育应继续作为教育的首要目标。之后我将介绍两个西方发展心理学的理论。这两个理论分别描述儿童，至少是在西方社会长大的儿童，是如何发展他们的社交能力及道德推理能力的。我会简单讨论这两个理论对于中国教育实践的意义。接下来我会讨论在全球化与科技驱动的职场中，哪些能力会有助于个人的事业成功。最后，我会介绍一下我们近年来的研究成果，来强调中国教育需要关注及保护儿童的长期健康发展。

中国儿童：从“乖孩子”到“蝇王”

从20世纪70年代末到现在，中国的下一代在北美的媒体及学术文献中的形象发生了很大的变化。1981 年,《纽约时报》一篇题为《中国如何培养乖孩子》的文章将中国幼儿园里的孩子描述为“沉稳、安静、听话,老师让做什么马上就做”(Butterfield, 1981)。他们当时的观察是,中国孩子很少像美国孩子那样“喧哗吵闹、好斗自私”,他们也很少表现出美国儿童常见的焦虑和紧张。该报道将中国儿童的这些好的品质归功于中国的育儿传统,比如父母通常和孩子很亲密、父母去哪里都抱着孩子,而不是把孩子放在婴儿车里推着走、用布裹紧婴儿、孩子两三岁前都是和父母一起睡等等。他们还注意到,中国托儿所老师会按部就班地安排孩子的活动,中国的家长和幼儿园教师也都热情、善良和尽职尽责。但同时这篇文章对中国当时的早教也含蓄地提出一些批评。比如他们指出,相比上托儿所和幼儿园的孩子,在家里带大的中国孩子看上去就比较娇惯和活泼。一些中国家长也担心幼儿园严格的管理制度可能会使孩子过于老实或缺乏创造力。报告还表示:“中国的孩子从小被教育要乖,结果是他们成年后会缺乏个性,凡事追求和他人一样,顺从权威。”

有趣的是,当越来越多北美中层和中上阶层的父母正在学习中国传统的育儿方式来建立子女与父母之间的亲密关系的时候,中国家长却在努力学习西方所谓的“科学”育儿方法来培养孩子的“独立性”。比如对婴儿做“睡眠训练”或是让 4 个月大的婴儿在自己的房间睡觉等。另外,随着中国的经济改革与社会变化,城市家长的价值观也发生了转变,由原来喜欢安静、害羞、听话的孩子到现在更喜欢善于表达和性格外向的孩子(Chen, Wang & Wang, 2009)。家庭结构的变化也对父母育儿方式和孩子的长期发展产生了深远的影响。2013 年,《科学》杂志报道了一篇由澳大利亚蒙纳士大学的研究人员做的一项研究。他们的研究发现,与同一时期出生但有兄弟姐妹的儿童相比，中国独生子女的特点是：不相信他人、不值得信赖、不愿意冒险和竞争、悲观、责任心差”（Cameron，Erkal，Gangadharan & Meng，2013）。参加这项研究的 421 名男孩女孩都来自北京，是在 1979 年中国独生子女政策生效前后的八年里相继出生的。同样，我们在上海针对 13 至 16 岁的青少年的访谈研究也发现他们大多数不信任他人并且对生活感到无能为力。

同样，到北美学校学习的中国孩子，也面临孤独的问题。我们对在加拿大高中读书的中国小留学生的调研发现，他们中的很多人常常感到孤独，一方面很难和寄宿家庭建立亲密关系，另外一方面在学校和同伴交朋友也很困难。放学后，他们通常待在自己的房间里，做家庭作业，或者在网上和中国的朋友聊天，或是玩网络游戏。由于我的研究关注小留学生和移民的社会融合问题，经常收到来自加拿大各省的社会工作者的邮件。他们的主要工作是帮助刚来的国际学生适应北美的学校与寄宿家庭生活。他们和我联系是希望我能够帮助他们理解一些中国学生的“行为问题”，比如不遵守寄宿家庭的规定、拒绝分担家务、不愿和寄宿家庭成员交流等。对于这些问题，我的理解是很多冲突与矛盾其实是由于文化不同和沟通不畅而造成的误会。但同时，2015 年发生在美国加州的一个比较极端的案例，也让我思考今天的教育多大程度上忽视了中国传统对道德品行的强调。

在这起发生在洛杉矶的案件当中，来自中国的 18 岁女孩刘一燕（音译），在一个公园里被一群同样来自中国的同学残忍地折磨了 5 个小时。他们都是在美国高中读书，但父母留在中国的所谓的“空降孩子”。受害者遭受了严重的生理和心理伤害。其中三名袭击者因绑架和暴力袭击罪被判处要在加州监狱服刑 6 至 13 年。这场袭击的直接起因不过是晚餐付账问题。但为什么一件小事导致如此严重的后果？深层的心理学和社会学的因素是什么？美国媒体的报道中，通常归结为这是“空降孩子”缺乏父母关爱及监督，因强烈的孤独感而导致的行为问题。用其中一名袭击者的律师 Rayford Fountain 说道：“他们非常孤独，只好与中国圈子里的其他孩子混在一起。没有成人监督，遇事也没人帮助，所以最终会走向失控”(Chang，2016)。在最初的听证会上，加利福尼亚高级法院的法官 Thomas C. Falls 将此案与威廉 · 戈尔丁于 1954 年写的小说《蝇王》进行比较。该书讲述了一群英国的孩子被困在一个偏远无人居住的岛屿上，远离文明，没有成年人的监护，他们虽然建立了自己的社会来试图自治，最终还是沦为野蛮和残酷的结局。

显然，年轻的孩子来到一个新的国家，没有父母的监督，很可能会面临一系列社会、情感及行为方面的问题，比如恐惧、孤独、过度依赖同龄人，甚至吸毒。但是，在以上案件中，积极参加到持续的对他人的暴力攻击行为，却表明参与者缺乏道德意识和法律知识，而且同情心泯灭。毕竟，洛杉矶不是《蝇王》中远离文明、无人搭救的岛屿；那些袭击者（袭击发生时均为 18 岁或以上）也不像戈尔丁小说中所描述的十来岁的孩子。虽然这是个极端的案例，我们还是必须思考一个更为广泛的教育问题：学校和家庭应该如何从小就引导孩子能够对自己的行为独立地做出符合法律与道德的决定？哪些道德及伦理原则可以引导孩子在不同的社会环境中都做出付责任的决定，无论他们是生活在自己的国家，还是移居其他国家？为了回答这些问题，我们有必要了解一下现代西方心理学中关于儿童道德发展的主要论述。

儿童道德发展

儒家教育强调的如何做人问题，是西方心理学中道德发展及道德教育领域所关注的问题。 西奥多·罗斯福曾说过：“如果只培养聪明的头脑，却不培养道德意识，教育就是在为社会埋下危机。”道德教育意味着帮助孩子获得必要的能力和美德，以确保其今后可以过上美好的生活，并为所在社会作出贡献。 与儒家教育倡导的“仁”、“义”、“礼”、“智”、“信”相似，西方传统的品德教育也旨在培养孩子的价值观与道德观，以此引导他们的行为。 但问题是：谁来指定这些价值观和道德观？ 或者说，由谁来定义社会中所有成员都要努力遵循的道德标准？ 不同的文化倡导不同价值观。例如，西方社会往往将个人权利和自由置于集体利益至上；而传统的东方社会则经常强调集体利益高于个人利益，并以此作为道德判断和行为的指导原则(Shredder，1997)。 从实用哲学的角度出发，约翰·杜威（1916）曾表示道德理念应该随着社会需求的变化而改变。

中国的道德观念的确随着社会的变化发生了巨大的改变。 2003年，中国道德教育开始包括个人主义、消费主义、如何与人相处及人文价值观等内容(Lu & Gao，2004；Zhu & Liu，2004)。 可以想象，个体主义与集体主义两种价值观在中国社会的并存，对儿童甚至成年人的道德观造成了一定的矛盾和混乱。 研究发现，中国年轻人的道德标准来自不同的系统，他们随意引用不同甚至相互矛盾的道德观点来解释和支持他们做出的符合自己实际利益的决定(Yan，2009；Zhao & Selman，2019)。 今天的中国儿童，尤其是那些生活在东西方文化之间的留学生或移民的孩子，成长过程中面临的一项重要的任务是学会如何处理不同的甚至相互矛盾的道德原则和社会规范，以此来指导自己的行为。 最重要的是，他们需要知道，中国传统文化强调的人的尊严、责任及相互帮助等价值是有普世意义的。 而教育的重要目的是帮助孩子培养在不同的情况下运用这些基本的原则做出自己的道德判断的能力。这个能力具体包括什么？教育如何培养孩子养成从道德角度衡量事物以及从他人角度考虑问题的习惯？西方心理学中以劳伦斯·科尔伯格及罗伯特·L·塞尔曼的理论为代表的道德发展理论对我们思考这些问题会有所启发。

正义推理能力的发展

科尔伯格关于正义推理发展的理论对北美社会的道德教育有深远的影响。在这里，我主要介绍我认为对中国教育实践具有重要意义的部分理论。科尔伯格的道德发展理论体系是以伊曼努尔·康德的道德哲学以及让·皮亚杰的道德发展理论为基础的。对于康德来说，人的道德推理/思考应该建立在一个最基本、客观，而且不能妥协的原则之上，这个原则即是个人对生命、自由和财产所拥有的平等权力。根据皮亚杰的理论，认知发展涉及儿童对一些基本概念的理解表现出来的思维的结构性改变，这些基本概念包括时间、空间、因果关系等。在道德领域，皮亚杰认为儿童的道德推理/思考在早期是建立在对其行为的后果的考虑上（比如是否会受到惩罚），只有年龄较大的儿童才会考虑到他人内心的想法。科尔伯格（1981,1984）关于人的道德推理能力如何发展的理论将康德和皮亚杰的理论融合在一起。他认为关于道德的心理学研究应该建立在人们关于普世认可的原则的判断。这些原则包括人的福祉、尊重，以及正义。他关于正义推理能力的心理学研究采用的是“道德困境”的方法。研究者对道德困境提出问题，从被访人的关于这些道德困境的看法判读其正义推理发展的水平。他使用的一个最著名的道德困境是关于一个穷人是否可以为了给垂死的妻子治病去偷窃药物。科尔伯格用有关道德困境的问题采访了70多个男孩。

经过15年的研究，科尔伯格（1981,1984）认为人的道德判断有三个层次。 第一层次为“前社会习俗的道德观”。 这一层次大多为9 岁以下的儿童，他们对好坏的判断建立在成年人的标准上，以及对遵守或违反成年人的规则所带来的后果的考虑上。 或者说，道德权威不在他们自身，而是他们之外的人。 而且他们的道理推理是基于行为的具体后果。 第二层道德判断是“社会习俗道德观”。 在这一阶段，年长一些的孩子逐渐开始内化他们所尊敬的成年人的道德标准。 这时，他们有了内化的道德权威，却不会去质疑这些道德标准。 他们的推理是建立在所属群体或社会的准则之上。 第三层被称为“后社会习俗道德观”。 在这一层次，一个人的道德判断是基于自己选择的基本原则，如： 个人权利、公义等等。 科尔伯格强调，从一个层次向更高层次的过渡，并不是因为人对于社会规则的了解更为深入，而是由于个人在与周围环境互动时所经历的认知结构的变化。 科尔伯格的理论受到了一些哲学家及心理学家的挑战，因为他的理论是建立在对于白人和男性的研究结果上，而且他的理论将情感视为次于理性思考的因素（如： Noddings，2002）。 尽管如此，科尔伯格的理论对于中国的道德教育应该有所启发，尤其是关于儿童道德发展方向的考虑，以及年龄和社会环境如何影响道德发展的问题。

换位思考的能力

在心理学的社会交往领域，同样受皮亚杰影响的塞尔曼认为，儿童社会心理能力的发展包括三个方面的变化： 理解人际关系的逻辑的能力（知识），解决冲突和加强关系的能力（方法），与他人建立深刻联系的动力和能力（重视度）。 这三种能力的基础是一个核心能力，即从不同的角度考虑情况、协调不同社会观点的能力。 幼儿阶段，他人的观点就是自己的观点。 比如： 幼儿相信，如果他们喜欢冰淇淋，那么每个人都应该喜欢冰淇淋。 随着年龄的增长，孩子逐渐懂得区分、理解并最终协调不同的观点（Selman，2007）。 塞尔曼认为，换位思考作为核心能力及其他三种相关能力的发展受到先天条件（生理）和后天教育（家庭、学校和社会）的影响。 为了提高孩子从不同角度思考问题的能力，成年人可以就生活中的实例、故事或是一个假设的场景，与孩子谈谈自己或他人的看法及感受（详见塞尔曼在本卷中的文章）。

为什么道德教育应该做为教育的首要目标?

科尔伯格和塞尔曼的理论对社会道德发展理论的主要贡献在于他们分别对正义推理能力和换位思考能力的发展轨迹进行了阐述。从这个意义上说，他们的理论科学地描绘了在北美的社会文化背景下，儿童生理成熟与道德思维和社会心理之间联系。 也可以说，在称科尔伯格和塞尔曼为发展科学家之前，我们应该先称他们为哲学家。 他们的理论在价值观上并没有保持中立，而是建立在他们所笃信的普世原则之上——对于科尔伯格，该原则是正义；对于塞尔曼，则是对人需要换位思考和协调不同观点这一原则的坚持。 这里的问题是，他们理论多大程度上符合中国儿童社会道德发展的情况?

以上这个问题不只是发展学的问题，还是社会学、历史以及存在哲学的问题。 我们近年在中国进行的调研，也是通过一系列社会道德难题（如是否应该帮助被取笑的新同学等）通过个人访谈或焦点小组的形式收集数据。 我们发现不仅中国城乡青少年在道德判断与道德选择上存在巨大差异，即便是在城市当中，来自不同学校和不同家庭背景的青少年对同一社会或道德问题也有着不同的认识（Zhao，Haste，Selman，& Luan，2014；Zhao，2015；Zhao & Selman，

2019)。 一般来说，中国学生（8 年级）的道德选择往往基于人应该善良、有同理心和助人为乐的价值观上。 相比之下，年龄稍大的青少年（11 年级）更倾向于强调自我保护的重要性（例如，避免惹麻烦和被人误解等）。 和 8 年纪的学生相比，11 年级的学生对于公共事务（如污染和食品安全）的兴趣相对较少，帮助他人的意识也相对较弱。 他们最关注的问题是如何在学习竞争中取得优势，日后能够考上好大学，因为父母、老师每天都反复提醒他们这一点。 用他们自己的话说，这是他们所面临的“社会现实”（Zhao，2015）。 但是，社会现实是由社会制度和个人的价值体系及其对外界压力的评估、接受或抵制所共同构成的。 换句话说，社会现实是个人和全体共同创造的。 一个健康和谐的社会必须建立在对道德教育的重视上，而道德教育需要建立在帮助儿童青少年发展正义思考和换位思考能力的基础上。

如何培养成功的世界人？21 世纪需要的技能

除了希望孩子健康成长，父母最关注的无外乎如何能培养孩子今后在事业上成功所需要的能力。 这些能力包括什么呢？ 上世纪 80 年代的中国流传着一句所有儿童都熟悉的俗语：“学好数理化，走遍天下都不怕。”随着 20 世纪 90 年代技术的蓬勃发展，无论是在发达国家还是在发展中国家，STEM（科学、技术、工程和数学）教育在全球都备受重视。 人们认为 STEM 教育不仅对学生个人的成功至关重要，还对整个国家的发展起到了关键作用（如 NSTC，2018 年）。 在美国，尽管目前只在中学教育阶段强调 STEM 课程，但从低年级开始加强科学和数学教育的呼声也日益高涨（Swift & Watkins，2004）。

但是，即使在科技界内部，也有批评声音认为把 STEM 课程作为教育的中心是把问题过于简单化的做法。 STEM 教育尽管重要，却不是教育的全部。 21 世纪的教育及职场发展需要结合对科学技术的高水平认知和对人类需要、需求及行为的深刻理解(Hill，2019)。这一观点最近被谷歌公司（可以说是 STEM 领域的领军机构）的一项研究证实（Strauss，2017 年）。 在这项名为“氧气项目”的研究中，谷歌工作人员研究了公司自 1998 年成立以来的招聘、解雇和晋升过程，希望了解最成功的谷歌员工所具备的特点。 他们的结论令所有人震惊。 在谷歌最杰出员工所具备的八大重要特点中，STEM 能力排在最后。 现在谷歌在招聘中最看重的能力包括：

1. 做一个好教练的能力；
2. 善于沟通与倾听；
3. 对人的洞察力；
4. 同理心以及对同事的支持；
5. 批判性思维；
6. 解决问题能力；
7. 综合复杂想法从中得出结论的能力。

在接下来一项名为“亚里士多德计划”的研究中，谷歌研究人员调查了其最佳团队的特点。 他们的结论再一次令人吃惊。 最好和最富有成效的想法并非来自那些专业知识最强的团队，而是来自于那些具有多方面“软实力”的团队。 这些软实力包括：平等、慷慨、对他人想法好奇、同理心以及情商。 最重要的是，一个成功团队必须让每个成员都感到自信，敢于表达想法，勇于犯错，他们想法得到了倾听和尊重。 报道该研究的《华盛顿邮报》总结说：“在一个瞬息万变的世界里，使你成功的并不是什么火箭科学。 更有可能是社会、科学、人文和艺术。 后者不仅能让你适应职场，而且让你了解世界。”这些来自职场的研究对于教育意味着什么？ 老师和家长应该如何帮助中国的下一代了解世界?

“8—C 能力”

英国教育家肯·罗宾逊爵士在其著作《让学校重生》中总结了学校应努力培养儿童的八个英文以 C 开头的能力(Robinson & Aronica, 2015)。这些能力包括:好奇心、创造力、批判精神、沟通能力、协作能力、同情心、镇定沉着以及公民意识。罗宾逊爵士长期对现代教育体系提出强烈的批评,认为其过于机械化,过分强调顺服与趋同。他提出世界各地的学校都应该努力培养孩子这八种能力。我的看法是,在这些方面中国儿童的成长尤其需要加强。在过去的 15 年里,我在中国及北美地区对华裔的家长和儿童做的研究都表明,虽然中国教育目前面临种种问题,但是恰恰因为这些问题,家长和老师对这些品质的重视和坚持尤为重要。当老师和家长如果没有意识到开发这些能力的重要性,同时不断对孩子施加压力,让他们顺从大人的旨意(比较常见的做法是反复对孩子强调他们需要在标准化考试中表现得好),孩子会产生无聊、焦虑,甚至更严重的生理及精神健康的问题。下面,我简单介绍一下罗宾逊爵士对这八种能力的解释以及他关于课堂教学的建议。

1. 好奇心:提出问题并且探索世界如何运作的能力

在课堂上,老师需要鼓励孩子在课堂上提问,帮助他们参与讨论的话题,而不是一味要求孩子保持安静。

2. 创造力:产生新想法并将其付诸实践的能力

创造力来自于对艺术和科学的想象。老师需要尽可能让孩子们去探索,允许他们犯错,鼓励他们表达自己的想法,而不是急于纠正他们。

3. 批判精神：分析信息与观点，形成有理有据的论点及判断的能力

在课堂上，教师需要更多地引导儿童批判性地分析信息，而不是单纯地介绍新的信息。老师需要教导孩子如何来利用信息，如何将其正确地融入到自己的生活中，如何辨别是非。

4. 沟通能力：通过不同媒介与形式，清晰自信地表达思想和情感的能力

教师需要鼓励孩子，并为他们提供一个安全的环境来传达思想、表达情感。教师还需要为孩子们提供机会，让他们不仅可以以书面及口头的形式交流，还可以通过艺术、舞蹈和戏剧等进行交流。

5. 协作能力：建设性地与他人合作的能力

与其鼓励孩子们互相竞争，老师倒不如邀请所有孩子，以两个人或是小组的形式，一起学习、玩耍，共同解决问题。老师还可以引导孩子在活动当中分享自己想法、尊重并听取他人的意见、学习从他人的角度考虑问题。

6. 同情心：同情他人并付诸行动的能力

同情心植根于同理心，而同理心则是从他人观点考虑问题的能力。学校需要建立一种充满同情心的、让所有孩子都感觉自己被接受的校园文化。教师要让学生们懂得关注彼此的感受，同时了解哪些行为是霸凌和偏见。老师自己也应该给孩子做出榜样，让他们看到如何关心他人的感受，尤其是对不开心的孩子。

7. 镇定沉着：能够了解自己内在的感受，与自己建立和谐平衡的关系的能力

了解、接受并信任自己的判断的人才会镇定沉着。老师需要帮助孩子去探索自己的内心世界，与自己的想法和感受建立联系，鼓励他们接受和表达或者必要时控制自己的情绪。

8. 公民意识：积极地参与社会活动并为社会发展做贡献的能力

老师可以带领学生了解社会状况，帮助他们作为未来公民的责任与义务。

中国孩子还需要的另外二个 C

根据我对中国儿童及家长的研究，我认为在罗宾逊爵士的“八C”之上应该再强调另外两个英文以 C 开头的能力：即自主选择与自信的能力。在上文提到的研究中，谷歌研究人员将这两中能力视作“软实力”的一部分，认为其对于个人成功及团队合作来说都非常重要。但是，我们对中国儿童的研究表明，只有当儿童有能力做出自主选择，并且对自己的判断表示自信时，他们才可以实现罗宾逊爵士所提出的 8C 能力。我们的研究还发现，由于西方心理学和教育理念的影响，中国城市中上阶层的父母充分意识到他们需要把孩子当作是独立的个体，需要尊重孩子的意见和愿望（Zhao，Selman，& Luke，2018）。许多父母允许并鼓励孩子自己选择食物、衣服、玩具、书籍、学校，甚至将来的职业方向。同时，他们也会为孩子设定必要的界限并提供必需的指导。然而，还是有许多父母，认为孩子（甚至青少年）年纪太小，没有经验，因此没有能力自己做决定，父母要替他们做好所有计划，安排好所有事情。

父母的这种做法有几种解释。首先，传统的父母大多认为教育的首要任务是教孩子学会控制自己的欲望和情绪（Desjarlais，Eisenberg，Good，& Kleinman，1995）。中国的大人经常鼓励孩子去关注他人的需求，而不是表达孩子自己的愿望和喜好。另外，这一代的父母在成长的过程中，大部分都经历了中国经济发展水平较低阶段，物质资源远没有今天丰富。他们童年时大多没有条件选择衣服、玩具和书籍。在培养自己的孩子的时候，这一代父母会在物质上给孩子提供最好的条件，但是未必有意识地给孩子提供自己做决定和从错误中学习的机会。同时，除了承担工作和家庭的压力，很多父母因为担心孩子在应试教育体制中的学习成绩而处于焦虑状态，在这些情况下，许多家长没有时间、耐心，或者承担风险的条件来为孩子提供做各种选择的机会。在这些社会文化与经济的多重影响之下，许多三四十岁的中国父母不得不经历一个深刻而漫长的自我反省的过程，来了解他们自己以及他们父母一辈的育儿观念和做法。在我们的研究中，一些善于自我反思的家长告诉我们，他们发现自己在日常生活中缺乏做选择和决定的能力，由于不会做出选择，他们的冰箱和壁橱里常常装满不需要的食物和衣服。这些父母把这个问题归结于童年的时候他们父母没有给他们机会去表达自己的愿望，根据自己的需要做出选择，反而让他们怀疑自己对事物的判断。他们会有意识地给自己的孩子以选择的机会，鼓励他们对自己判断力的信心。

焦虑的父母还有可能通过另外一种方式来剥夺孩子对世界进行探索的机会、打击孩子信心、进而影响他们长期的心理健康。这种方式就是不断向孩子灌输一种我称之为简单化的生活逻辑。为了督促孩子努力学习，大人会反复地告诉孩子："如果你这次考试考不好，你就不能上一所好的初中。那你就考不上好大学，就找不到好工作，你一辈子就完了。"在这种逻辑下，孩子会害怕犯错，不敢承担风险，自然没有勇气去探索和发现自己的兴趣与潜力。短期之内，孩子可能因为害怕结果而努力实现父母和老师的要求；长此以往，哪怕成功考上名校的学生，也会面临焦虑和抑郁的风险，因为他们会觉得由大人写好脚本、按照父母和老师的期望活着的人生毫无乐趣。

结论

在我们考虑父母和老师应该做什么来培养善良、快乐和成功的孩子的这一问题的时候，我们也要考虑，为了孩子的健康成长，我们不应该做什么。英国著名哲学家、数学家、历史学家和诺贝尔奖获得者伯特兰·罗素认为教育往往削弱儿童的生命力。他认为由于在教育当中成人对儿童的权威性从某种程度上不可避免，成年人必须对孩子抱有一种彻底的敬畏态度。与其考虑如何去塑造孩子，成人应该在每个孩子身上感受到某种“神圣的、无法定义的、无限的、独特的、极其珍贵的”东西(Russell，1971)。罗素的这一教育理念与我们常见的教育方式形成鲜明的对照。我们在现代的教育制度里看到的是不同孩子被放在一个狭小的竞技场里，用同样的标准反复地比较，分出胜利者和失败者，再比较，再分类，直到每个孩子都变成伤痕累累的失败者。好的教育是关于如何帮助每个孩子成长成为他/她自己。孩子对失败的恐惧和焦虑从来不是通往幸福和成功的道路；个人的挫折感也就不会带来健康和谐的社会。教育不是让每个学生为了考试高分、大学的录取书、令人羡慕的高薪孤独地奋斗，在焦虑和绝望中挣扎。要培养善良、快乐和成功的孩子，教育应该继续以教孩子做人为首要目标，让学生和老师在平等自由的交谈中，学生在与彼此合作学习的过程中，发展10C的能力，了解自己、他人和世界。教育最终的目的是让孩子们发现自己的潜能，学会和他人建立深刻的关系，为社会做出自己独特的贡献。这样，他们才会经历人生种种起伏挫折，仍然充满生命的活力。

参考文献

Butterfield, F. (1981). https://www.nytimes.com/1981/01/05/style/how-china-raises-its-well-behaved-children.html.

Cameron, L., Erkal, N., Gangadharan, L., and Meng, X. (2013). Little Emperors: Behavioral Impacts of China's One-Child Policy. Science, 339 (6122), 953 - 957.

Chang, C. (2016). Sentenced to prison for assault, teenage 'parachute kids' deliver warning to adults in China. LA Times. February 17, 2016. https://www.latimes.com/local/lanow/la-me-ln-parachute-kids-sentencing-20160217-story.html.

Chen, X., Wang, L., & Wang, Z. (2009). Shyness-sensitivity and social, school, and psychological adjustment in rural migrant and urban children in China. Child Development, 80, 1499 - 1513.

Dewey, J. (1916). Democracy and education. New York: Dover Publications.

Desjarlais, R., Eisenberg, L., Good, B., & Kleinman, A. (1995). World mental health: Problems and priorities in low-income countries. New York, NY: Oxford University Press.

Hill, C. (2019). STEM Is Not Enough: Education for Success in the Post-Scientific Society.

Journal of Science Education and Technology, 28, 69. https://doi.org/10.1007/s10956-018-9745-1.

Kohlberg, L. (1981). The philosophy of moral development: moral stages and the idea of justice (1st ed.). San Francisco: Harper & Row.

Kohlberg, L. (1984). The psychology of moral development: the nature and validity of moral stages (1st ed.). San Francisco: Harper & Row.

Lu, J., & Gao, D. (2004). New directions in the moral education curriculum in Chinese primary schools. Journal of Moral Education, 33(4), 495 - 510.

National Science and Technology Council (NSTC) (2018). Chartering a course for success: America's strategy for STEM education.

https://www.whitehouse.gov/wp-content/uploads/2018/12/STEM-Education-Strategic-Plan-2018.pdf.

Noddings, N. (2002). Educating moral people. New York and London.: Teachers College, Columbia University.

Russell, B. (1971). Principles of Social Construction. New York, Routledge.

Swift, T. M., & Watkins, S. E. (2004). An engineering primer for outreach to K - 4 education. Journal of STEM Education: Innovations and Research, 5 (3/4), 67 - 76. http://www.greenframingham.org/stem/research/item2_engr_k4_outreach.pdf.

Roberson, K. & Aronica, L. (2015). Creative schools: The grassroots revolution that is transforming education. London, UK: Penguin.

Selman, R. L. (2007). The promotion of social awareness: Powerful lessons from the partnership of developmental theory and classroom practice. New York: Russell Sage.

Strauss, V. (2017). The surprising thing Google learned about its employees — and what it means for today's students. Washington Post, December 20, 2017. https://www.washingtonpost.com/news/answer-sheet/wp/2017/12/20/the-surprising-thing-google-learned-about-its-employees-and-what-it-means-for-todays-students/?utm_term=.d038a6160904.

Yan, Y. (2009), The Individualization of Chinese Society, vol. 77, Oxford: Berg.

Shweder, R. A., Much, N. C., Mahapatra, M., & Park, L. (1997). The "Big Three" of morality (autonomy, community, divinity) and the "Big Three" explanations of suffering. In A. Brandt, & P. Rozin (Eds.), Morality and Health, 119 - 172. New York: Routledge.

Yang, Y. (2016). The 'Lord of the Flies' bullying case that's sending three Chinese 'parachute kids' to Calif. Prison. Washington Post, February 18, 2016. https://www.washingtonpost.com/news/morning-mix/wp/2016/02/18/the-lord-of-the-flies-bullying-case-thats-sending-three-chinese-parachute-kids-to-calif-prison/?noredirect=on&utm_term=.690051115e52.

Zhao, X. (2015). Competition and compassion in Chinese secondary education. New York: Palgrave MacMillan.

Zhao, X., Haste, H., Selman, R. L., & Luan, Z. (2014). Compliant, cynical, or critical: Chinese adolescents' explanations of social problems and individual civic responsibility. Youth & Society, 49(8), 1123 - 1148. doi: 10.1177/0044118X14559504.

Zhao, X., Selman, R. L., & Luke, A. (2018). Academic competition and parental practice: Habitus and change. In M. Mu, K. Dooley, & A. Luke (Eds.), Bourdieu and Chinese Education (pp. 144 - 174). NY: Routledge.

Zhao, X., & Selman, R. L. (2019). Bystanders' responsibilities in a situation of teasing: A Dual Dynamic Analysis approach for understanding culture, context, and youth moral development. Qualitative Psychology.

Zhu, X., & Liu, C. (2004). Teacher training for moral education in China. Journal of Moral Education, 33(4), 481 - 494. doi: 10.1080/0305724042000315608.

周兢

华东师范大学学前与特殊教育学院副院长、教授；

华东师范大学 ESEC 儿童语言研究中心主任；

世界学前教育组织中国委员会主席；

教育部高等教育自学考试指导委员会教育专业委员；

高迪安&哈佛大学教授国际合作教育科研中心理事。

9. 对我国学前儿童的英语教育作定位思考

周 兢

华东师范大学

自20世纪90年代以来，我国幼儿英语教育的问题一直是幼教界关注的热点，迄今尚未达成共识。社会现实状况让我们看得到的是，无论学术界对此争论如何激烈，越来越多的父母要求幼儿园开设英语教学，越来越多的幼儿园在开设英语课，同时也有越来越多的业余英语培训班以各种诱人的广告词吸引着家长和孩子。这样的现实状况，要求我们的幼儿教育工作者予以真正的关注，并需要跟进真正的研究，简单的判断已经不能解决中国幼儿教育的这个新问题。

思考中国学前儿童英语学习热的问题，我们首先需要冷静地分析一下这样的现象产生的社会文化环境。这些年来，科学技术的飞速发展和改革开放程度的扩展加深，使得中国人的经济生活和社会文化生活都产生了巨大的变化。伴随着世界范围内经济全球化的趋势，多元文化的潮流正在推向经济迅速崛起的发展中国家。作为亚洲经济龙头的中国，已经成为引人注目的发展中的多元文化社会。因此，我们今天讨论中国学前儿童的英语教育问题，需要立足于变化了的中国社会环境作深入思考。

一

如我们所知，多元文化社会的一个鲜明特征，就是语言的多元化倾向。 因为在一个有着不同人群和不同文化信息存在的社会环境中，人们需要有不止一种的语言作为交流的手段，尤其需要能够用于全球性沟通的共同语言。 近年来，中国和亚洲一些国家地区，语言多元化的倾向越来越引人注目。 英语在中国和其他发展中多元文化社会的地位，其实就是这样应运而生并且不断地得到提高的。 从这样的角度看中国学前儿童英语学习现象，我们不难理解，这是中国社会发展变化的产物，也是由中国正在发展中的多元文化社会倾向所决定的。 从现在到未来的若干年，家长送幼儿去学英语，家长要求幼儿园开设英语教学，这样的现象恐怕具有不可逆的趋势，不会因我们的争议或者制令而消失。 值得中国的幼儿教育工作者认真思考的是，如何为中国文化环境中的学前儿童英语学习定位，如何指导我们的幼儿积极有效地学习英语，如何让孩子的英语学习不影响并对母语学习产生促进作用。

我们认为，中国的学前儿童英语学习应当有一个基本原则： **在学好汉语普通话的前提下学习英语**。

在一个多元文化的社会中，除了母语以外的任何语言都可能成为人们学习的第二语言，因此我们在这里讨论学前儿童学习英语，实际上也就有着讨论中国儿童早期第二语言学习的意义。 从语言研究的角度来看，这样的问题属于双语学习和双语教育的范畴。 研究告诉我们，学前阶段是人的母语的口头学习关键期，错过了这个关键期，人的语言发展会受到不可弥补的影响；而人的第二语言学习并不像第一语言学习那样具有特别的发展关键期（Snow，2002）。多年来，持续的儿童语言研究结果让我们了解到，学前儿童学习第二语言或者外语，除了语音之外，其他诸如语法、语义和语用方面的发展，不一定会比大年龄的儿童学英语更具有优势。与此同时，研究也告诉我们，第二语言学习会给人的发展带来一定的促进作用，比如人的语言发展领域与认知和社会性发展领域关系密切，对有机会学习第二语言的人来说，学习第二语言也将有益于他们的认知和社会性发展（Gleason,2001）。因此，我们承认英语对儿童语言发展和其他方面发展的价值，但希望不要盲目地无限夸张英语学习的意义。

充分考虑中国的发展中多元文化社会特点，我们需要认定的是，中国目前没有“均衡”的双语学习或者双语教育环境。为中国儿童的充分发展着想，学前阶段儿童的母语——汉语普通话的学习，应当毫无疑问地放在语言教育的第一位来加以考虑。需要中国幼儿教育工作者引起重视的是，任何影响儿童母语发展的第二语言教育计划，都有可能导致儿童发展的严重失误；某些有违于我国语言教育政策的教育安排，不仅做法极其愚蠢，而且对儿童终身发展的危害可能非常深远。诸如在某些较发达地区兴起的所谓“全英文学校”，人为地构造以英语为第一语言的“教育环境”，将儿童隔离于我们的自然母语学习环境，这样的现象不仅有违儿童发展基本规律，而且背离中国教育方针政策，需要警惕关注并加以督导。因此，在让幼儿学好母语的前提下，为幼儿提供多元文化的语言环境，引导幼儿学习英语，这是我们开展幼儿英语教育的首要观点。

基于上述的观点，我们认为，学前儿童的英语教育目标应当主要放在以下三个方面：

第一，培养幼儿英语学习的兴趣，提高运用语言进行交往的积极性。儿童的语言研究告诉我们，儿童语言的第一动力是语言学习动机。当母语学习有着天然自发的动机的时候，第二语言的学习在多数情况下需要环境因素的引发。对学前儿童来说，最好的引发就是他们的兴趣，孩子有兴趣就会有积极性学习，就会在交往过程中运用。学前儿童通常在学习运用第二语言时很大胆，不会因为自己讲错而觉得难为情，我们就应当利用这样的优势，为幼儿提供使之不断产生并保持兴趣的英语学习环境。让幼儿在学习英语的过程中觉得新奇、快乐、有趣，没有任何枯燥乏味感。这样的英语学习兴趣和伴随的交往动机，将对他们未来的第二语言学习产生重要的影响。

第二，帮助幼儿建立初步的英语语音感，增长他们的语言敏感性。如前所述，人的语音觉知在学前阶段形成，同时第二语言语音觉知也比较容易地在这个时期获得。正因为如此，学前儿童的英语学习应当具有非常鲜明的特点，即引导幼儿在唱唱念念说说英语的过程中，自然而然地获得英语语音感，增长对这样一种不同于母语的语言的敏感性。这种在早期语言关键期建立的语言敏感性，将有助于儿童擅长分辨区分不同语言的语音，知道语言和语言之间的差别。可以这么认为，学前阶段的英语学习，不能将要求幼儿学会多少词汇、句型放在首位，更不应当把英语国际音标等因素作为教学的任务。与之相反的是，幼儿主要的英语学习应当只是“接触”英语语言，获得一定的英语语言感受，从而在早期建立起语言的敏感性。实际上，这种在早期获得的对另一种语言的敏感性，会在儿童大脑中潜移默化地留下痕迹，对他们的母语和第二语言的学习都可能起到良好的作用。

第三，引导幼儿透过英语感悟不同文化的存在，从小获得文化多元的基本概念。 就今日发展着多元文化的中国而言，很多家长要求让孩子学习英语，很多幼儿园积极开设英语课程，实际上潜藏着为孩子适应多元社会变化做准备的心理。因为任何一种语言都与文化有着不可分割的联系，儿童在学习语言的同时，也在不知不觉地学习文化。学前阶段儿童对文化的感悟，主要是通过与成人和同伴的互动来实现的，因此我们应当要求让孩子在活动中学习英语，通过原汁原味的英语儿歌、故事、游戏、戏剧等，来感悟不同文化的人和事的特殊性。通过英语的窗口，去眺望和想象不同的人们生活的世界，这样有益于我们的幼儿从小建立起文化多元的基本概念。

以这样的基本定位来要求学前儿童英语教育，我们认为在中国现有的情境条件下，有条件的幼儿园可视英语学习为语言教育的一个有效组成部分。在努力发展幼儿的汉语普通话的前提下，花比较少的时间组织孩子学习，为幼儿创造一个有趣的英语学习环境，让幼儿快快乐乐地接触“英语”，为未来的学习做好准备。

二

讨论了我国学前儿童英语教育的基本定位之后，我们需要进一步思考目前幼儿园英语教育存在的问题。在过去的 10 年里，中国幼儿教育工作者已经发现，似乎突然之间就有众多的幼儿英语教材涌现到我们的面前。审慎地选择教材并有效地组织教学，成为幼教界不得不面对的一个新课题。究竟如何从纷繁众多的教材中选择出比较适合的材料，如何通过正确的教学途径让我们的孩子获得有效的学习经验？有一些基本的原则必须坚持。

经历过 90 年代中国幼儿教育改革，我们曾经对幼儿园语言教育的“全语言”基本原则有了认识。这里需要说明的是，第二语言学习有一些特殊的规律，但是从语言教育的角度看来，母语教育和双语教育的基本观念是相同的。因此，我们需要提醒幼儿教育工作者，在开展幼儿园英语教学时，应当遵循全语言教育的六个基本原则。

第一，儿童的语言学习是整体性的学习。 在吸收当代儿童语言研究的诸多成果的基础上，研究者们认为，儿童从出生起就已经具备了学习作为人的全部语言的基本条件，儿童语言发展的过程是以完整的方式进行和呈现出来的，因而儿童语言的认知学习应当是完整的学习，在早期的语言教育应当不仅重视儿童的听说能力的发展，同时也要注意创造环境，有利于他们的萌发读写能力的准备。

第二，儿童的语言学习是自然而然的学习。 全语言的提倡者注重儿童语言发展的规律，认为儿童是通过与人互动的方式学习使用语言的，主动理解是儿童学习语言的特点。因此早期教育机构要为幼儿提供学习各种语言的机会和资源，让幼儿被充满语言和文字信息的环境所包围。同时采用“自然学习模式”进行语言教育。这个自然学习模式包括四个部分，即示范、参与、练习或扮演角色、创造表达（Holdaway,1986）。

第三，儿童语言学习是有效的和有用的学习。 研究发现，有效的语言学习不是“正确的”或者是“标准的”，有效的语言学习是连接个人生活经验和社会的学习。对幼儿来说，当他们的语言学习是有用的时候，当他们能够用语言来沟通的时候，这种学习才对他们产生意义。他们会集中注意力在交流的话题上，会关注从交流的口语或者从阅读的图书中发现有关的语言信息；当他们用口头语言及书面方式来表达自己所学习的事物时，儿童便成为寻求并建构有意义沟通的学习者。因此，教育者要注意引导幼儿在情景中学习语言，脱离了情境的语言对儿童来说是没有特殊的意义的（Harste，et al. 1985）。

第四，儿童语言学习是整合的学习。 全语言教育的新观念告诉人们，人的学习是符号的学习。从早期语言教育的角度来看幼儿学习语言符号系统，实际上包含了作为学习对象来学的和作为工具用来学习其他内容的双重功能。全语言的研究者吸取了维果斯基的理论观点，认为任何符号系统学习的原理都是相通的，因而建议将不同的符号系统交叉运用在儿童学习的过程中。例如在语言学习中并用艺术、戏剧、音乐和舞蹈符号手段，这种打破学科限制的学习，不仅有利于儿童语言的认知学习，而且有利于其他相关领域内容的学习（Goodman & Kenneth，1986；Fisher，1991）。

第五，儿童语言学习是开放而平等的学习。 在全语言教育观念中，教师和儿童是构造愉快学习过程的共同体。从教师方面来说，教师有比较充分的专业自主权，这些主要表现在他们熟悉学习和教学理论，设计课程内容和选择教材，并且根据他们对儿童的了解做教学活动设计。从儿童方面来说，在教育过程中儿童和教师的关系是合作学习者的关系，而非上对下的关系（Goodman，1986）。教师的责任是为儿童创设一个良好的的语言学习环境，而且在儿童之间营造一个非竞争的学习共同体。尤其要注意的是，当儿童有权利去作自我选择的时候，学习的效果会最好（Fisher，1991）。

第六，儿童的语言学习是创造的学习。 语言的学习应用兼具了守成与创新双方面的特点。所谓守成是指，语言是社会约定俗成的产物，一个社会文化环境里的通行语言一定是有共同的定义的。但是语言也是不断的创新的产物。在全语言研究者的眼睛里，儿童学习语言的过程中是没有“错误”可言的，有的只是他们的“尝试”和“创新”。只有尝试了，才会在下一次获得正确的表达方式，尝试是创新的前奏和必由之路。教育工作者应当充分肯定和鼓励儿童语言学习的创新精神（Harste,1984）。在一些提倡全语言的幼儿园里，教师将幼儿看成是小小阅读者和作者，给幼儿充分的天地去实践和建构自己的语言能力，不在乎幼儿可能说错，不要求孩子表达完美，而用期待的态度鼓励和赞赏幼儿的语言表现愿望（Raines & Canady，1990）。

以这样的原则标准反思我国学前儿童的英语教育现状，目前在我们的实践层面存在着一些最基本的问题，具体反映在两个方面：

***教师教学过程中的语言输入*。** 教师的语言输入从来都是第二语言学习的关键因素，早期儿童英语学习也不例外。就我国幼儿英语教学状况来说，目前的教师英语输入有这样几个情况：（1）教师的英语输入数量不足。其中部分的原因是受到教师的英语水平限制，许多教师因原有英语水平不足而无法用英语自然地与幼儿交往互动；另外，也有教学观念和方法问题造成的英语输入问题，比如许多流行教材实际上属于传统的学科模式，教学过程中要求幼儿反反复复地跟读某一句对话或者几个单词，机械练习和重复的背后掩藏着严重的英语输入匮乏问题。（2）教师的英语输入质量不高。同样因为教师自身或者教学材料的关系，我们的幼儿英语课堂中存在着英语不够标准的问题。从语音的角度看是这样，从语用的角度看更需要注意。一些中文式英语，即过去人们在相声小品中常常嘲笑的“Chinglish”现象，目前在我们的幼儿英语学习中大量存在。值得我们警惕的是，即使是外国教师执教的幼儿英语，也可能存在上述的问题。外籍教师的教学方法和语言水平，同样也因为个人文化和教育背景等因素而存在极大差异。

***儿童学习过程中的语言运用*。** 儿童的语言运用是语言学习的驱动力，在学习过程中直接着影响他们的语言学习效果，第二语言的学习尤其如此。对学前儿童的英语学习来说，幼儿能否获得与语言

输入相匹配的语言运用机会，决定着幼儿是否真正获得英语学习效果并产生持续学习动机兴趣。 考察我们目前的幼儿英语学习现状，存在的问题主要有三：（1）幼儿语言运用的机会较少。 即使是在教师英语输入比较好的英语教学课堂上，往往也存在着教师说得多而孩子说得很少的问题；（2）幼儿语言运用的类型偏少。 受到教师教学主导的倾向影响，幼儿的课堂英语基本处于回答问题状态，主动发起并自然运用不同类型语言的机会比较少；（3）幼儿运用语言交往的情境不足。 在大多数幼儿英语教学环境中，都存在着偏重集体活动而忽略个别交往或者小组交往情境的创设。 因此，幼儿的英语学习活动缺乏真正操练运用所学语言进行交往的机会。

为了解决上述问题，我们认为中国儿童的英语教学要考虑“最佳配套条件”（optimal condition）（Snow，2002），建议采用以下几点措施：

1. 选择与新教育观念相符的教学材料，认真考证教材教法是否与目前我们的幼儿教育课程改革方向一致，应尽可能地考虑幼儿园的英语教学与中文课程融为一体，成为整体课程的有效组成部分，由此使得儿童的英语学习成为符合全语言发展需要的有效学习。

2. 多使用较高水平的英语 CD、录音录像带和其他教学辅助设备，努力营造幼儿听标准自然的英语学习环境，弥补现有英语教学中语言输入的不足，提高语言输入的数量和质量。

3. 积极开展不同形式的英语教师培训活动，将师资培训的重点放在英语教学观念和教学方法上，同时在此基础上进行英语口语的培训。 选择外籍教师为幼儿教英语的机构，也需要对外籍教师的英语水平和教师资格进行考察论证。

三

儿童的学习生活是相互之间存在联系的系统，因此在讨论我国学前儿童的英语教育的时候，我们无法将之与幼儿园的课程割裂，需要从课程的角度来进一步探究幼儿园英语教育问题，思考幼儿的英语学习与幼儿每天经历其中的学习生活之间的关系。将幼儿英语学习纳入幼儿园的课程范围考虑，并视之为幼儿园课程教学的有效组成部分，我们的英语教学才有可能帮助儿童获得有效发展。

这里我们想具体说明，如何将幼儿园的英语教学纳入课程作为儿童整体学习的有效组成部分。如果一个幼儿园小班下学期正在进行“扮家家”的一个课程单元，围绕这个课程单元的核心内容，我们提供给儿童符合他们生活经验的学习内容，并且对儿童的各个领域能力发展提出了要求，通过游戏和活动来建构提升儿童的学习经验。那么我们可以选择与之相配合的英语“My family”单元，主要抓住“家—family”和“我家—my family”重点展开活动，因为这里有与中文课程相关的概念。分析这样两个相对独立又可构成整体的中文和英文单元，我们可能发现：(1) 幼儿在学习英语过程中，所理解的家庭人际关系、亲情感受和爱的表达方式，与他们的中文学习内容是一致的。因此幼儿在中文的“扮家家”课程单元中获得的经验可以成为他们英语学习的支撑。当然，如果该英语单元与相近的其他课程单元配合，亦可连接幼儿相似或者相关的学习经验。(2) 从语言要求上来说，英语表达的要求低于中文；但幼儿在学习过程中的认知水平是相同的，他们的理解和形成概念的水平也是与中文相应的，这些都有助于他们的英语学习。(3) 我们还应当确信，幼儿通过吟唱英语歌谣感受英语的语音语调和节奏韵律，通过聆听英语故事掌握英语最基本词语和句型，还通过英语玩游戏尝试运用英语表达和交往，幼儿可以自然而然地获得他们用英语表达的能力。

因此，基于有关儿童语言学习理论、第二语言学习理论以及儿童发展与教育的理论，我们希望学前儿童的英语教育在教学过程中形成三个方面的连接：

一是英语学习与汉语学习的连接。 一个人无论学习多少种语言，都会需要通过认知系统实现概念的符号化过程，这里就实际存在着同种概念由不同语言符号表征的问题。 就中国文化情境中的学前儿童学习英语来看，在他们学习英语时，大部分儿童的母语学习水平大大高于第二语言水平，因此帮助连接第二语言与母语之间的学习，将有利于儿童对英语学习内容的理解和运用，可以产生事半功倍的学习效果。 假定今天幼儿学习了中文的童话故事《三只蝴蝶》，这时英语学习内容是儿歌“Butterfly”，那我们可以充分相信幼儿，他们掌握英语儿歌的速度一定非常快。

二是英语学习与生活经验的连接。语言的学习是与社会生活分不开的，也是在社会交往中实现的。 这个通识也适用于幼儿的英语学习。 有效的和有用的英语学习，必须与幼儿的生活经验相联系。从事学前儿童英语教学的教育工作者需要时时关注，自己的教学对象所具有的生活经验，努力在教学过程中调动他们的生活经验。 那种脱离儿童生活的英语，那种死记硬背的英语教学，都不可能对幼儿的英语学习产生好的作用。

三是英语学习与整合课程的连接。将英语教学纳入幼儿园的整合课程，同样有助于解决上述两个问题，与此同时，整合课程中的英语学习还将产生真正全语言发展和教育的效果。 因此，学前教育机构需要考虑儿童中文学习的主题和英语学习主题的连接，关注在中文学习的基础上整合英语学习内容，使之产生双方面支持和共同发展的效应。 即使是缺乏研究整合课程中英语教学的人力的幼儿园，也需要提醒从事英语教学的人员，密切关注幼儿园正在进行的整合课程，将英语教学内容尽可能地与当前课程内容配合。

总之，我国学前儿童的英语教育还处于匡正观念、探索路径的阶段。 正因为如此，需要更多的热心于儿童语言教育的同行携手共同研究，解决我们的社会发展中出现的幼儿教育新问题，真正为幼儿的全面和谐发展创造越来越好的教育环境。

参考文献

Gleason, J. B. (Ed.) (2001). The development of language. (5th ed.) MA: Allyn & Bacon.

Fisher, B. (1991). Joyful learning — A whole language kindergarten. Porstmouth, NH: Heinemann.

Goodman, K. (1986). What's whole in whole language? Porstmouth, NH: Heinemann.

Harste, J. C., Woodward, V. A. & Burke, C. L. (1985). Language stories and literacy lessons. Porstmouth, NH: Heinemann.

Holdaway, D. (1986). The structure of natural learning as a basis for literacy instruction. In Sampson, M. (ed.). The pursuit of literacy: Early reading and writing. Dubuque, IA: Kendall/Hunt.

Raines, S. C & Canady, R. J. (1990). The whole language kindergarten. NY: Teachers College Press.

Snow, C. E. (2002). **Looking Closely at Second Language Learning, Unpublished interview in HGSE News**, Harvard Graduate School of Education, USA.

10. 早期儿童语言发展与脑发育研究的进展

周　兢　李传江　张义宾

华东师范大学

有关早期儿童语言习得与发展，在近半个世纪语言学和心理学几代学人的研究中，获得了一系列的理论研究成果。各种不同流派的普遍共识是，早期儿童的语言习得必须建立在大脑的生理基础上，并在与环境的交互作用下逐渐发展。但是，儿童语言发生与发展的交互作用过程究竟是怎样形成和建立的，换言之，儿童语言习得与脑发育的内在关系机制是什么，一直以来仍然是研究中的一个“黑箱”。进入21世纪之后，由于非侵入神经成像研究技术与方法的迅速发展，使得各种关于儿童的研究超越了外部行为观察与推测的原有现实，开始允许我们建立基因与行为之间的神经生理学的中介连接[1]，从而产生更为敏感与有效的研究范式。因此，早期儿童语言发展与脑神经发育机制“黑箱”的逐渐打开，已经呈现出走向光明的突破性研究状态。本文拟综述近年来该领域的研究进展，试图回应我们学界研究的若干重要问题，以期推动我国早期儿童语言发展与教育的深入探讨。

1. 儿童语言发展的脑生理基础

自有儿童语言研究以来，人们普遍认为语言是人类特有的功能，因为人类具有更为复杂和高级的大脑。 早期的研究发现，人类的语言主要由大脑左半球负责，并且具有一种“不可逆决定论”的观点。 因为在有关新生儿言语加工的研究 [2] 中发现，儿童左半球偏向于复杂的语音，提示语言的左侧化在出生时即已存在；而有关脑损伤儿童的研究又证明，大脑左半球切除的儿童，在句法任务中的语言功能障碍较为严重。 这些研究结果引发人们的进一步兴趣，究竟儿童语言发展的脑生理机制是什么呢？ 儿童语言的发展与大脑发育的哪些部位之间的关系更为密切？

首先，新近研究告诉我们，人类的大脑在进行语言加工时，并不只是左半球负责语言的理解与产生，事实上语言加工过程中大脑左右半球活动联系紧密。 有关研究发现，婴幼儿的大脑在一些语言任务中表现出和成年人同样的激活区域，特别是在被人们视为经典大脑语言区的布洛卡区和颞上回，他们的左侧脑区激活强度显著高于右侧脑区 [4] ；单双语儿童在这些脑区的激活上同样具有一致性，比如语音处理上激活颞上回，单词处理上激活左额下回 [5,6] 。 但是，诸多研究证明语言脑区的左侧偏侧化并不意味着右脑没有参与工作，在句子处理和语音语义信息分析的任务上，脑的右半球同样得到了激活 [7,8] ；双语儿童进行语言转换的时候，经典语言区和认知脑区（前扣带回、背外侧前额）都会激活 [9,10] ；人类在进行语篇及句子理解的过程中，会不断调动大脑中的语义地图(semantic maps)，而这个语义地图在左右脑均有所体现，进一步说明人类语言活动离不开左右脑 [11] 。

其次，新近研究提出了语言习得的神经网络结构的观点。 传统理论认为，儿童语言发展的大脑语言区，大多是单一的语言区。例如（1）运动语言中枢：位于额下回后部（44、45 区，又称 Broca 区）。（2）听觉语言中枢：位于颞上回 42、22 区皮质，该区具有能够听到声音并将声音理解成语言的一系列过程的功能。（3）视觉语言中枢：位于顶下小叶的角回，即 39 区。该区具有理解看到的符号和文字意义的功能。（4）运用中枢：位于顶下小叶的缘上回，即 40 区。此区主管精细的协调功能。（5）书写中枢：位于额中回后部 6、8 区，即中央前回手区的前方。以往我们对语言的神经基础的认知停留在，语言是一个由布洛卡区、韦尼克区以及联结二者的弓状束组成的简单模型。随着神经科学和认知神经科学的发展，研究者[12]逐渐认识到，各种心理活动特别是一些高级复杂的认知活动，比如语言的产生，都是由不同脑区共同合作构成的神经网络来组织实现的。个体语言网络的脑皮质发展可以分为两个阶段：在第一个阶段（出生到 3 岁），婴幼儿的语言脑区遵循从下往上的发展路径，两侧颞叶迅速发展；在第二个阶段（3 岁到成年），从上往下的发展路径逐渐显现，左侧前额的功能选择和结构连接性逐渐增强。更多来自新近神经科学的研究，比如对失语症的影像学研究、弥散张量成像研究、功能性磁共振成像研究、皮质和皮下组织的电生理研究等，增进了对大脑语言神经网络的复杂性认识。Fujii 等[13]研究者提出，语言是通过两种不同的路径进行加工的，背侧通路和腹侧通路，背侧通路的核心是上纵束/弓状束，其与语音加工密切相关；而语义加工则主要与腹侧通路（主要包括额枕下束和颞骨内面网络）有关。此外，他们还发现了联结辅助运动区和布洛卡区的额骨斜束(frontal aslant tract)，其在言语的发生和驱动中发挥着重要的作用。当然，由于脑网络分析技术的不成熟以及多模态数据采集和认识的不足，如何整合语言脑结构和功能的网络模型，如何解释相应的语言产生及发展等都有待进一步研究，传统语言脑区的观点尚未能完全被替代。

再次，新近研究认为，早期儿童的脑发育状况可以预测他们未来的语言发展。近年来，一系列研究聚焦探讨婴幼儿大脑结构的发育与未来语言及认知能力发展之间的关系。研究者[14]利用功能性磁共振成像(functional magnetic resonance imaging，fMRI)技术研究发现，正常婴儿6个月时的右侧杏仁核容量与2—4岁的接受性语言和表达性语言能力相关，但12个月时候右侧杏仁核容量与语言能力不相关，据此认为婴儿初生的前6个月，会调动杏仁核组织参与处理环境中的语言信息；而到1岁时，婴儿大脑的其他脑区将更多参与到语言活动中来，大脑的杏仁核组织结构在婴幼儿语言习得中发挥着重要作用。一些有关孤独症儿童研究中，和上述研究有类似的结论认为，早期儿童大脑的左侧杏仁核体积越大，语言能力越好；大脑右侧杏仁核则反之[15]。因此认定早期儿童大脑的杏仁核体积与未来语言能力之间具有较强的联系。另外，一系列研究发现：婴儿语音学习的大脑活动水平能够预测14和30个月时的语言能力[16]；婴儿脑的语言活动水平可以预期他们5岁时的语言发展水平及其前的读写能力[17]；婴儿阶段的大脑语言加工图景，还可以预测儿童8岁的语言和认知水平[18]。此外，也有研究[19]证明，2岁孤独症儿童单词加工的脑电水平，能够预测儿童4岁和6岁时的接受性语言能力、认知能力和适应性行为。因为早期儿童大脑发展状态可以预测儿童的语言发展水平，研究正继续致力于通过观察儿童早期大脑活动探测婴儿脑的阅读障碍易感基因，试图通过神经成像研究进一步确定阅读障碍易感基因的不同功能，以及可能引发早期大脑发展中出现异常的神经迁移或者轴突的增长，预测可能具有阅读困难风险的儿童并为之准确鉴定提供证据，从而对美国学校阶段存在5%—

17%的发展性阅读障碍儿童进行早期干预[20]。

有关儿童大脑发育与语言发展提供相关神经生理机制的研究，让我们看到了早期儿童大脑发育对儿童语言发展和教育不可忽略的重要意义，值得所有的研究者和教育工作者重视。

2. 儿童语言发展关键期与脑发育的机会窗口期

有关儿童语言发展关键期的概念，在 Lenneberg 等[21]所著的《语言的生物学基础》中正式提出，得到 20 世纪的儿童语言学研究的普遍认定。语言发展关键期的主要观点是，早期阶段是人的一生中比其他任何时期都更容易习得语言的时期。语言发展关键期的证据，一方面来自当时神经生理学的发现，认为人类进化的结果决定了孩子一出生就具备了语言学习机制，而人类大脑中掌管语言学习的布洛卡区、韦尼克区在 4—12 岁处于灵敏时期，此时被存储的语言会被大脑认为是“母语”，因而可以获得很快掌握并灵活运用；语言发展关键期学说还建立在一系列语言发展不利儿童的研究上，例如对脑损伤儿童与语言恢复关系的研究发现提出过了一个时间点，儿童的语言康复效果非常难；对语言环境受到剥夺的儿童语言行为的研究，发现儿童身处于无语言环境错过了童年时期，后来的语言发展受到严重影响；还有对来自于移民家庭儿童第二语言学习的研究，都再三证实学龄前阶段是儿童语言发展关键期的存在。

有关早期儿童脑发育的研究，向我们揭示了从婴儿期起快速的发育过程。婴儿阶段儿童的神经元发育极为迅速，大脑皮质突触发展意味着突触的增殖和迅速产生，意味着学龄前阶段儿童处于大脑神经细胞的黄金发展时期[22]。同时研究也告诉我们，这个黄金发展过程中大脑不同功能的神经细胞发展速率不同，可能对应儿童发展的不同领域。在早期儿童脑发育过程中，实际存在着不同的“机会窗口”，大脑机会窗口期正是神经细胞快速连接和髓鞘化的过程[23]。机会窗口期对每一个孩子是公平存在的，决定孩子发展水平的主要条件，是在适当的机会窗口期给予适当的某种发展需求的良性刺激，儿童就可能获得该方面的良好发展。

联系脑发育机会窗口期的研究，我们认为在儿童语言发展范畴，大脑机会窗口期正是语言神经细胞快速连接和髓鞘化的过程，由此引发再次思考有关儿童语言发展关键期的问题。

第一，儿童脑发育的机会窗口期对应了语言发展不同方面的敏感期。尽管现有研究尚未能完全准确记录每一种语言成分发展的准确时间，但是连接儿童大脑活动的语言研究告诉我们，儿童语言发展的不同范畴如语音、语义和句法习得的关键期存在差异。研究[24]发现，儿童语音学习的关键期出现在出生后的第一年之内，具体而言是出生后 6—12 个月；而儿童母语学习的句法习得成长的关键期是在 18—36 个月，儿童可以快速习得各种句法要素；儿童的词汇发展的大脑机会窗口期在 18 个月时，这个时期的儿童词汇量有一个突飞猛涨的表现，但是需要说明的是，研究同时告诉我们，儿童词汇发展有持续性增长发展的态势，个体可以在任何年龄学习新的词汇并不完全受到年龄的影响。

Kuhl[25]认为，从早期婴儿语音学习的角度去看，儿童语言的发展有赖于两个条件：一是在大脑机会窗口期的学习；二是母语神经条件的存在，两个方面相互影响存在于儿童发展过程之中。例如，婴儿出生后的 6 个月内，他们的大脑神经环路和整体结构发展，能够允许他们汲取周围环境中的语音和声音韵律模式，在这样的机会窗口期进行的语音学习，会对儿童言语知觉经验产生影响并改变他们未来的语言学习能力。在不同的大脑发育机会窗口期给予儿童学习的机会，儿童将会形成反映自然语言输入的神经网络，这些初始的神经网络的形成会对新语言的学习产生影响[26]。当我们认识到儿童语言发展具有一定的窗口期，理解整个学前阶段尤其是1岁前，语言环境及经验刺激对儿童语言神经突触和神经网络迅速发展的意义，我们有必要在这个敏感期提供给幼儿适当的语言刺激和环境促进他们的语言发展。如图1 [27] 中语言神经组织在8个月以前基本呈直线式的迅速发展轨迹，8个月左右达到发育的高峰期；高级认知神经细胞在1岁左右达到发展的高峰期，其后发育速率开始稳定而下降。

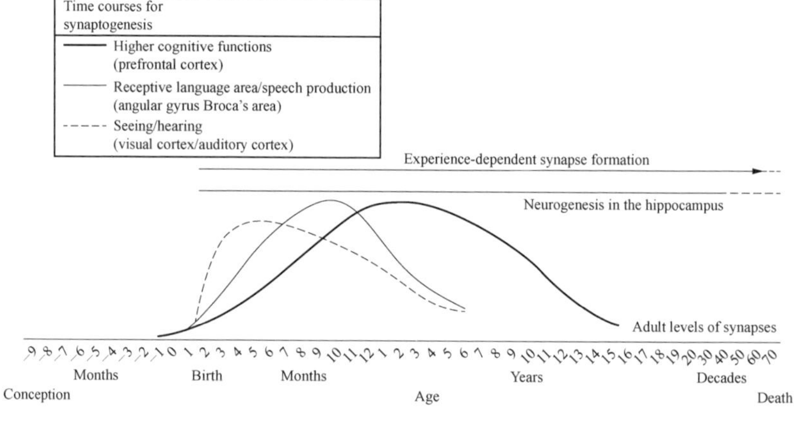

图1　人类大脑的发展

第二，儿童脑发育的可塑性允许儿童在语言发展关键期的补偿性发展。大脑可塑性是大脑受到经验的塑造，在结构和功能上发生改变的能力。来自一系列特殊儿童的语言研究指出，早期的语言学习经验会对大脑的解剖结构产生影响，从而补偿原有的语言发展的不利条件。Mayberry等 [28] 使用fMRI对从出生到14岁聋人手势语（手势语作为第一语言）习得的研究发现，手势语习得的年龄与脑前侧语言区的激活水平呈现线性负相关，而与视觉区域激活水平呈正相关。对某些听觉障碍儿童而言，通过早期阅读和读写学习，有可能会改变他们的大脑结构和大脑激活水平。读写会发展语音意识、发展口语能力和促进言语加工，而通过阅读习得，特定的脑区（左后侧颞叶皮质———视觉单词形成区）会对已习得文本的正字法刺激做出反馈。Dehaene 等[29]也通过 fMRI 技术发现，读写可以增强这些大脑的活动水平。其一，增加了视觉皮质的组织水平，特别是左后侧颞叶皮质和与视觉相关的枕叶皮质；其二，句子的书写使得整个左半球的口语网络得到激活，或者说通过阅读增加言语的发展；其三，读写通过促进语音区（颞平面）发展，完善了口头语言的加工。进一步的相关研究[30]指出，儿童经验的获得会引发脑结构和功能的变化，与任务相关的脑区在经过训练之后会得到增强，而与任务无关的脑区的激活程度则逐渐减弱。脑并非一成不变的实体，现代神经科学已经揭示，它会随着发育而改变；但更为重要的是，它会随着环境输入和学习者经验的获得而改变。因此，教育支持在儿童脑发育的过程中发挥着重要的作用[31]。但是，需要特别指出的是，已有研究[32]发现，在大脑机会窗口期和语言发展关键期的学习非常重要。比如不同年龄的手势语习得，在观察与语言加工相关的大脑枕叶皮质组织浓度的变化时，研究发现了手势语习得年龄对它产生了不同影响。因此，我们需要特别指出，利用儿童大脑的机会窗口期，在儿童语言发展关键期提供儿童语言发展特别需要的支持，帮助儿童重塑脑和语言发展，这是非常重要的观点。

3. 儿童双语学习与“双语脑”的发展

有关儿童双语学习的问题，最近几年受到越来越多的研究关注，尽管研究[33]证明儿童第二语言学习与语言发展关键期并不同步，即使过了第二语言学习的敏感期，大脑仍然具有一定的可塑性。但是更多研究揭示，早期儿童的双语学习会影响大脑的功能活动，甚至影响大脑的结构。因此，我们需要面对这个方面的问题，做出比较正面的回答。

首先，我们回答的问题是，双语是否有利于儿童的脑发育?

“双语认知优势效应”背后的脑研究，近年来一直是儿童语言研究的热点问题。已有的许多行为实验研究发现，双语儿童在一些言语和非言语认知任务，尤其是执行功能任务上，表现优于单语儿童，这种现象被称之为“双语认知优势效应”[34,35]。有关双语对儿童大脑发育产生影响具体表现的问题，近十多年来的研究发现，早期儿童双语能力对大脑的影响主要体现在执行功能脑区功能和结构的变化上。研究发现，双语的使用能够促进儿童执行功能脑区的不断激活，使得儿童执行功能脑区的认知控制和灵活性等功能得到了强化。Kovelman 等[36]在一项语义判断任务中发现，即使两组儿童在任务表现上没有差异，但双语儿童比单语儿童更多地激活了背外侧前额叶和额下回，而背外侧前额叶与工作记忆和抑制控制等认知功能有关。他们的研究表明，双语经验强化了儿童大脑的认知控制和灵活性的功能。

许多研究关注，双语对儿童大脑结构产生的影响。有研究者[37]采用高分辨率磁共振扫描技术发现，多语儿童在下顶叶脑区灰质密度上显著高于单语儿童。还有研究[38]发现，基底核尤其是尾状核也会受双语经验的影响，因为尾状核在语言转换中发挥着重要作用。研究者[39]发现，双语者的左侧尾状核灰质密度显著高于单语者。Hosoda 等[40]在报告中指出，经过一段时间的第二语言词汇学习的训练干预，双语者的尾状核灰质容量比其他脑区显著增大。

其次，我们需要回应早期双语学习经验与儿童脑发育的关系问题。有关研究提出双语脑是否和单语脑相同的问题，探讨儿童语言和认知脑机制的关系，试图回应早期双语经验是否会改变大脑这样一个核心话题。研究从探讨初次习得二语年龄如何影响语言神经组织激活问题入手，有研究者[41]将7—10岁正常儿童分为双语和单语两组，与正常成年人相应单语组和双语组比较，考察不同年龄不同语言经验组在语句处理上的脑区激活状况。双语儿童组的研究对象，又包括了早期双语儿童（出生接受二语环境）和晚期双语儿童（4—6岁接受二语环境）。双语儿童和双语成年人在左侧经典语言区的激活均显著增强。更重要的发现是，早期双语儿童通过调动经典语言区进行二语句子处理任务，而晚期双语儿童改变了大脑管理高级执行功能的脑区来处理句子任务，更强地激活了前额叶。

让我们进一步研究探讨早期语言学习经验是否会影响儿童阅读神经系统的发育，并试图说明单语儿童和双语儿童的阅读神经系统发育是否不同的问题。Jasińska等[42]采用脑成像技术对比了6—7岁儿童、8—10岁儿童和成年人的阅读时的大脑激活模式。他们发现了经典语言区，比如左侧额下回(left inferior frontal gyrus，LIFG)和颞上回(superior temporal gyrus，STG)随着年龄增长而发生的变化，双语者更多地激活了双侧LIFG和STG和认知脑区（背外侧前额叶等前额脑区）。这种双语“神经信号”(neural signature)表明，早期第二语言学习经验会改变儿童阅读神经系统，促进儿童阅读能力的发展。

最近的脑神经成像研究，不仅发现在语言任务上双语者的表现优于单语者，而且发现双语者使用认知控制网络上更加有效，任务表现更好[43]。Arredondo等[44]发现，早期双语经验可以改变儿童注意控制的前额脑区功能，单语儿童在解决注意控制的任务中更多地激活和使用右侧额叶，而双语儿童更多地激活左侧额叶，尤其是左侧前额下回，表明了双语儿童在处理一般注意控制任务中调动了语言脑区。他们认为双语经验和早期认知交互发展和影响，使得大脑左侧前额叶的功能有了变化。Abutalebi等[45]比较了单语者和双语者在非言语冲突监控任务上的表现，发现他们都激活了前扣带回这一参与认知控制的脑区，但是双语者更加有效，同等水平的冲突监控任务中需要更低程度的脑激活水平。

及至如此，我们仍然要回答这样的问题：双语学习为什么会有利于儿童的脑发育？主流研究认为，双语者在执行功能行为任务上具有优势，主要得益于他们能够获得额外的或过度的抑制控制训练，不断抑制来自干扰语言的刺激和反应。这主要是因为许多心理学行为研究发现：双语者在只使用一种语言时，两种语言都被激活并进行竞争。脑科学从内在神经机制解释“双语认知优势效应”，认为我们需要关注双语选择和控制机制和认知控制机制是否依赖类似的神经网络。研究发现，当个体对两种语言进行转换和控制时，背外侧前额皮质将被激活[10,46]；而个体在解决执行功能任务时，背前额皮质也将被激活，它是执行功能的核心脑区[47]。亦有研究证明，基底核在双语选择中发挥重要作用[48]，而基底核在执行功能中同样扮演着重要角色[38]。总之，研究者往往使用语言转换的范式来研究双语控制机制，发现左额下回、双侧前额叶背侧、前扣带回和尾状核等区域似乎与双语词汇竞争抑制功能有关[49]。而认知控制属于执行功能的一部分，有研究者[9]认为它主要由5个重要脑区负责：左背外侧前额叶、前扣带回、尾状核和缘上回或顶下小叶。

研究[50,51]表明，双语者具有的优势来源于语言学习给予他们大脑的超水平锻炼，在两种语言选择和竞争时，在个体完成执行控制任务时的脑区和神经网络产生出多重激活的运作经验，促使人脑的执行功能积极参与。双语学习和使用者在两种语言之间的选择，不断激活他们的执行功能脑区，使得他们的执行功能控制能力得到增强，在神经生理学基础上为“双语者执行功能优势得益于双语选择和竞争机制”。

在儿童双语学习与脑发育关系问题上，还存在一个涉及现实的关键问题：什么时候开始双语学习最为有利?

回应这个问题，我们必须关注有关儿童语言发展关键期与脑发育机会窗口期的研究，也必须关注第二语言学习不一定存在关键期的研究结果。更多研究证明的是，初次接触第二语言的时间或者说暴露于双语环境的年龄影响着儿童的双语能力发展[52]。有研究[53,54]认为，5 岁以前接触双语学习，是保证双语发展的最佳时间。同时，必须考虑儿童双语学习的环境因素、社区和家庭是否具有大量的、系统的、多途径的双语因素存在，这三大特点的语言环境是良好的第二语言学习环境的主要体现。Kovelman 等[55]提出“一双手套并不适合所有人”的观点，同时强调全语言环境的教育策略更适合 3 岁以前接受第二语言的儿童，能够有效提高儿童的语言和阅读能力；如果 3—4 岁儿童初次接触第二语言，可以考虑全语言教育环境结合使用自然拼读法教育策略，确保儿童的解码能力和阅读能力得到更好的成长。此外，还需要提及儿童可能通过学习企及的双语熟练程度以及因此造成对儿童发展的影响可能。研究[56]发现，双语熟练程度调节着儿童执行控制任务的表现，第二语言越熟练，其执行控制的行为表现越好；Mechelli 等[57]发现双语儿童二语熟练程度愈高，其大脑左下顶叶脑区的灰质密度愈高。这些研究从另一方面说明，双语学习对儿童大脑发育有利，何时学习以及如何学习，将更多地影响着儿童大脑功能可塑性的效能，值得我们再三斟酌深思。

4. 儿童语言发展与“社会脑”的发育

在研究儿童语言发展与脑发育的时候，研究者[58]发现，即使是非常小的婴儿，他们感知语言的能力的变化，极大地受到周围语言中所含声音的频率分布的影响。婴儿学习语言时，令人神奇地能够运用从与社会互动的经验中积累的分析模式，区分语言环境中的语音语调因素，并逐渐学习语音要素和语言词汇；于是早期与婴儿进行语言互动的成人，如果能够给予孩子充足的良性的语言刺激，就可以在帮助孩子语言发展的同时，支持孩子成长起一个“社会脑”[59]。

研究认为，6 个月之内的婴儿可以称之为“世界公民”，因为他们能够辨别世界上所有语言的不同声音；而 10—14 个月的婴儿学习语言已经受到社会文化的影响。Kuhl 等[60]的一项研究聚焦 9 个月大的美国婴儿社会互动与语言学习，研究对象被分为 4 组：一组婴儿的老师用汉语普通话与婴儿一起在地板上读书、玩玩具；另外两组婴儿分别看视频上的人说普通话和听普通话录音；第四组是对照组，这组婴儿不听普通话，而是由一个美国研究生用英语和婴儿一起读同样的书，玩同样的玩具。研究结果发现：①经过 1 个月共 12 次的活动，听真人说普通话的美国婴儿学会了识别普通话音位，这组婴儿的汉语普通话听力水平达到在中国环境中汉语普通话婴儿 11 个月的水平。②通过电视或录音接触普通话的婴儿，完全没有学会识别普通话音位，他们的音位分辨能力与对照组婴儿相当。③对照组婴儿未接触汉语普通话语音，正如预期的一样，他们对汉语普通话音位分辨能力在研究前后没有差异。这个实验充分说明了只有在自然情境下的语言互动才能促进婴幼儿语言的产生与学习，成人与婴儿的母语互动，决定了婴儿对母语的敏感度。

社会互动学习决定着孩子的“社会脑”成长，也决定着孩子的语言发展。那么在儿童的“社会脑”和语言同步发展过程中，社会互动的哪些成分可以更好地支持儿童语言学习[61]？这是目前研究的新的方向问题。能够给读者提供的有效建议，包括了以下几点：

第一，给儿童提供良性的社会互动经验，利用语言来构造积极的互动过程。一些研究者发现，父母需要构建温暖的社会互动环境，与婴儿一起读图画书、看玩具的时候，婴儿会跟随父母的言语所指而改变眼神轨迹，而且也会跟随父母的眼神轨迹而改变自己的表现[62,63]。Brooks 等[64]的研究表明，出生后头两年中，幼儿如能跟随成人目光的指向，那么他们所掌握的词汇会比不能跟踪目光移动的儿童更多。研究据此认为社会互动中的注视与说话之间存在的联系非常有意义，亲子之间需要亲密接触的互动，而不是电子媒体这种被动的互动方式。Kemp[65]研究证明，父母经常与孩子亲子阅读，为孩子大声朗读故事能够有效促进儿童大脑和语言的发展：父母在家经常给孩子朗读故事，亲子阅读的频率较高，或者说在家经常接触阅读的儿童，其大脑负责语义处理的脑区更加活跃，这一区域对于发展语言文字乃至自主阅读都极其关键。这项研究还发现，与图像有关的大脑区域也被激活，这使儿童能够“看到故事”，同时也支持了此前的理论：视觉化对于理解故事和发展阅读技能至关重要。因此，在父母与儿童的社会互动中，亲子阅读被视为有效建立“社会脑”和语言关系的一种途径方式。

第二，儿童的社会性游戏是儿童语言与社会脑同步发展的最佳实践区。近年的研究告诉我们，游戏活动所产生的作用，在于激活儿童大脑神经元，帮助儿童大脑在发育关键窗口期建立神经元之间的联系，构建起良好的大脑发展地图。新的游戏理论将儿童游戏与脑发展连接起来，探讨基于游戏的儿童活动与脑的发育关系，即儿童游戏过程受到大脑活动影响以及游戏能否促进大脑发展的问题[66]。研究[67]证明，儿童积极参与的游戏活动，形成一种互为促进的大脑活动过程，出现类似于自我引导地进行大脑重塑的现象。游戏专家们[68]认定：儿童游戏、脑的发展和丰富的环境之间存在着一种互益的关系；游戏是一种神奇灵活的、不可预知的，并且具有创造性反应的进化潜质的力量；通过丰富环境因素的介质，产生促进儿童大脑可塑性及其与现实连接的作用。因此，游戏是儿童学习的重要方式途径，通过脑科学的研究，进一步得到了确认。当我们关注儿童的语言发展和“社会脑”发育的时候，我们知道儿童所参与的社会性游戏中，需要实践体验成人通过搭建鹰架教给他们的种种能力。儿童需要在玩娃娃游戏时遵守游戏规则，他们需要与同伴商量娃娃家的游戏计划，他们需要记住各自所扮演的角色。在游戏进程中，他们需要关注每个角色都做了什么，并加入一段每个人都感兴趣的剧情。这些看似玩耍的游戏，却在寓教于乐地要求儿童有效运用语言和积累“社会脑”的经验。

第三，为儿童创建有效学习的语言发展和“社会脑”发育环境。儿童“社会脑”的概念，其实还包括社会、学校和家庭环境，以及社会经济状况对儿童脑发育乃至全面发展的影响因素。迄今为止，所有研究都认同的一点是，儿童“社会脑”成长的不良环境，将有害于儿童脑发育和全面发展。这个不良环境有可能但并非绝对由经济因素决定。美国国家儿童发展科学咨询委员会对影响儿童脑发育提出三种压力经验分类方法[69]。研究指出，现实社会生活中存在着三种影响儿童发展的压力经验：积极的(positive)、可忍受的(tolerable)和毒性的(toxic)。在这一分类框架中，“压力”是指压力反应系统的生理学表现，而不是指刺激物的自然属性或客观测量和获得的压力。虽然诸多研究仍在探讨压力发生的机制，已有概念已经在生物学的基础上建立起来。积极的压力是指适度的、短暂的心律、血压和压力激素水平的加强。可忍受的压力是指这样一种生理状态：它可能对大脑结构产生潜在的损害，但能从支持性的环境、促进性的、可适应的相互关系获得缓冲。毒性压力是指强烈的、频繁的，或延长的、缺乏成人支持和缓冲保护的、对儿童神经反应系统的不良影响[70]。就语言发展与“社会脑”成长而言，我们希望对中国的读者说，仔细检查儿童生长的环境因素，规避毒性压力，提供良性压力，真正为儿童创建积极有效的学习和发展环境。

总之，我们需要支持儿童的语言发展，我们也需要支持儿童的大脑健康发展，这是儿童教育最重要的任务和挑战。

参考文献

[1] Braver TS, Cole MW, Yarkoni T. Vive les differences! Individual variation in neural mechanisms of executive control [J]. Curr Opin Neurobiol, 2010, 20(2): 242-250.

[2] Hellige JB. Hemispheric asymmetry: what's right and what's left [M]. Cambridge Harvard University Press, 1993.

[3] Day PS, Ulatowska HK. Perceptual, cognitive, and linguistic development after early hemispherectomy: two case studies [J]. Brain Lang, 1979, 7(1): 17-33.

[4] Petitto LA. Cortical images of early language and phonetic development using near infrared spectroscopy [J]. Educ Brain, 2010: 213-231.

[5] Petitto LA. Revolutions in brain, language and education [R]. Vatican City Pontifical Academy of Sciences, 2003.

[6] Petitto LA, Baker S, Baird A, et al. Near-infrared spectroscopy studies of children and adults during language processing [C]. Cambridge International Workshop on Near-Infrared Spectroscopy, 2004.

[7] Beeman MJ, Bowden EM, Gernsbacher MA. Right and left hemisphere cooperation for drawing predictive and coherence inferences during normal story comprehension [J]. Brain Lang, 2000, 71(2): 310-336.

[8] Vigneau M, Beaucousin V, Hervé PY, et al. What is right-hemisphere contribution to phonological, lexico-semantic, and sentence processing? Insights from a meta-analysis [J]. Neuroimage, 2011, 54(1): 577-593.

[9] Abutalebi J, Green D. Bilingual language production the neurocognition of language representation and control [J]. J Neurolinguistics, 2007, 20(3): 242-275.

[10] Buchweitz A, Prat C. The bilingual brain flexibility and control in the

human cortex [J] . Phys Life Rev, 2013, 10(4): 428 - 443.

[11] Huth AG, de Heer WA, Griffiths TL, et al. Natural speech reveals the semantic maps that tile human cerebral cortex [J] . Nature, 2016, 532 (7600): 453 - 458.

[12] Skeide MA, Friederici AD. The ontogeny of the cortical language network [J] . Nat Rev Neurosci, 2016, 17(5): 323 - 332.

[13] Fujii M, Maesawa S, Ishiai S, et al. Neural basis of language an overview of an evolving model [J] . Neurol Med Chir (Tokyo), 2016, 56(7): 379 - 386.

[14] Ortiz-Mantilla S, Choe MS, Flax J, et al. Associations between the size of the amygdala in infancy and language abilities during the preschool years in normally developing children [J] . Neuroimage, 2010, 49 (3): 2791 - 2799.

[15] Munson J, Dawson G, Abbott R, et al. Amygdalar volume and behavioral development in autism [J] . Arch Gen Psychiatry, 2006, 63 (6): 686 - 693.

[16] Kuhl P, Rivera-Gaxiola M. Neural substrates of language acquisition [J] . Annu Rev Neurosci, 2008, 31: 511 - 534.

[17] Cardillo GC. Predicting the predictors: individual differences in longitudinal relationships between infant phonetic perception, toddler vocabulary, and preschooler language and phonological awareness [D] . Seattle University of Washington, 2010.

[18] Molfese DL. Predicting dyslexia at 8 years of age using neonatal brain responses [J] . Brain Lang, 2000, 72(3): 238 - 245.

[19] Kuhl PK, Coffey-Corina S, Padden D, et al. Brain responses to words in 2-year-olds with autism predict developmental outcomes at age 6 [J] . PLoS One, 2013, 8(5): e64967.

[20] Ozernov-Palchik O, Gaab N. Tackling the 'dyslexia paradox' reading brain and behavior for early markers of developmental dyslexia [J] . Wiley Interdiscip Rev Cogn Sci, 2016, 7(2): 156 - 176.

[21] Lenneberg EH, Chomsky N, Marx O. Biological foundations of language [M] . New York Wiley, 1967.

[22] Huttenlocher PR, Dabholkar AS. Regional differences in synaptogenesis in human cerebral cortex [J] . J Comp Neurol, 1997, 387(2): 167 - 178.

[23] Schiller P. Early brain development research review and update [J] . Exchange, 2010(11): 26 - 30.

[24] Kuhl PK. Brain mechanisms in early language acquisition [J] . Neuron, 2010, 67(5): 713 - 727.

[25] Kuhl PK. Early language acquisition cracking the speech code [J] . Nat Rev Neurosci, 2004, 5(11): 831 - 843.

[26] Kuhl PK, Conboy BT, Padden D, et al. Early speech perception and later language development implications for the "critical period" [J] . Lang Learn Dev, 2005, 1(3): 237 - 264.

[27] Shonkoff JP, Phillips DA. From neurons to neighborhoods the science of early childhood development [M] . Washington, D. C. National Academies Press, 2000: 188.

[28] Mayberry RI, Chen JK, Witcher P, et al. Age of acquisition effects on the functional organization of language in the adult brain [J] . Brain Lang, 2011, 119(1): 16 - 29.

[29] Dehaene S, Pegado F, Braga LW, et al. How learning to read changes the cortical networks for vision and language [J] . Science, 2010, 330 (6009): 1359 - 1364.

[30] Casey BJ, Tottenham N, Liston C, et al. Imaging the developing brain what have we learned about cognitive development [J] . Trends Cogn Sci, 2005, 9(3): 104 - 110.

[31] Sousa DA. 周加仙，译. 心智、脑与教育：教育神经科学对课堂教学的启示 [M] . 上海：华东师范大学出版社，2012。

[32] Pénicaud S, Klein D, Zatorre RJ, et al. Structural brain changes linked to delayed first language acquisition in congenitally deaf individuals [J] . Neuroimage, 2013(66): 42 - 49.

[33] Li P, Legault J, Litcofsky KA. Neuroplasticity as a function of second language learning anatomical changes in the human brain [J] . Cortex, 2014(58): 301 - 324.

[34] Costa A, Sebastián-Gallés N. How does the bilingual experience sculpt the brain? [J] . Nat Rev Neurosci, 2014, 15(5): 336 - 345.

[35] Calvo A, Bialystok E. Independent effects of bilingualism and socioeconomic status on language ability and executive functioning [J] . Cognition, 2014, 130(3): 278 - 288.

[36] Kovelman I, Baker SA, Petitto LA. Bilingual and monolingual brains compared a functional magnetic resonance imaging investigation of syntactic processing and a possible "neural signature" of bilingualism [J] . J Cogn Neurosci, 2008, 20(1): 153 - 169.

[37] Della Rosa PA, Videsott G, Borsa VM, et al. A neural interactive location for multilingual talent [J] . Cortex, 2013, 49 (2): 605 - 608.

[38] Stocco A, Yamasaki B, Natalenko R, et al. Bilingual brain training a

neurobiological framework of how bilingual experience improves executive function [J] . Int J Bilingua, 2012, 18(1): 67 - 92.

[39] Zou L, Abutalebi J, Zinszer B, et al. Second language experience modulates functional brain network for the native language production in bimodal bilinguals [J] . Neuroimage, 2012, 62(3): 1367 - 1375.

[40] Hosoda C, Tanaka K, Nariai T, et al. Dynamic neural network reorganization associated with second language vocabulary acquisition a multimodal imaging study [J] . J Neurosci, 2013, 33 (34): 13663 - 13672.

[41] Jasińska KK, Petitto LA. Age of bilingual exposure predicts distinct contributions of phonological and semantic knowledge to successful reading development [R] . Seattle Society for Research in Child, 2013.

[42] Jasińska KK, Petitto LA. Development of neural systems for reading in the monolingual and bilingual brain new insights from functional near infrared spectroscopy neuroimaging [J] . Dev Neuropsychol, 2014, 39 (6): 421 - 439.

[43] Kroll JF, Bobb SC, Hoshino N. Two languages in mind bilingualism as a tool to investigate language, cognition, and the brain [J] . Curr Dir Psychol Sci, 2014, 23(3): 159 - 163.

[44] Arredondo MM, Hu XS, Satterfield T, et al. Bilingualism alters children's frontal lobe functioning for attentional control [J] . Dev Sci, 2016 Jan 6. [Epub ahead of print] .

[45] Abutalebi J, Della Rosa PA, Green DW, et al. Bilingualism tunes the anterior cingulate cortex for conflict monitoring [J] . Cereb Cortex, 2012, 22(9): 2076 - 2086.

[46] Rodriguez-Fornells A, De Diego Balaguer R, Münte TF. Executive control in bilingual language processing [J] . Lang Learn, 2006, 56 (S1): 133 - 190.

[47] 倪媛媛，李红. 从生理机制探讨心理理论与执行功能的关系 [J] . 西南师范大学学报自然科学版，2010，35(5)：75—79.

[48] Ullman MT. The neural basis of lexicon and grammar in first and second language the declarative/procedural model [J] . Bilingualism, 2001, 4 (2): 105 - 122.

[49] Abutalebi J. Neural aspects of second language representation and language control [J] . Acta Psychol Amst, 2008, 128 (3): 466 - 478.

[50] Abutalebi J, Green DW. Neuroimaging of language control in bilinguals

neural adaptation and reserve [J]. Bilingualism, 2016, 1(4): 689-698.

[51] Weissberger GH, Gollan TH, Bondi MW, et al. Language and task switching in the bilingual brain bilinguals are staying, not switching, experts [J]. Neuropsychologia, 2015(66): 193-203.

[52] Petitto LA. New discoveries from the bilingual brain and mind across the life span: Implications for education [J]. Mind Brain Educ, 2009, 3(4): 185-197.

[53] Petitto LA, Kovelman I. The bilingual paradox how signing-speaking bilingual children help us to resolve it and teach us about the brain's mechanisms underlying all language acquisition [J]. Learn Lang, 2003, 8(3): 5-19.

[54] Petitto LA, Kovelman I, Harasymowycz U. Bilingual language development learning the new damage [R]. Ann Arbor Society for Research in Child Development, 2003.

[55] Kovelman I, Salahuddin M, Berens MS, et al. "One glove does not fit all" in bilingual reading acquisition using the age of first bilingual language exposure to understand optimal contexts for reading success [J]. Cogent Educ, 2015, 2(1): 1006504.

[56] Thomas-Sunesson D, Hakuta K, Bialystok E. Degree of bilingualism modifies executive control in Hispanic children in the USA [J]. Int J Biling Educ Biling, 2016.

[57] Mechelli A, Crinion JT, Noppeney U, et al. Neurolinguistics structural plasticity in the bilingual brain [J]. Nature, 2004, 431(7010): 757-757.

[58] Maye J, Werker JF, Gerken L. Infant sensitivity to distributional information can affect phonetic discrimination [J]. Cognition, 2002, 82(3): B101-B111.

[59] Kuhl PK. Early language learning and the social brain [C] //Cold Spring Harbor symposia on quantitative biology. New York Cold Spring Harbor Laboratory Press, 2014: 211-220.

[60] Kuhl PK, Tsao FM, Liu HM. Foreign-language experience in infancy effects of short-term exposure and social interaction on phonetic learning [J]. Proc Natl Acad Sci USA, 2003, 100(15): 9096-9101.

[61] Meltzoff AN, Kuhl PK, Movellan J, et al. Foundations for a new science of learning [J]. Science, 2009, 325(5938): 284-288.

[62] Brooks R, Meltzoff AN. The importance of eyes how infants interpret adult looking behavior [J]. Dev Psychol, 2002, 38(6): 958-966.

[63] Brooks R, Meltzoff AN. Connecting the dots from infancy to childhood a longitudinal study connecting gaze following, language, and explicit theory of mind [J] . J Exp Child Psychol, 2015(130): 67-78.
[64] Brooks R, Meltzoff AN. The development of gaze following and its relation to language [J] . Dev Sci, 2005, 8(6): 535-543.
[65] Kemp C. MRI shows association between reading to young children and brain activity [N] . APP News, 2015-04-25(4).
[66] McFadden D, Train K. Mixed MNL models for discrete response [J] . J Appl Econometrics, 2000, 15(5): 447-470.
[67] Konner M. The evolution of childhood relationships, emotion, mind [M] . Cambridge Harvard University Press, 2010.
[68] Sutton-Smith B. The ambiguity of play [M] . Cambridge Harvard University Press, 1997.
[69] Shonkoff JP, Boyce WT, McEwen BS. Neuroscience, molecular biology, and the childhood roots of health disparities building a new framework for health promotion and disease prevention [J] . JAMA, 2009, 301(21): 2252-2259.
[70] 周兢，陈思. 建立儿童学习的脑科学交管系统——脑执行功能理论对学前儿童发展与教育的启示 [J] . 全球教育展望，2011，40(6): 28—33.

致谢

塞尔曼博士和斯诺博士感谢孙千惠、于双辰、李静喻、王越、王艺璇、何海晴对第一章和第二章内容所做的贡献。 两位作者同时感谢哈佛大学教育学院 CEREC Lab 陈思、梅子雯、赵易、何思伟、胡以同、何堃蕾、冯卓、Skyler Yin 和陈皓一为本书内容所做的翻译和校对。 此外，塞尔曼博士感谢何海晴和王露橙完成的翻译工作。

后记

顾文元

经过三年的积淀，历时十个月的筹备，《国际教育专家论“早教”--来自哈佛大学、卡尔加里大学、华东师范大学的研究》（以下简称《国际教育专家论“早教”》）终于与读者见面了。在此，我想对为本书撰写十篇高质量论文的四位国际顶尖教授，为本书拨冗写下序言的专家学者，为本书的中英文翻译进行质量把关的哈佛大学及卡尔加里大学师生团队，为本书的顺利出版提供诸多帮助的“高迪安集团早教研发中心”及出版社的领导和编辑，以及关心本书的所有朋友，致以我诚挚谢意。

始怀胎十月，三年乳哺，回乾就湿，多少辛勤。来自哈佛大学、卡尔加里大学、华东师范大学的四位教授，将其生命的精华都调动了起来，凭借其在学界数十载的沉淀以及对儿童早期教育的热忱，协力孕育出了《国际教育专家论“早教”》这个初生的婴孩。从适宜孩子阅读的绘本到早期儿童语言发展与脑发育的研究，该书涵盖了十个重要教育话题，旨在为幼儿家长、早教工作者及教育家打开一扇窗，帮助他们更好地为培养出关爱他人、德才兼备、认真负责的全球公民做好准备。读罢全书，我的内心感慨万千，久久不能平静——每个大人在看完这本书之后也许都会反思，与其说我们能够教给孩子些什么，倒不如问问我们能从孩子身上学到些什么。

其实，高迪安集团对于教育的投入在许多年前就已经开始了。2014 年 3 月，高迪安集团参加了于纽约联合国总部举办的“第 34 届联合国教科文组织协会世界联合会年度国际大会”，并被授予“世界和平贡献奖”。同年 7 月，出席了于长春举办的“2014 年亚欧教育论坛”，并被联合国教科文组织协会世界联合会授予了“促进多元文化交流杰出贡献”荣誉证书。为了积极引进优秀的国际化教育资源，推动优质儿童早期教育的发展，集团于 2015 年成立了“高迪安集团早教研发中心”，于 2016 年与哈佛大学教授团队展开合作并成立了“高迪安 & 哈佛大学教授国际合作教育科研中心”。

我们坚信，教育的意义，本质上就是“用生命影响生命”。让幼小的心灵盛开真爱人文之花，展露勃勃生机，成为世界所需要的栋梁之才，这正是我们出版这本书的根本目的。

值此书出版之际，将我在“2014 年亚欧教育论坛”演讲全文在此分享，让我们不忘初心，砥砺前行。

英国皇家礼仪培训

萃取多元文化精华，努力构建人文家园

——在2014“亚欧教育论坛”上的演讲

尊敬的各位领导，女士们、先生们，老师们、同学们，各位上午好！

在座的都是教授、学者、学术界的专家。我站在这里就好像回到了课堂，内心忐忑又深感荣幸，请允许我再次向各位致敬！

首先，非常感谢大会主办方——中国教科文组织协会联合会对我的邀请。高迪安集团很荣幸能够作为唯一的一家企业代表，参与2014亚欧教育论坛，并将象征东西方文化交融的艺术瑰宝——“海马龙”，赠送给世界多元文化教育中心。

大家一定很好奇，海马龙是什么？它有什么含义？出处是哪里？在这里，我想先给大家讲个故事。15世纪初，大明王朝永乐帝一位年轻的亲王十分崇尚马可·波罗，于是他便沿着丝绸之路来到西方，并在法国停留。他通过惊人的天赋与高超的艺术造诣逐渐成为了国王查理六世的御用金匠，他还遇到了平生至爱。为了见证其美好的爱情，年轻的亲王将西方文化中海神的坐骑“海马”与东方文化中尊贵的化身“神龙”相结合，创造出了代表和平、包容、睿智的海马龙。不仅收获了爱情，同时也赢得了世人的敬仰。

这虽然是一个传说，但也是我心中的一个梦。今天论坛的主题是“促进多元文化交流，提高教育国际化水平”。一个具有社会责任的企业，应该通过品牌背后的企业文化，积极地参与到多元文化教育与交流中。今年3月，高迪安集团在联合国总部获颁“世界和平贡献奖”，并代表联合国教科文组织协会中国联合会代表团，向联合国赠送了象征“和平、包容、睿智”的文化艺术瑰宝——“海马龙·和平印鉴”。高迪安集团作为将中国人文地产品牌推向全球的先行者，走出了“向世界展现真实中国”民间外交的创新一步。

在座的各位一定看过很多著名的建筑物，奥地利的美泉宫、德国的新天鹅堡、俄罗斯的克林姆林宫、法国卢浮宫……这些建筑之所以成为经典，正是因为它们本身具有多国文化交融的独特魅力。有鉴于此，我们在集团人文地产发展的道路上，始终秉承多元文化交流和融合的理念。在建筑设计上吸收了多国文化，整个社区的景观和配套设施也处处体现了多元文化元素。我们打造了一座公益性园林“香梅和平御园”（Anna Chan Chennault Peace Royal Garden），以美国著名将军陈纳德，中国名门之后、侨界领袖陈香梅夫妇命名。我们在御园内成立了他们的纪念馆及“香梅书苑”，弘扬他们在东西方文化友好交流中的事迹和精神。而我们独创的文化艺术瑰宝——“和平艾琳娜”、“海马龙”、“海马凤”，赋予园林更生动和优雅的文化韵味，其所传递的“和平、和谐、和美”的精神适用于教育、文化、建筑、民生等领域，具有普遍的人文价值。

以人为本，以家庭、社区为载体的多元文化教育，正成为全球的一种大趋势。我们顺应趋势，通过积极引进国际学校，为社区提供教育文化方面的资讯，提供国际化的培训课程，整合多种资源，以利提升社区的教育文化水准。

文化延续着民族的精神血脉，不仅需要薪火相传、代代守护，更需要冲破传统束缚、大胆创新。我认为，这不仅是今天论坛所彰显的责任，也是我们企业家的使命和目标。

我家里有两个八岁的女孩，有一次在和平艾琳娜前的许愿池许愿，只见她们双手合十，闭上眼睛喃喃自语，我问了我的小女儿：“你们许了个什么愿？”她先是愣了一下，然后淡淡地说：“希望我们两个以后永远不会吵架了。”

多么和谐美好的一幕！去除纷争，追求和平，包容互爱，大度和睦……如果世界都能像孩子的愿望那样纯真，我们一定能够开创一个“和平、和谐、和美”的未来！

谢谢大家。

（作者系高迪安集团董事长）

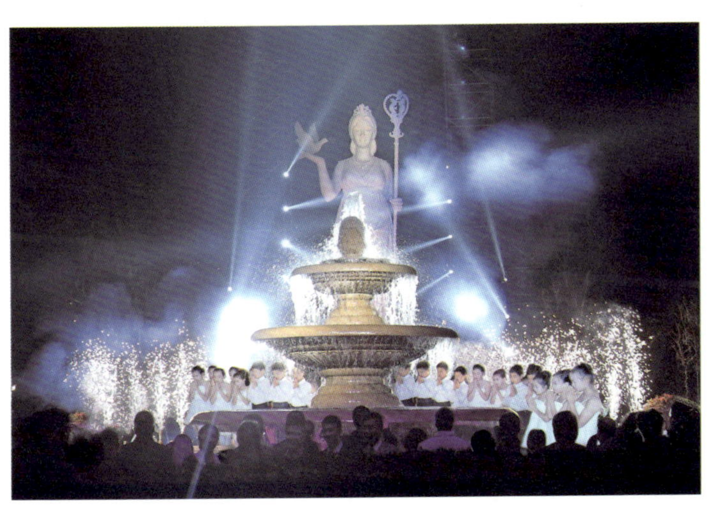

小天使在艾琳娜雕塑及和平许愿池前许愿

Square of Yulong Kindergarten

Heart-shaped Gesture of “9 · 9 True Love”

Outdoor rainbow playground of Yulong Kindergarten, with a natural lawn

Playground for children

Professional basketball court and tennis court

British royal etiquette courses

Afternoon tea in Yulong palace

Afternoon tea in Yulong palace

Equestrian lessons in Anna Chan Chennault Peace Royal Garden

Equestrian lessons in Anna Chan Chennault Peace Royal Garden

Skylight Swimming Pool in Yulong Palace

Premiere of three humanistic and artistic treasures in the United Nations Haïmalong, Haïmafong and Irene

9 · 9 gallery of celebrities

Foreword

Early childhood is a time of remarkable growth with brain development at its peak. The Sustainable Development Goal 4 proposed by the United Nations, i. e. to "ensure inclusive and equitable quality education and promote lifelong learning opportunities for all", has given prominence to early childhood education. As indicated by Target 4. 2, all the nations are expected to, by 2030, ensure that all girls and boys have access to quality early childhood development, care and pre-primary education so that they are ready for primary education. Early childhood education, as the start of lifelong learning and a vital part of national education and social welfare, is inextricably linked with the growth of tens of thousands of children, the well-being of tens of thousands of families as well as the future of a nation. With a view to catering to national needs and gearing itself to advanced global education standards,

Goldian Group has placed a premium on international education, early childhood education in particular. In consequence, the "Goldian Group ECE R & D Center" (herein referred to as the "R & D Center") was established in 2015 and "Goldian and Harvard Professors' Educational Research and Practice Center" was founded in 2016. The goal of the "R&D Center" is to form multilateral strategic cooperative partnership with leading universities, organizations and institutions in the world, assimilate more pedagogical experience as well as educational theories from the field of early childhood education, lead research on the holistic development of a child's social, emotional, cognitive and physical needs in order to build a solid and broad foundation for lifelong learning and wellbeing. All the research results of the "R&D Center" will be applied firstly to the Irene Bilingual Kindergarten and Center for Humanities and Arts, with a view to making them a pioneer of early child education in the world at large.

Since the start of collaboration, the professors from Harvard University, the University of Calgary, East China Normal University, along with the "R&D Center", have launched many intriguing research programs. Predicated on their academic specialization and research interest, the professors have delved into such thematic areas as bilingual education, cognitive development, language development, reading development, literacy, multicultural education, education equity and inclusion, child social development and education, child psychology, second language acquisition and early childhood education in China. After three years of whole-hearted dedication, they have gradually turned their research into the book, *International Working Group's Research on Early*

Childhood Education — A volume contributed by Harvard University, the University of Calgary, East China Normal University, and intend to publish both English and Chinese versions for educators, parents and education researchers in the world.

The book is divided into ten chapters. With thought-provoking case studies and meticulously structured theoretical frameworks, the book has indeed brought up a new prospect for global early childhood education. The professors and educators who have contributed to this book include: Catherine E. Snow, the Patricia Albjerg Graham Professor at the Harvard Graduate School of Education (HGSE); Robert L. Selman, the Roy E. Larsen Professor of Education and Human Development at the HGSE and Professor of Psychology in the Department of Psychiatry at Harvard Medical School; Xu Zhao, the Associate Professor of the University of Calgary and former Doctor of Harvard University; Jing Zhou, the Professor of College of Preschool and Special Education of East China Normal University and Chairman of World Preschool Education Association of China.

Regarding ECCE as a way to nurture caring, capable and responsible global citizens, we believe that it is one of the best investments a country can make to promote human resource development, gender equality and social cohesion, and to reduce the costs for later remedial programs. Throughout the years, Goldian has made unremitting efforts to promote early childhood education. Be it software or hardware, it is committed to gathering the best resources. Well goes a Chinese saying, "Good tools are prerequisite to the successful execution of a job." It is in our sincere wish that the book, *International Working Group's Research on Early*

Childhood Education — A volume contributed by Harvard University, the University of Calgary, East China Normal University, can become a blessing to the global cause of early childhood education. We hope that one day all the children, regardless of their nationality or gender, can have access to quality early childhood enlightenment and fully understand the quintessence of true love and humanities.

Goldian Group ECE R&D Center

Goldian Holdings Co. Limited

Preface

QIAN Wenzhong

"If you do not start to educate your baby until the third day since its birth, you are already two days late."

Well said Pavlov, the world-renowned psychologist, whose words once again remind us of the critical importance of early childhood education.

Early Childhood Education (ECE) is a concept that can be traced back to the epoch of Enlightenment, which generally refers to the education and parenting of infants and young children from birth to the age of six.

As indicated by one of the major works on ECE, *The Education of Karl Witte*, what matters most for children is education. Just as the dawn of their intelligence starts to break, only by developing their intelligence as soon, as much and as correctly as possible can they turn into talents.

The essence of education is to respect life, cherish nature, inspire benevolence and awaken the souls. In a word, to take care of the seeds buried in the heart of children.

Early childhood education is the enlightenment of life. It is of great significance for it lays the foundation of a child's life. Imagine when you are putting on a shirt, doing up the first button correctly is the very first step.

Over the years, I have been invited to interpret the classics such as *the Three-Character Classic* for the audience of the CCTV Lecture Room. I want to give my life to children, to enlightenment and to education.

Therefore, I am very pleased to learn that the book, *International Working Group's Research on Early Childhood Education — A volume contributed by Harvard University, the University of Calgary, East China Normal University*, is about to be published soon.

Reading the manuscripts is quite an intriguing experience. I am especially impressed by the research on "Cross-discipline cross-language (CDCL) Instructional Framework" from the perspective of picture books; the analysis of different interactions of children by selecting different books to read with them; the interpretation of the goal of "raising good, happy and successful children" from the angle of bilingual education, brain development research and promotion of children's social awareness, etc. All these themes on ECE are not armchair strategy but guidance to real life.

Only by being "concrete" can it become "vivid and profound". *International Working Group's Research on Early Childhood Education — A volume contributed by Harvard University, the University of Calgary*, *East China Normal University* is such a concrete, vivid and profound book for enlightenment.

It indeed gratifies me to know that the impressive book is soon to be published and that it is the presented by "Goldian and Harvard Professors' Educational Research and Practice Center" after several years of hard work.

Goldian Group, as a comprehensive enterprise based in Hong Kong, China, was once awarded "World Peace Builder" at the United Nations Headquarters. In its endeavor to push forward the program of "humanity education" and adhere to the spirit of "true love and humanity", it has brought into existence three ingeniously-designed humanistic and artistic treasures — Haïmalong, Haïmafong and Peace Irene. What is also noteworthy is its groundbreaking initiative of launching *the Irene* 9 · 9 *International True Love Day* five years ago, the first global festival that commemorates "true love and humanity". Mr. Dhirendra Bhatnagar, President of WFUCA, once depicted the festival as a "Nobel-style effort and contribution".

As a staunch advocate for the spirit of humanity, Goldian Group seeks a higher platform where it can fully develop its potential.

This explains the establishment of "Goldian and Harvard Professors' Educational Research and Practice Center". Convinced that quality early childhood education is inextricably linked to the future of a country, Goldian Group attempts to apply advanced and scientific ECE theories to the Irene Bilingual Kindergarten, with a view to blazing a trail in the field of education where "true love and humanity" is taken as the core value.

Humanity and life are per se the source of everything in this world, be it living space or mode of life, be it the nature that surrounds us or the way of thinking that we are used to.

Humanity is where the living water starts; life is the beat of the world that never stops.

Life is a way of no end, while humanity is a practice.

Circling back to the book, *International Working Group's Research on Early Childhood Education — A volume contributed by Harvard University*, *the University of Calgary*, *East China Normal University*, we could say that it is the byproduct of true love, humanity and education.

There is no end to the voyage of humanity or the way of life. It is in my genuine wish that Goldian Group will stick to its humanistic practice and explore more possibilities on the way of life.

(Wenzhong Qian: Scholar, Professor of Fudan University, Speaker at CCTV's Lecture Room)

Contents

Catherine E. Snow

Snow has conducted extensive research on early childhood education, with a special interest in bilingual and low-income children. She is the Patricia Albjerg Graham Professor at the Harvard Graduate School of Education. She has chaired three National Academy of Sciences committees that produced influential reports: *Preventing Reading Difficulties in Young Children* (1998; available in Chinese), *Assessing young children: Why, what and how* (2008), and *Science Literacy: Concepts, Contexts, and Consequences* (2016). She is a member of the National Academy of Sciences and of the American Academy of Arts and Sciences, and a former president of the American Educational Research Association.

Robert L. Selman

Robert L. Selman is the Roy E. Larsen Professor of Education and Human Development at the Harvard Graduate School of Education and Professor of Psychology in the Department of Psychiatry at Harvard Medical School. His research focuses on ways to promote various forms of social awareness as they are related to educational achievement, ethical development, psychological wellness, and youth intercultural participation, most recently in conjunction with digital media.

Selman has been: The recipient of a Career Scientist Award from the National Institute of Mental Health (USA); a trustee of Devereux

Advanced Behavioral Health; and a Scholar in Residence at the Russell Sage Foundation. He is a Fellow of the American Psychological Association, the Association for Psychological Science, the American Orthopsychiatry Association, and the American Educational Research Association.

1. Cross-discipline Cross-language (CDCL) Instructional Framework: A Prototypical Unit Using the Picture Book 'HUG'

Robert L. Selman and Catherine E. Snow

Harvard University

I. An Overview of the CDCL Framework

The Cross-discipline/Cross-language (CDCL) Instructional Framework is a conceptual model designed to help educators of young children in preschools promoting early bilingualism and biculturalism learn how to develop their social and scientific knowledge as they also begin to learn to be bilingual. We will focus on the case of Chinese-English bilingual programs in China, recognizing that the details would have to be adjusted for other language pairs or, indeed, even for this same language pair in a different social context. Nonetheless, we propose some principles and approaches that we hope will have general applicability.

Our general framework is supplemented by a set of instructional strategies and curriculum activities that address six "content and skills" domains considered central to early childhood development and in particular specified by the Chinese Ministry of Education. These are health, social skills, math, language, art, science (see Figure 1). The CDCL framework specifies how each of the six domains can be addressed to ensure skills in two languages — with social skills (and social awareness) featured in a primary role because of their central place in very young children's lives. The framework uses stories and story-telling, both to ground the curriculum and to provide reference points for all the children to be able to talk about their understandings of a shared experience with each other, as well as to understand it on their own. The stories provide children (and their teachers or parents) with descriptions of social relationships to which they need to pay very close attention. With this basis of shared understandings, the children can learn about the content and practice the skills relevant to each of the other five areas.

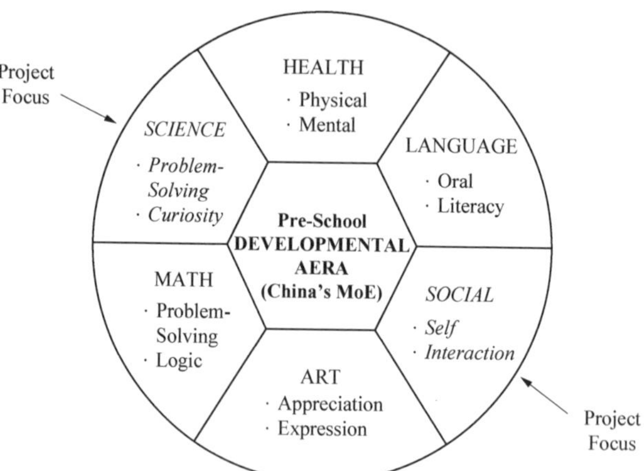

Figure 1 Below is a description of the Chinese Ministry Framework for Preschool Education

For example, as can be seen in Figure 2, below, the CL/CD approach always incorporates two languages (in this specific case, Chinese and English) while focusing on two aspects of the world in which young children live. In any story selected, one of those aspects is the language of the social world. The other may be any one of the other five domains in the content framework. (Language is both one of the targeted domains and the medium for access to all the domains.) As an example, the second area (or domain) is science (see Figure 2). In reading a book about transportation, information about vehicles and what makes them move (human power for bikes and skate boards, internal combustion engines for cars and motorcycles) can be presented. Some children may be engaged in this text because they simply love front-loaders or motorcycles. Others may show less natural engagement with this story topic. However, having stories discussed and/or explained to children with a focus on both the scientific **and** the social-emotional aspects of the story allows different children different points of entry. Those not so fascinated by the world of machines can come to understand the experience of trucks, buses, and other vehicles as extensions of their own basic human need for agency and self-efficacy (to get around, to see things, to meet others).

Furthermore, when a young child wants to know what makes the trucks move, whether they themselves have the skills to move them (agency), they also need to know from the story **who** will allow them to do so while still insuring they, the children reading or listening to the story, will stay safe (safety) and will retain the support of their parents (identity). These basic social foundations of human psychological development (safety, self-efficacy, and social identity) may manifest in different ways across different cultures, but are always central to the optimal promotions of children's health, education, and welfare.

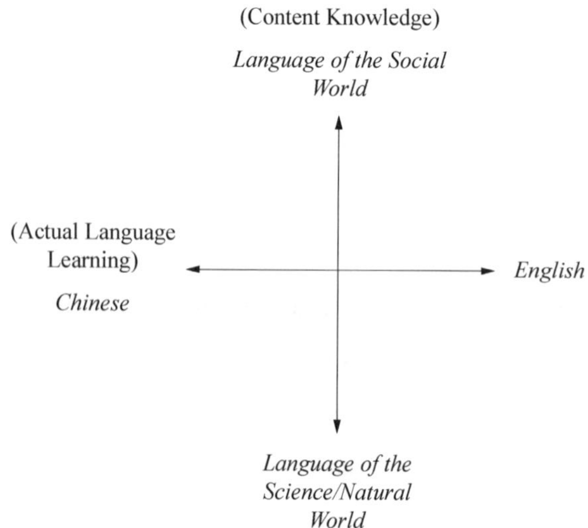

Figure 2 Conceptual Framework that emphasizes language as a vehicle for communication (Chinese and English) and language as a way for young children to navigate their social world.

Why highlight social skills and the language of the social world in early childhood education?

Social development in early childhood lays the basic foundation for ethical and civic behavior later in life. Therefore, social skills always need to be integrated with each of the other five domains. This is done not only through the management of the social interactions in the classroom, but also by ensuring the formal curriculum integrates social learning with new content knowledge and skills across content areas.

The primary medium for promoting social development, especially for young children, is language. Children develop language initially to accomplish social goals (making connections with others, directing others' attention, giving and receiving help). As young children develop their language skills, they also develop a more nuanced and better articulated set of social goals for themselves (and for others) through the words they use to communicate with others (Ninio & Snow, 1996). Subsequently children also start using language to accomplish cognitive goals — to learn new things, to satisfy their curiosity. They do that best, and most happily, when they have strong, positive, trusting relationships with the adult 'experts' from whom they seek knowledge (Harris P et al., 2018).

Language provides a powerful tool for children who want to play with a friend, ask for a toy, or tell someone how they feel. Thus, social competencies develop hand in hand with language skills and social linguistic competences. Learning language is requisite for social development, and early communication skills create opportunities for an early entry into social interaction and sociability. Furthermore, in a curriculum such as the one we propose, that is organized around shared books, social relationships can always be "read into" the curriculum content in any of the domains on which the text focuses (Selman, 2017; Snow, 2002).

How do we best teach children to be bilingual?

Research evidence suggests that the most efficient condition for second language learning is initial exposure to content in one's first language, and then to the same stories/information/themes/vocabulary words in the second language. Therefore, one approach is to start the content instruction in children's native language. Once the background information becomes familiar and students approach mastery, they can be immersed in the second language context (Snow, 2017).[①] It is important to realize, though, that this approach is topic-specific. We are not endorsing postponing the introduction of the second language until a particular level of mastery in the native language has been achieved. Rather, we suggest introducing information about a particular, engaging, and circumscribed topic (e. g., modes of transportation and the engineering challenges they offer, or playground equipment and the opportunities for play they create) in the native language; only after the children have achieved some depth of familiarity with the topic in their native language should that same information be introduced in the second language.

How this would work

We illustrate the principles informing our framework by presenting here a prototype unit, anchored in the picture book *Hug*, by Jez Alborough, designed for children from 2 to 5 years old in bilingual kindergartens in China. Each session introduces a variety of instructional subunits, including *warm-up*, *discover the story*, *discussion*, *explore*

① On the other hand, a standard approach in Chinese "international schools" is often actually the opposite — to start with 100% immersion in the second language and slowly increase the amount of time in native language up to 50%. There are pros and cons to both approaches in bilingual classrooms, which also vary with the larger social context.

beyond the story, and *family engagement activities*.

Each unit contains suggestions for achieving each of the four fundamental pedagogical principles of the CDCL Framework：

- Find engaging stories, activities and materials
- Identify the social language world of the child as one "anchor"
- Build in discussion-oriented activities to promote competence in oral language and critical thinking
- Design units to include parent involvement activities

Each unit selects key vocabulary words for students to learn in each language. For example, to go along with the book *Hug*, even though it has no words in print or text, here are some vocabulary words that can be taught and learned, depending on the age of the student：

- 森林 forest
- 草原 grassland
- 长颈 giraffe
- 河马 hippo
- 变色龙 chameleon

About the story, *HUG*, the picture book written by Jez Alborough we use as an example：

Bobo, a young chimp, happily sets about alone to take a walk in the jungle (see picture below). As he meets different kinds of animals, he notices that the young of each species he encounters is being hugged by his/her parent. Seeing his jungle friends cuddling and snuggling with their parents, from time to time, Bobo says "Hug." The first time, this can be interpreted as an observation —

just a description of the scene. As he goes on, though, seeing more and more such pairs, and presumably realizing that he is alone, his sadness and agitation grow. Eventually, Bobo sees his mother and they hug in joyful reunion, after which he happily revisits all the other animals with hugs.

Although this widely loved book contains only three words, it conveys an intriguing and engaging story about love and attachment. Most importantly, it can be interpreted from various points of view. Children can discuss the social world of primary attachments and cross species friendship through language, and better understand the material, physical, logical, and aesthetic world in which Bobo (and we) live through their study of math, art, science and health.

For example, to the sophisticated "reader" of this story, it may seem clear that at the start of his walk through the jungle, Bobo is simply pointing out that the first mother/child dyad encountered, two elephants, are hugging. However, as he continues to walk, the depiction of Bobo, especially his facial expressions, suggest a progression of emotions: Bobo feeling a bit sad and lonely (see Picture 1), then increasingly distressed, until he and his mother see one another, and his expression, mood, and feelings change dramatically (as signified by the large print or font size and smiling faces in Picture 2).

These feelings are universal, not only in humans, but across much of the mammalian kingdom. Although few words are printed in *Hug*, many words are needed to complete Bobo's story, consider different perspectives on it, and relate it to the listener's life. It is this aesthetic device, i.e., leaving aspects of the story unspecified so that tellers and listeners can fill it in, that we, as educators, can use to promote cross language/cross domain development, both of skills and knowledge. This is one of the devices that will help young children become sophisticated readers and story tellers, and that will nurture their educational, ethical, and aesthetic development.

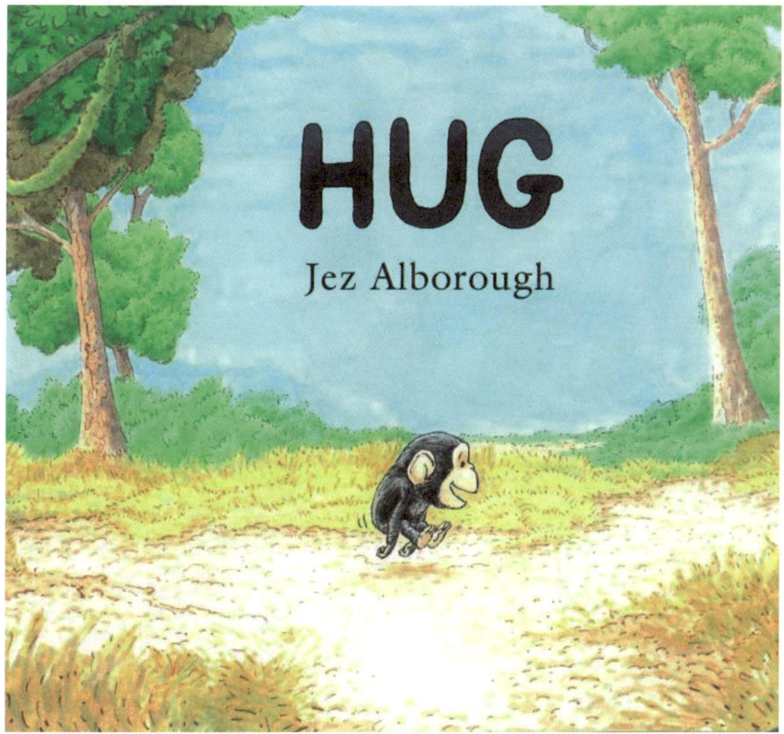

ISBN: 10 0-7636-1576-5

Picture 1

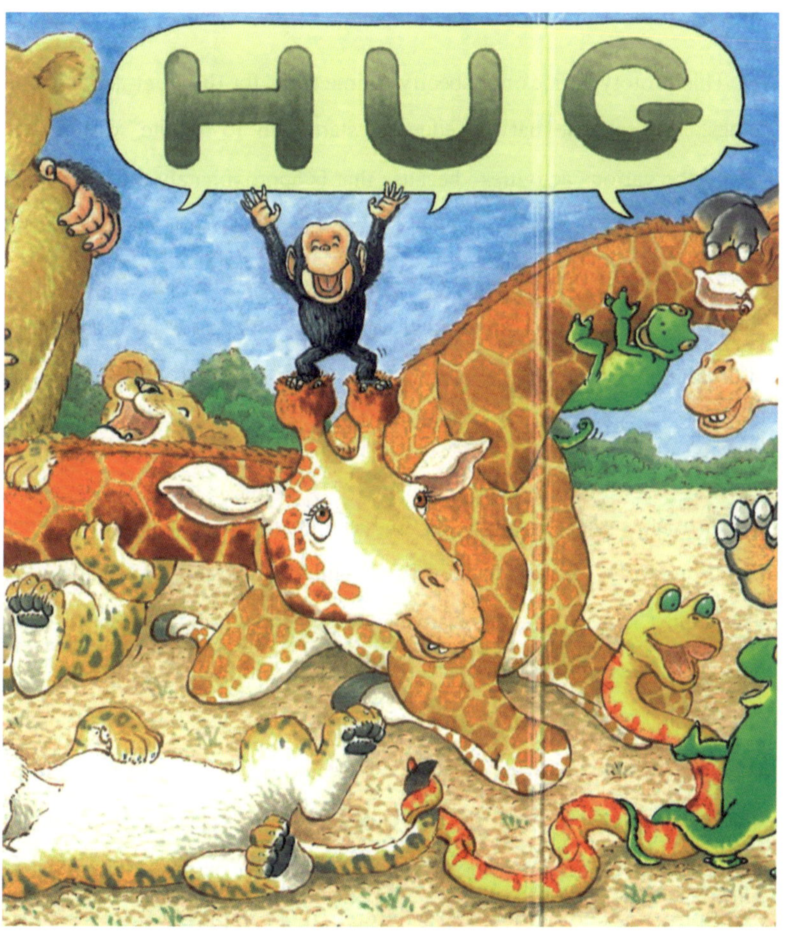

Picture 2

II. The Cross Language/Cross Discipline Instructional Model:

How to distribute the instructional time

This prototype does not specify a time limit for different activities or themes. We suggest that the educator start with 15-minute sessions for each of the various activities, because that is approximately the amount of time that most 2-or 3-year-olds can concentrate. Instructors can adjust the length of sessions according to the needs of individuals and groups; 20 – 25 min sessions are very appropriate for 4-year-olds, or even for younger children after they have been socialized into classroom practices.

How to create a language enriching classroom or home

Instructors are encouraged to ask open-ended questions about discussion-worthy topics, to be open to children's responses, and always to remember that, while there are never right or wrong answers to truly contestable questions, there are better and less good answers.

Parental engagement is an important factor in building an enriching language/literacy environment for children. Topics discussed both at home and at school will be associated with a richer web of social relations, and with more varied language forms. If parents know what is going on at school, they can reinforce those topics, activities, and language forms at home in the language of the home.

How to present age-appropriate teaching materials

A variety of activities are provided in this unit. Instructors may address the selection/content/instruments/order of the activities based on their best understanding of their students' developmental levels.

How to coordinate the Chinese and the English lessons

We suggest that for each unit teachers teach the same content in two languages, in Mandarin first and English later. Educators are encouraged to use Mandarin and English at separate times, for example, discussing Bobo's emotions in Mandarin on Monday and then teaching the same content in English on Tuesday, or alternately reading the book several times in Mandarin during one week and then returning to it in English the next week. We teach Mandarin first so that children can understand the content deeply in their mother tongue, before learning the English words/structures to discuss the same content. Also, to allow for the consolidation of new knowledge in each language, schedules should leave a certain amount of time as an interval between Mandarin and English classes on any given topic. The optimal interval (a few hours? A day? Several days?) is a worthy topic of further research.

We suggest that the content covered in Chinese and English be the same but that teachers choose a somewhat different range of activities for the two lessons. So, for example, if the activities engaged in after discussing the book in Chinese include reproducing the story with puppets and building a model of a jungle as an art activity, the activities engaged in after the English reading might include acting out the actions of the different animals as the teacher reads the story (which is less challenging than the full reproduction of the story), then reproducing one of the animals by drawing, painting, or molding in clay.

Teachers who use this prototype are encouraged to choose the activities that suit their class best, making modifications as needed, while maintaining a focus on reaching the overall teaching goal.

Recap of basic principles

Teachers are the experts. Considering the children's ages and the paucity of words in this particular book, teachers are encouraged to tell the story as the first activity. However, we recommend that teachers be straightforward with the children; let them know that it is just the teacher's own understanding and that children are perfectly welcome to have their own thoughts and understandings.

At the end of each session children will benefit from opportunities to retell the story in their own words, with the support of the pictures in the book and with any necessary scaffolding from the instructor. Instructors can encourage their students to develop their own interpretations of the story content and to learn to understand and appreciate one another's understandings (Selman, 2003).

Play is the context for learning. It is critical to integrate 'play' into the learning process. We encourage teachers to involve 'play' as much as possible in the process of learning, as play is children's nature. Children learn while playing (Vygotsky, 1967).

Parents have a crucial role. As family engagement is one of the four primary principles in our pedagogical framework, we include in every curricular unit a design for family activities (see example at the end of this prototype). Family engagement is important in child development, and language support from families in the home language is crucial in negotiating the time constraints inherent in bilingual programs (Bowlby, 1982). Thus it is the responsibility of the kindergarten to provide the kinds of activities that can enhance children's learning in the home language, e.g., sending the books to be read in the classroom home in the home language, suggesting other books on the same theme and with some of the same vocabulary words for parents to share with their children.

In addition, it is the responsibility of the kindergarten personnel to make sure that parents understand their role: supporting and enriching the home language and the child's knowledge base in the home language. If parents start speaking the second language to their children, that undermines the principles underlying this program.

References

Bowlby, J. (1982). Attachment (2nd ed., Bowlby, John. Attachment and loss; v. 1). New York: BasicBooks.

Harris, P. L., Koenig, M. A., Corriveau, K. H., & Jaswal, V. K. (2018). Cognitive foundations of learning from testimony, Annual Review of Psychology, 69, 251 – 273. (2018)

Ninio, A., & Snow, Catherine E. (1996). Pragmatic development (Essays in developmental science).

Selman, R. (2003). The promotion of social awareness : Powerful lessons from the partnership of developmental theory and classroom practice. New York: Russell Sage Foundation.

Selman, R. (2017). Fostering Friendship: Pair Therapy for Treatment and Prevention. Taylor and Francis.

Snow, C. (2002). Reading for Understanding. RAND Corporation.

Snow, C. (2017). Early literacy development and instruction: An overview. Routledge.

Vygotsky, L. (1967). Play and Its Role in the Mental Development of the Child. Journal of Russian and East European Psychology, 5(3), 6 – 18.

2. Cross-discipline Cross-language (CDCL) Instructional Framework: A Prototypical Unit Using the Picture Book 'SEESAW':

Catherine E. Snow and Robert L. Selman

Harvard University

SeeSaw is a children's picture book that has been published in several languages. We use it here to explore the use of a traditional read aloud as a context for demonstrating an approach to early childhood education we call the Cross-discipline Cross-language (CDCL) Instructional Framework. The CDCL framework is appropriate for use in any bilingual preschool or kindergarten context. Here we consider how it might be used in a Chinese kindergarten that has adopted English as its second language.

The Chinese Ministry of Education defines six domains that early childhood education (ECE) should address (see Figure 1). While we accept the importance of all six, we consider two of these domains to be of particular relevance to young children, and to offer great affordances to the educator. Thus, without in any sense excluding the other domains, we concentrate here on science and social skills, domains for which

SeeSaw is a particularly apt vehicle.

The Seesaw Story is about a young giraffe on the playground who wants to play on a seesaw with his friends, but runs into a problem because he is so much heavier/bigger/larger than them. It is clear that this story offers a rich array of potential social themes (playing together, making friends, being alike and being different) and at the same time ample opportunity for science exploration (weight, density, balance). We display below the lesson sequence that highlights both these options for a Chinese-English kindergarten setting.

Our approach to developing a set of lessons from *the Seesaw Story* is a prototype for how to develop useful curriculum within the CDCL framework. Specifically, the steps are:

- Locate social relationships as an important focus of the story.
- Specify the language forms, in both Chinese and English, that are most urgently needed to discuss the content of the book, in this case both its social and its scientific content. In other words, identify key vocabulary words for each story, present those words in Chinese (the stronger language) first, and subsequently in English.
- Develop collaborative activities designed to expand the themes of the book, so that the children can exercise autonomy in pursuing their own ideas (designing a playground, testing weights on a balance beam, acting out the narrative plot) while creating opportunities to use their new vocabulary and explore the new ideas they are encountering.
- Carefully observe what sorts of topics and activities engage children and encourage their ongoing development of the native language (here Chinese) and the second language, in this case English, as a

source of input into ongoing practice improvements.

- Seek out other books to read with the children that expand the theme and to the extent possible repeat the key vocabulary. These might include, for example, books showing different kinds of playgrounds and games children play, nonfiction books about giraffes, books about very big things and very small things.

One example

To demonstrate more concretely how the CDCL framework would be put into action, we present here an extensively worked out lesson plan for using *the Seesaw Story*, as a prototype for developing other content. The prototype we developed using this story is presented below.

Picture 1 The Seesaw Story

The Seesaw Story — A prototypical unit

DAY1：The Language of the Social World — Chinese

❖ **Get Ideas Going**

Vocabulary of the unit

一起 (together)	合作 (collaboration)	帮助 (help)	开心 (happy)	伤心 (sad)

* These target words will be repeatedly used and emphasized by the teacher.

- ➢ Activity 1：Preview characters：animals
  - ■ Use flashcards to preview animals mentioned in the story：长颈鹿 猴子 小狗 小老鼠
  - ■ Looking through the pictures in the storybook, ask children to identify, name, and describe the animals involved (e. g. "刚刚我们学会了几种小动物的名字，那么哪些小动物在我们的故事里呢？你能在这张图画里找到他们吗？""长颈鹿是什么样子的呀？小老鼠呢？")
  - ■ Talk about animals：What's your favorite animal? What does your favorite animal look like?
- ➢ Activity 2：Preview the setting：playground
  - ■ P6－7 Identify the structures on the playground：跷跷板 滑梯 秋千
  - ■ Talk about games on the playground：Are there other structures on the playground? What do you do when you go to a playground? What's your favorite activity on the playground?

❖ **Discover the story** (read aloud)

- ➢ Show the cover to children and ask them to describe what they see. Who are the main characters? Where are the characters? What do you think the story is about?
- ➢ Instructor reads aloud, adding more vocabulary words referring to thoughts, emotions, and perspective taking
- ➢ Dialogic reading：check children's comprehension and encourage children to speak up, describe the pictures, ask questions, and provide alternative interpretations
- ➢ Script for reading-aloud：

今天我们来讲一个长颈鹿和跷跷板的故事。我们一起看这幅图，<u>猜一猜，这是一个什么样的故事呢？</u>长颈鹿说："今天我要去公园，到公园的广场上去玩。"

长颈鹿来到了公园里。公园里有（**point to the pieces of playground equipment and wait for the children to name them**）跷跷板，滑梯和秋千。长颈鹿看到了公园里有这么多游戏可以玩，他心里有什么感受呀？（**keyword**：开心）我们大家一起做一个笑脸好不好？长颈鹿看了看四周，说："我现在不想荡秋千，我想去玩跷跷板。"

但是现在长颈鹿遇到了一个难题，你们说是什么难题呢？长颈鹿想，一个人怎么玩跷跷板呢？我需要和别人一起玩跷跷板。长颈鹿可以和谁一起玩跷跷板呀？他看到了小老鼠。小老鼠或许愿意和长颈鹿一起玩跷跷板。现在长颈鹿要怎么做呢？

"你好，小老鼠！"长颈鹿说，你愿意和我一起玩跷跷板吗？长颈鹿邀请小老鼠一起玩跷跷板，小老鼠要怎么回答呢？小老鼠说，"好啊，听起来很有趣呢！"所以呀，小老鼠愿意和长颈鹿一起玩跷跷板。"嗖"的一下，小老鼠就跳到跷跷板上了。你们猜，下面会发生什么呢？小老鼠和长颈鹿能够开心地一起玩跷跷板吗？

"哎呀！"小老鼠说，"我们不能一起玩跷跷板，因为你太重了。看，我只能一直停在上面，不能继续玩。""我没有那么重，"长颈鹿说，"是你太轻了。看，我不能往上，只能坐在下面。"

那么现在他们遇到了一个难题，这个难题是什么呢？遇到难题的时候他们要怎么办呢？小老鼠小心地从高高的跷跷板上爬下来，然后看到了小猴子。小老鼠有了一个好主意："或许你可以问问小猴子，小猴子个头比我大，也比我重，或许你可以和小猴子一起玩跷跷板。小老鼠为什么要提出这个建议呢？小老鼠知道长颈鹿想玩跷跷板，他这么做是为了帮助长颈鹿，让长颈鹿开心。长颈鹿听到这个建议，会怎么做呢？

…

长颈鹿想和朋友们一起玩跷跷板，但是没有成功。他现在很伤心，很难过。"没有人可以和我一起玩跷跷板了。"长颈鹿说。看到长颈鹿伤心的样子他的朋友们要做什么呢？小老鼠，小猴子和小狗狗想帮助长颈鹿，于是他们想了一个好办法。是什么好办法呢？他们要一起合作来解决这个难题。生活中有些事情不是我们一个人可以完成的，要和别人合作才可以呢。

小猴子开心地说："我们几个一起坐在跷跷板上就不会太轻了。"小狗狗和小老鼠叫道："你也不会太重了。"长颈鹿开心地说："这样我们就可以一起玩跷跷板了。"

❖ **Explore beyond the book**

➢ Activity 1：Social perspective taking and problem solving
Read the story again, check children's comprehension of the story, and ask the children to take the characters' perspectives (questions embedded in the read aloud), incorporating the key words：

- ■ Page 12, the mouse finds out he isn't able to play seesaw with giraffe. What did the mouse say? ("you're too heavy, I can't play with you") How does the giraffe feel when he hears that? Is that a nice thing to say to a friend? If you were the mouse, what would you say or do?
- ■ P14, what did mouse say or do? (he invites monkey to play with giraffe) Is that a nice thing to do? How would you describe the mouse's behavior? (virtues: helpful, nice, caring, etc.)
- ■ Page 26, giraffe is sad. Why is giraffe sad? What did giraffe's friends say and do? (they came up with a great idea) What would you say or do if a friend is sad?

➢ Activity 2: Draw and Tell

- ■ Draw a picture of one time when you and your friend played on a playground (encourage children to think about past events), or a picture of you and your friend playing on the playground in the future (prompt children to envision and plan for the future)
- ■ Incorporating the keywords (一起 合作 帮助 开心 伤心), describe to your partner: what are you playing with? Were you happy or unhappy? Why? What did say to each other?

DAY2: The Language of the Social World — English

❖ **Get Ideas Going**

Vocabulary of the unit

together	collaborate	help	happy	sad

❖ **Discover the story**

❖ **Explore beyond the book**

DAY3: The Language of the Science World — Chinese

❖ **Get Ideas Going**

Vocabulary of the unit

大 小	重 轻	高 矮	上 下

➢ Activity: measure and describe

Supplies: *Objects to compare*: teacher's chair vs. children's chair; eraser vs. pencil; picture book vs. dictionary etc.

Measurement tools: electronic scales, rulers

Instruction: the teacher introduces the vocabulary in pairs and show corresponding objects. Then, the teacher ask the students to "feel the word" by holding or measuring the objects and then describe their feeling.

❖ **Discover the story**

➢ Activity： read aloud with focus on science content

➢ Script for reading-aloud：

P. 1： 今天我们再来讲一遍长颈鹿和跷跷板的故事，看看大家会不会有新的发现呢？ 记得我们刚刚学过的词，看看大家能不能在今天的故事里找到他们？

P. 4： 长颈鹿到公园的广场上玩。 在广场上，长颈鹿看到了很多玩具。 看！ 有跷跷板、秋千、滑梯。 长颈鹿说：”现在我不想荡秋千，我想玩跷跷板。”

P. 5：”但是一个人怎么玩跷跷板呢？ 我需要和别人一起玩跷跷板。”长颈鹿想。 确实是这样，不是吗？ 你可以想象一下，当长颈鹿一个人坐到跷跷板上的时候会发生什么吗？ （**wait for children's response and provide feedback, if there is any.**）幸运的是，他这个时候看到了小老鼠。 她或许愿意和长颈鹿一起玩跷跷板。

P. 6： 于是长颈鹿走过去说：“你愿意和我一起玩跷跷板吗？”“好啊，听起来很有趣呢！”小老鼠说。 嗖的一下，小老鼠就跳到了跷跷板上了。 你们猜猜，小老鼠坐上跷跷板之后会发生什么呢？

P. 7：“哎呀！”小老鼠说，”我们不能一起玩跷跷板，因为你太重了。 看，我只能一直停在下面，不能继续玩。”“我们有那么重，是你太轻了。 看，我不能往上，只能坐在下面。” 小老鼠小心翼翼地从高高的跷跷板上爬下来，然后看到了小猴子。”或许你可以问问小猴子，”小老鼠对长颈鹿说，”小猴子的个头比我大，也比我重，或许你可以和小猴子一起玩跷跷板？”

P. 8—13： ……

P. 14： 小伙伴们想帮助长颈鹿，于是他们想了一个好办法。 如果你是长颈鹿的朋友，你会想什么办法来帮助他呢？

P. 15： 看！ 小伙伴们一起跳到了跷跷板上。 小猴子说：”这样我们几个就不会太轻了。”“你也不会太重了！”小老鼠和小狗狗说。 就这样，跷跷板取得了平衡，小伙伴们可以一起开心地玩跷跷板了！

❖ **Explore beyond the book**

➢ Check for basic comprehension：

Can you rank the characters in the book by weight? Who is the heaviest? Who is the lightest?

➢ Check for deep comprehension：

Supplies： small seesaw, finger puppets with different sizes and weights (e. g. bunny, lion, frog, dinosaur, panda)

Instruction："Now, if you have a chance to invite more animals to play the seesaw, who will you invite? Who do you think should be playing with whom?"

<table>
<tr><td>
Activity: Students are divided into groups of four. Each group is given a small seesaw and several finger puppets. Children do experiments within their groups (ideally to try to achieve balance on their seesaw) and then share their findings with the class.

Extension for older students: besides adding several animals on one side of the seesaw, what else do you think we could do to get them play happily?
</td></tr>
<tr><td>
DAY4: The Language of the Science World — English
[WILL REPEAT ACTIVITIES IN DAY 3, BUT IN ENGLISH]
❖ Get Ideas Going
Vocabulary of the unit
<table>
<tr><td>big
small</td><td>heavy
light</td><td>tall
short</td><td>up
down</td></tr>
</table>
❖ Discover the story
❖ Explore beyond the book
</td></tr>
<tr><td>
DAY 5: Integrating the Social and Science World across Languages
❖ Review
➢ Review key social and science vocabulary in both Chinese and English using flash cards
➢ Retell the story, most likely in Chinese, but students are allowed to use English words if they can. Students are encouraged to use the key vocabulary they have learnt in the unit.

❖ The Power of Collaboration — A creative activity
➢ Group set-up: Students are divided into groups of four. Each child is given one crayon of a single color and the four children in the same group will have different colors. Each group will only get one piece of paper.
➢ Instruction: "Please draw a picture of the playground of our school. Please collaborate/work together with your group members to make your picture colorful! After your group completes the drawing, you will describe to the class what you have drawn and how you did it as a team."

❖ The Beauty of Languages
➢ Synonyms and acronyms will be taught in Chinese and English.
</td></tr>
</table>

Beyond *The Seesaw Story*

As a next step, we need to find books that are most likely to place a heavier emphasis on one of the six domains in the Ministry developmental areas framework, and so have themes, topics, vocabulary words (content) and skills that fall within that area. In the *Seesaw* story, the two domains are the language of the social world and the language of the scientific world, in the case of this story, the rules of physics. In future story selections, we will search for books about each of the other four domains (math, art, health, and language.) This model can be seen in the picture below.

6 settings/ 6 hi-lited content domains	Going to the play-ground	Going to the library	Going to the grocery	Going to the museum	Going to the computer room	Going to the clinic
Social	XX	XX	XX	XX	XX	XX
Language	X	XX	X	X	X	X
Math			X			
Art				X		
Science and technology					X	
Health						X

For example, a story about a trip to the symphony or the theater will emphasize the developmental area (domain) of art, including music and drama. As such, both the story selected and the activities that are constructed will focus on both appreciation of art (knowledge of art) and artistic expression (artistic skills). A trip to the doctor's office, will emphasize knowledge about health, for example, why it is important to wash our hands before eating, and skills (how to brush one's teeth). In addition, the health stories will also focus on mental health, that is knowledge about ways to stay happy, engaged, alert, as well as the skills one can use (for example, sharing with parents one's worries).

While any story we choose will be able to touch upon each and all of the six domains, we recommend as children grow older, improve upon their oral language, begin the task of reading comprehension, and engage in the world outside their families as social beings, to have a "specific developmental area approach." For instance, if the class of five year olds seems to be having challenges with sharing or teasing, stories about these topics told bilingually are very appropriate. Words are very important for these issues, so a bilingual program will want to help children be conversant with these topics in both languages.

And, of course, one can revisit previous stories which will have new meanings to children as they grow older. As an example, we can revisit the *Seesaw* story we used earlier to help children learn basic words about their social world and their science world. At age four or five, we can retell the story to include themes and topics that may now be in the child's experience, for example, feeling left out, or feeling different (after all Giraffe is rather taller than all giraffe's friends).

References

Bowlby, J. (2005). A secure base: Clinical applications of attachment theory (Vol. 393). Taylor & Francis.

Children's wall art-wooden animal letters. Retrieved August 1, 2017, from Alphabet Gifts: http://www.alphabetgifts.co.uk/Childrens-Wall-Art/Sevi-Animal-Letters

Jalongo, Mary Renck (2000). Early Childhood Language Arts: Meeting Diverse Literacy Needs through Collaboration with Families and Professionals [M]. Second Edition.

Numbers song let's count 1 – 10 new version. (2012, May 16). Retrieved August 1, 2017, from You-tube: https://www.youtube.com/watch?v=85M1yxIcHpw

Primary colors song for kids/Secondary colors song for kids. (2015, April 27). Retrieved August 1, 2017, from You-tube: https://www.youtube.com/watch?v=bmquqAP2w_8

Selman, R. (1971). Taking Another's Perspective: Role-Taking Development in Early Childhood. Child Development, 42(6), 1721 – 1734. doi: 10.2307/1127580.

Selman, R. (2007) The Promotion of Social Awareness. Russell Sage Foundation, N. Y. C.

Snow, C. (2002). Reading for Understanding: Toward an R&D Program In Reading Comprehension. Santa Monica, CA: RAND

Wood, D., Bruner, J. S., & Ross, G. (1976). The role of tutoring in problem solving. Journal of child psychology and psychiatry, 17(2), 89 – 100.

Zhao Minghui, Kou Aili. (2016). Analysis of Color Words Age Suitableness and Writing Strategies of Preschoolers Literature [J]. Journal of Pingxiang University. Vol. 33. No. 2.

泥娃娃. (2009, July 12). Retrieved August 1, 2017, from Youtube: https://www.youtube.com/watch?v=DPIDWnfz

Appendix: Figure 4

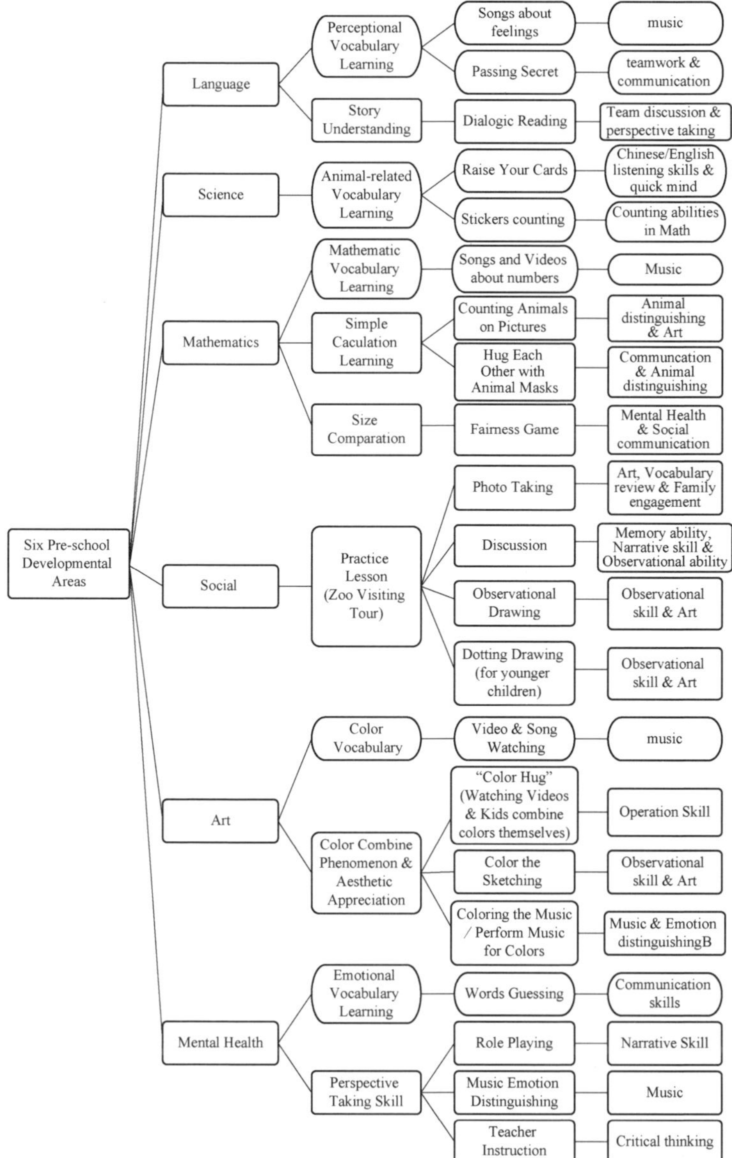

Figure 4 From ministry pre-school developmental areas to actual curriculum design to specific activities (content knowledge domains and skills: A hierarchical model)

2. Cross-discipline Cross-language (CDCL) Instructional Framework: A Prototypical Unit Using the Picture Book 'SEESAW':

3. The Development of Social Awareness in Young Children: Some Reasons for the Promotion of Social Perspective Taking Skills

Robert L. Selman[1]

Harvard University

Regardless of the culture or country of which they are citizens, all caring and dedicated parents want their children to grow up to be successful, not only at work but also within the family. They want their children to learn to have good friends, and to have close and respectful relationships with others. They want their children to understand *why* it is important to make and maintain these close relationships. They want their children to be able to respectfully resolve conflicts both at home and outside their home. And they want their children to compete successfully in the social world. We call children's understanding of their parents'

[1] **Robert L. Selman** is the Roy E. Larsen Professor of Education and Human Development and Professor of Psychology in Psychiatry at Harvard University. Currently, he studies the developmental and cultural antecedents of the capacity of children and youth to form and maintain positive social relationships, as well as ways to prevent negative educational, social, and health outcomes.

social expectation — the developing awareness of the reasons why strong social relationships are an important feature of human development—the growth of *social awareness*.

Today, almost everyone is aware that *children* see the social world in a way that is different from the way in which adults tend to view it. Parents and educators of young children work hard to socialize their children and students to abide by the rules of the culture, that is, the family culture, the peer culture, the school culture, and the national culture. Parents and educators can do much to promote the kind of social awareness they think will be best for their children and best for their country.

However, even though, cultural values play a crucial role in what parents in a society want their children to say and do in social situations, what may not be so obvious is that when children are not following the rules of the larger culture, they are not simply unaware of certain facts, or values or understandings about the social world they will inherit. They also have their own (childlike) theories as to how to interpret the social events in their lives: among them, social affection, emotion, engagement, conflict and disagreement.

Often, it is at a young age that children's own "deep theories" about social relationships are actually more like those of other children all around the world than they are like those they will soon learn from their parents and teachers and other important members of their life in their own culture. This is because at this time of life, children's ways of interpreting social experiences are largely based on the early limitations in their language and neurological development, and are strongly constrained by biological, or what we call developmental, factors, e.g., their "naturally" limited social-cognitive development. Their social-cognitive skills will grow naturally with age, but how far, fast, and well they will develop requires social nurturing.

One very important set of social-cognitive skills that develops "naturally" with age, we call *social perspective taking skills*. Those skills that help children understand what (and why) the people around them are thinking, feeling, and doing in social interactions with themselves or with others. Social perspective-taking (SPT) skills usually accumulate over time, and the quality of SPT has the influence of a wide range of socio-cognitive skills as the child grows into an adolescent, but these social skills start off as quite simple and naturally unable to be differentiated from other social cognitive skills when the child is young. That said, they are both developmental in nature, meaning they will emerge with time, but also very malleable, and sensitive to healthful (or unhealthful) social inputs by people who and circumstances that influence the child. Put another way, SPT skills are a key part of all social awareness and socialization processes. They are the basic or core social-cognitive (developmental) foundations of social relationships.

And yet, as important a part of natural human development processes as they are, they are not learned automatically. They still often learned or acquired only with effort and under healthy social conditions: to acknowledge the point of view of another person, to be able to explicitly articulate that point of view, to understand why someone else's perspective may be different from their own, and then to be able to position the point of view of another with respect to its genesis in that person's life experience, history, or current circumstances, and how when others disagree with them, how their differences influence one another. All this is challenging social-cognitive work.

As such, early in life social perspective taking skills are closely tied up with language development, which as these language skills develop, allow young children to better express their points of view. And later on, when the child is in elementary, middle, and high school, these skills can play an important role in the support of students' academic skills, such as deep reading comprehension of, for example, civic or historical academic material. And the benefits of SPTs skills in the later years should extend beyond the arena of reading and writing. Indeed, they arguably could serve to help students understand that key issues relevant to the lives of adolescents—such as the pervasiveness of technology—have multiple sides and can be reasoned about with more nuance than is typical of what occurs in the middle-grades classrooms or years.

However, returning to our focus on the early origins of social perspective taking skills, the preschool and kindergarten years, the time when it is most heavily influenced by the affordances and constraints of early language, early cognition, and early brain development, developmental psychologists have identified important, and universally identifiable, developing "organizational changes" in social perspective taking skills; each successive reorganization in SPT skills at these early ages can be thought of as a new level of social awareness. At these younger ages, as the child reaches each new and exciting level of *social* awareness, he or she develops a new theory, a personal discovery, about the nature of people, their social motives, and their social interactions.

Each new theory each child discovers thus constructed strongly influences the child's social judgment, social ability, and social maturity. I have prepared this essay to provide teachers and parents with a background in this theoretical perspective, and to provide educators, in particular, teachers, on ways to run effective classroom discussion groups in the early grades of school that will take advantage of the malleability of these social perspective taking skills to strengthen their students' social-cognitive abilities.

THEORETICAL BACKGROUND

Research about the ability to put the self in another's place and view the world from another's position has its roots in the work of George Herbert Mead (1934) and further work has been done by Jean Piaget (1947) and others. "Piaget has described the stages of cognitive development in the child's conception of the physical universe (for example, such categories of universal experience as time and space) and has shown that these conceptions develop systematically and are closely related to overall cognitive development, that is, the development of the way the child reasons in general. In this way, perspective-taking skills are dependent upon, and a part of, the child's logical or cognitive development. Yet even when the more basic cognitive development occurs in a child, enabling her to understand the physical and even social world to some degree, it does not guarantee that these more sophisticated social-cognitive skills will follow along. For Piaget, the development of social-cognitive skills and their application to such social practices as moral reasoning required healthy and open discussion of the social world, not only with parents and authorities in their lives, but also with peers.[①]

Social perspective taking studies of children from toddlerhood all the way through young adulthood show that there is a sequence of levels through which individuals pass in their understanding of the relationship between their own and others' points of view. Each level emerges from the preceding level and paves the way for the next one. Children may go through the levels of awareness at different rates but always in the same order, even though, in each culture the meanings children make of the relationships and the social strategies they use to deal with challenges that arise in social relationships, differ in important ways.

In our view, in general, children's social perspective taking changes as they move through each level in ways that are often closely related to their age. This is so because, as mentioned earlier, the levels are greatly influenced by the natural developmental processes including language and cognitive development.

We can think of each level as a new social perspective taking skill and that skill enabling a range of social competencies. In early childhood, which is our focus here, we can often distinguish three important levels/skills (first person skills, second person skills, and third person skills) in

---

① We have done research in social development, and specifically on social perspective-taking ability for over 50 years. Our work has been described in a number of books and empirical research papers over the past 50 years. A good summary can be found in my 2007 book, **The Promotion of Social Awareness: Powerful Lessons from the Partnership of Developmental Theory and Classroom Practice**. New York: Russell Sage (Outstanding Book Award, American Educational Research Association Section on Moral Development and Education). For the practical origins of this work, and some of the stories we used in both the research and practice, see Selman, R. L. and Byrne, D. (1974) *First Things: Social Development.* Guidance Associates, Harcourt, Brace, Jovanovich, Inc., New York, (primary grades.)

the development of social perspective taking, remembering of course that these social cognitive skills are only one of many factors that comprise or influence children's overall social awareness. We can illustrate what we mean here by some sample responses to the following typical social dilemma a young child might face, in which the social perspective taking skills of the child who hears or sees it play a large part in determining what that child will recommend doing in a social situation:

> Tom and Greg are young boys who are trying to figure out what to get their friend Mike for his birthday. Greg has already bought some checkers for Mike, but Tom cannot decide whether to get Mike a football or a little toy truck. The boys see Mike across the street and decide to try to find out what he would like for his birthday.
>
> Greg and Tom ask Mike about trucks and football, but nothing seems to interest him. He is very sad because his dog, Pepper, has been lost for two weeks. Mike's family has put an advertisement in the paper for Pepper, but there seems to be no chance of getting him back. When Greg suggests that Mike could get a new dog, Mike says it wouldn't be the same as having Pepper. He says he does not even like to look at other dogs because they make him miss Pepper so much. Nearly crying, he leaves to go home.
>
> Tom still does not know what to buy for Mike. On their way to the toy store, Tom and Greg pass a store with a sign in the window — "Puppies for Sale." There are only two puppies left and both are cute. Should Tom get Mike a puppy for his birthday? Greg remembers what Mike said about not liking to even look at other

dogs, but Tom thinks he would be happy with the puppy because it would be his. Greg thinks that getting a puppy might make Mike sad and spoil his birthday. The story ends as Tom says, "I know what I'll do."

We then ask children, individually or in small groups the question; What do you think Tom will do, and why do you think Tom will do that? How young children think about this story, and specifically what they suggest Tom might be thinking, depends to some degree on the rules of the culture within which the child lives. But it also depends, independent of the culture, on the social perspective-taking skills they are able to use in their reasoning. Although children vary in their responses, we often find some typical ways they express their social awareness at each of four age-levels, roughly defined. (Please keep in mind that whether or not you agree with the direction of the kind of action the child recommends in the following examples, it is the social reasoning, the level of social perspective taking skills being used that we are examining here.)

The toddler and early preschool levels. *Children at this age do have social perspective taking skills, but they are seldom easily verbalized, and it is hard for them to reflect on these skills or their relationships with others. They often have difficulty telling us how they distinguish between their own view and those of others. For that reason, among others, they appear to reason as if their point of view is* the true *perspective, not because they think their view is right and others are wrong, but because they are somewhat unaware or unable* *to express the ways that others may have a different social perspective. For instance, it is not uncommon for a young child to say in response to the puppy dilemma, "Tom should give Mike a puppy. I like puppies. Puppies are fun." He does not consider the possibility that Mike may not want a new puppy to replace him. Or, they might say, I don't like dogs, so I won't get Mike a puppy. Of course, what children decide to do, either hypothetically in discussion, or actually, is only partially a function of this world view. The child's personality, things that may have occurred recently, parents' socialization efforts, and the powerful rules of the culture all play a part in what the child might actually do, but so does the general world view of the child that their social perspective taking skills allows at this and each of the following three age-levels.*

The *late preschool and early kindergarten grades levels.* *By this age, children begin to more clearly understand, be socially aware, that they and other people can possibly have different social interpretations of the same social situation, depending upon a growing list of factors, e. g., how much information each has, what the other people in their family believe or tell them, etc. We can think of this awareness as the primary emerging social perspective taking skill of early childhood. However, they still have a hard time putting themselves in another's place because they do not realize that another person can think about what they are thinking. A typical child at this level may respond to the puppy story like this, "Mike said he doesn't want a puppy. Tom likes puppies, but he shouldn't get one for Mike."*

The late kindergarten, and early elementary grade levels. *The child becomes aware that people think or feel differently from one another, not only because they have different (objective) information, but also because they have different (e. g., subjective) values. This can be thought of as the second social perspective taking skill of childhood. The child can put himself in other people's shoes, and, in doing this, he can begin to see how he or she may appear through their eyes. He understands that one person can think about another's views. A child at this level may answer, "If I were Mike, I'd want a puppy. Maybe Mike just doesn't know how he would feel if he had a new dog."*

The early and *later elementary grades, and middle school levels.* *The child realizes that both he and other people are thinking about each other's views at the same time (i. e., simultaneously). The child can view his own interactions with people as if he were a bystander watching himself and others. This is a big jump in level and a very important new social perspective taking skill. A child at the level of mutual perspective taking may say, "Well, if Tom gets Mike a puppy and Mike doesn't like it, Tom still knows Mike will understand that he was only trying to make him happy." At this level the child understands that people can be simultaneously and mutually aware of their own and others' motivations.*

Please keep in mind that at each age level, each new social perspective taking skill, associated with each age level, does not replace earlier skills, it integrates the earlier developed social skills so that the child becomes more and more competent at understanding the complexities of the nature of other persons, themselves, and their relationship to one another. In so doing the child develops an increased level of social awareness.

Four Important Social Awareness Competencies that are supported by the promotion/development of social perspective taking skills:

Earlier I noted that social perspective taking development is an important underlying ingredient in the development of other social skills and forms of awareness that may be more easily observable. Here are four worth mentioning.

- ***Solving social problems.*** *In the old days, (now we all have cell phones) when two people get separated in a busy store without having planned where to meet, each person must think about what the other is thinking. If a person plans to meet someone else at a park but forgets to specify which park, both people must do some perspective taking. Many games of strategy depend upon a player's ability to figure out the opponent's potential behavior. In social problems of coordination and competition, an essential element for success is the ability to take another's perspective.*

***An Example of the use of Social Perspective Taking in Solving Social Problems*:** Problem solving in a social situation often depends on taking other people's points of view.

ALEX:

"Wait a second, Billy. I told Timmy that I'd bring home his felt pens so he'll have something to do while he's sick."

BILLY:

"Okay, where are they?"

ALEX:

"Oh, gee, I forgot to ask him. Probably in his desk.

Nope, not here. Phooey, I can't search this whole room. I guess I'll have to tell him I couldn't find them. He'll sure be disappointed."

BILLY:

"Wait. Let me think. Hmm, if I were Timmy, where would I leave my pens? I bet I know. He likes to work in the art corner. Maybe he left them there.

I was right. Here they are."

Analysis: There are many times when the use of one's best level of perspective-taking ability means the difference between solving and not solving a problem. For example, in the **Solving Social Problems situation**, Alex was aware of Timmy's enthusiasm for drawing, but Billy went even further. He actually put himself in Timmy's place to solve the problem. This means that Billy was showing that he was using mutual perspective taking in his problem solving and reasoning.

• ***Understanding others' feelings.*** *The young child who gives his mother bubble gum for her birthday is not necessarily being selfish or unfeeling. He may just believe that because he likes bubble gum, everyone does. In order to take another person's feelings or interests into account before he acts, the child must recognize that others have different perspectives on social situations and may have feelings different from his own.*

An Example of Using Social Perspective Taking in Understanding Feelings: A child who is able to take another's point of view can understand, be sympathetic to, and share the feelings of others.

TEACHER:

"Okay, kids, you can have twenty minutes free period before we get back to math."

HELEN:

"Let's try to finish the puzzle, Jane. We're almost done."

JANE:

"Okay, there's probably time. Maybe we can finally get it."

HELEN:

"Uh-oh, there's Brenda. I bet she'll want to work on it too. She's such a pest!"

JANE:

"Aw, she's not so bad."

BRENDA:

"Hey, can I work on the puzzle with you guys?"

HELEN:

"No, we don't want you to help us."

JANE:

"Brenda, Helen just means that the two of us have been working on this puzzle for a long time, and we'd like to finish it all by ourselves. Maybe we can do something later."

BRENDA:

"Okay, okay."

HELEN:

"Why'd you tell her that?"

JANE:

"Well, think about how you'd feel if someone just said, 'I don't want you around."

"You wouldn't want your feelings hurt. Besides, if you'd just give her a chance, you might find out she's not so bad."

Analysis: In the situation, where social perspective taking is very important to **Understanding Feelings**, Jane was able to put herself in each of the other girls' shoes and she used this ability to good advantage in her relations with both Brenda and Helen. Helen may have the same capabilities, developmentally speaking, but her actions indicated that she was not exercising them, *at least in this situation.* Jane is using a social perspective-taking skill that usually develops at the early or late elementary grade level.

• ***Making fair judgments.*** *When a child is asked, "If someone came up and hit you, what would be the fair thing to do?" he may say, "Hit back," and give as his reason, "Because I want to," or, when he's a little older, "He deserves to get punished." When faced with the necessity for judging fairly, the young child may be unable to take the perspective of others and consider the conflicting claims of each person. However, if he could do this, he might answer the question with, "Think how he feels, why he might be doing it. Maybe he doesn't mean to."*

An Example of Social Perspective Taking in Judging What is Fair: Moral decisions are often based on the ability to take the points of view of other people who are involved in the situation or dilemma.

BOB：

"Watch it, Tom! Don't go pushing me or I'll knock your block off."

TOM：

"Take it easy, Bob. I didn't bump you on purpose. It was just an accident."

BOB：

"Well, just watch it, that's all!"

JERRY：

"Boy, what a temper! How come you didn't punch him one? I would have."

TOM：

"Aw, he just got mad cause he thought I bumped him on purpose. No sense in getting in a fight over that."

Analysis： In the example, from **Judging What is Fair**, Bob did not consider Tom's intention when he accused Tom of starting a fight. The inability to distinguish the intention from the accidental behavior of others is often characteristic of the earliest level of social perspective taking. Tom, on the other hand, was aware that Bob misinterpreted his motives. This understanding rests on the ability to realize that others are capable of understanding (or in this case misunderstanding) the thoughts and reasons of self. Because Tom's level of social reasoning in this situation was higher than Bob's, he was able to avoid a fight.

- ***Persuading and Communicating with Others.*** Parents are familiar with the problem of trying to understand what a young child means when he refers to "this" or "that"： while on the other end of the phone or in another room. The child has not considered the fact that the listener cannot see what is meant by "this" or "that." The ability to communicate one's point of view is important in a child's attempt to persuade others when he believes that he has a good idea or when it is necessary for him to clarify his ideas in a social situation that has become confused. To communicate or persuade effectively, children must be able to try to consider the needs and wishes of his listener, even if their estimates are not correct. It is the focus on trying that is the aim of our approach.

An Example of Persuading and Communicating: *A child who wants to get his ideas across needs to take the listener's point of view.*

ART:

"Hey, Gloria, let me use the screwdriver. You're done."

ANDREW:

"Hey, wait a minute. I need it."

GLORIA:

"How am I supposed to decide who gets it next?"

ART:

"Well, I have to use it for my whole project."

ANDREW:

"Why don't you just figure out who needs it the most? Art's got a lot to do, but I can't work on my project at all until I do this one little thing. You wouldn't want me to have to wait around for a whole hour while Art does his project, would you?"

Analysis: Social perspective taking is especially important when one has to be convincing. In the situation that calls for **Persuading and**

Communicating others, Art and Andrew each tried to persuade Gloria to give him the screwdriver. Art argued only on the basis of his own wants. Andrew tried to give equal consideration to each point of view. This demands a very sophisticated social perspective-taking ability, a skill that develops at an age a bit farther along than the early childhood years.

In Conclusion: Here Are Five Important Theoretical Ideas About Social Perspective Taking to Keep in Mind:

1. Social perspective taking skills can be understood to proceed in a sequence of levels of development for the young child but it is not automatic.

As a teacher, (or a parent) you may have questions about this social-cognitive developmental process. It is not often a major focus of elementary education, but it is often a focus on preschool and kindergarten education. If all children pass through the sequence in the same order, then what is there to teach? Why teach something that will develop whether or not it is taught? In fact, can one really teach SPT skills? These are important questions. In order to answer them, it is helpful to know a little more about the nature of social perspective-taking development.

2. It is when the child has a firm command of one level of social perspective taking, i. e. an earlier emerging skill, that she or he is ready to move to the next level.

Just as children need to exercise the specific skills they acquire in the classroom — their reading, language arts, and math — they must also exercise their social and logical thinking abilities. Through exercise and application, the child begins to become aware of the social problems that challenge the adequacy of his level of social reasoning.

3. Although the application of a level of social perspective-taking ability is not automatic, with enough 'exercise' we would hope that sophisticated social perspective taking skills could be "written" into one's social awareness/behavioral scripts and happen almost "automatically."

Children may have the skill to put themselves in another's place, but they may not perceive the need to do so. They may struggle with a communication problem without realizing that perspective taking would help solve the problem. One purpose of programs or curricula designed to promote social skills is to stimulate children to use whatever skills they have in the appropriate contexts. The use of perspective taking in the areas touched upon in a program with this focus may increase the child's effectiveness as a communicator, empathizer, moral reasoner, and social problem solver.

4. Do not define children with the sequence of developmental levels. When they seem to be stuck in a level, they need adults' help to get to the next level.

While the levels or social perspective taking skills I have described can be found in how they are taking perspectives in any given situation, at the same time it is important to realize that each of the levels we have described and exemplified is only typical of certain ages. In this sense, besides the forces of normal or typical brain and biological development, movement from level to level is thought to occur through two basic social-cognitive mechanisms — social conceptual conflict and exposure to reasoning at a level slightly, but not too far, above the child's own level. Social conceptual conflict means that if a child is made aware of conflicting social outcomes based on his own level of reasoning this may stimulate development toward the next level. The teacher's role is to facilitate this challenge to each student's level of reasoning. The most natural method for exposing children to reasoning one level above their own, as well as for challenging their own reasoning, is peer group discussion.

5. It also needs to be noted that the movement from one level of insight to the next is a long-term process. Findings indicate that movement from one level to the next may take several years or more. Teachers should not expect to see great leaps from level to level of social perspective taking skills in the space of a few months. And the ages I have given are only averages and are focused on what most children at those ages can reflect upon and say, not so much on what they may actually do. A child may move into a level earlier or later than the guidelines suggest — and sometimes children's developmental level may not be stable. Children should be allowed to proceed at their own pace in an orderly way, although the type of discussion herein suggested may facilitate child's use of optimal development.

And One Final Thing to Remember About the Social World of the Developing Child:

Around the world, educators who understand the crucial role they play in fostering children's social perspective-taking may come up against certain barriers to their explicit teaching of these skills: For instance, parents may seem to be desperate to see "immediate" and "straight-forward" progress in their children's academic performance so that teachers may feel their professional knowledge/experience which takes social competencies into account does not match the parents' expectations of the children. This puts pressure on teachers to emphasize academic subjects and topics, often to the exclusion of everything else. However, children also need to develop social understanding. They need to improve their understanding of the thoughts and feelings of others. Is there a valid way to teach this, just as we teach reading and writing?

But there now is also a growing concern around the world with the social and emotional development of children and with the role of the teacher in the promotion of these social skills. In attempting to find educationally sound approaches to this tension, developmental psychologists have discovered that one important basis for the maturation of social understanding that is also important for academic growth is the child's increasing ability to relate his or her own point of view to the perspectives of other people.

But, please keep in mind that my primary aim in writing this essay is not to advocate for the acceleration of social awareness competencies or of the social perspective taking skills that underlie them, but to consider the ways, through practice in thinking about and discussing social dilemmas, that barriers to children's natural social awareness development will be removed. Using this approach allows children to practice their newly developing social skills in a safe environment, and helps children learn to apply their strengthened social reasoning across a wide range of social situations, social problems, and social relationships. In so doing, it is quite possible that in the future the child who is developing these social skills now will be the adult who will not only improve his or her success in life but also the success of the society in which he or she lives.

References

Mead, George Herbert. *Mind, Self, and Society.* Chicago: University of Chicago Press, 1934.

Piaget, Jean. *The Moral Judgment of the Child.* New York: The Free Press, 1965 (reprint of 1932 edition).

Selman, R. L. *The Promotion of Social Awareness: Powerful Lessons from the Partnership of Developmental Theory and Classroom Practice.* New York: Russell Sage, 2007.

Selman, R. L. and Byrne, D. (1974) First Things: Social Development. Guidance Associates, Harcourt, Brace, Jovanovich, Inc., New York, (primary grades.)

4. How to Promote Children's Social Awareness through Guided Discussions of Social Dilemmas Found in Humanistic Stories

Robert L. Selman

Harvard University

Whether or not she or he recognizes them as such, every caring parent, grand-parent primary-grade teacher, pediatrician, or counselor provides lessons for young children in both socialization practices and the importance of morality. They may praise a child for being fair, for keeping his or her word, or for obeying a social rule in order to reinforce desired behavior. They may scold or punish a child in order to effect a positive change in young children's social behavior: for not telling the truth, for taking someone else's property, or for breaking a rule. Both types of approaches influence children's social behavior, especially in the moment. But what happens when no one in authority is watching — when no one is there to praise or scold? What are some things a teacher or parent can do to help strengthen a child's inner moral convictions — and make them stick?

The Natural Development of Children's Rules of Fairness Reasoning

Compared to cultural psychologists, who like to describe and understand the importance of the different moral and social rules children from different backgrounds adopt as they are socialized into their own society, developmental psychologists tend to study what is most generally common among children at a certain age-related phase in their development into society, even though their societies may differ. That is what I mean by, and why I have used the term, Natural, so readily in this essay. Researchers in developmental psychology have clearly shown that the better the child's *fairness reasoning ability*, the more likely she or he is to act in a social and moral way — even though such good behavior cannot be guaranteed. When no one is around to monitor him or her, a child whose moral reasoning includes a concern for the welfare of others is more likely to do the "right" thing more consistently than is one whose primary reason for sharing or showing empathy is about not getting into trouble. We can safely say that unlike their cultural psychology cousins whose focus is on the importance of what social norms are particular to a child in the context of a family, a community, a society, the researcher with a strong developmental orientation seeks to identify what norms are socially universal, even while acknowledging that in this diverse human world and across the centuries, significant changes in values have occurred.

To start, developmentally speaking, very young children are unaware or only vaguely aware of the fairness rules in their society, whether these rules are general or particular. It is "natural" for instance that all everyday preschool age children tend to begin to learn and look upon fairness rules in the adult world as something most generally to be obeyed, primarily to avoid punishment for doing things that the adults in their lives do not approve of, or think is unfair to others, mainly the people with whom they regularly interact socially, those in their family or local peer group.

As they get a little bit older, across what we often call the elementary grades, most all children will begin to develop a sense of fairness built upon a new and key fairness rule, "The same for you and the same for me." Having lived in the social world, and observed how they and others react to each other, these youngsters start to develop their own fairness rules, beyond what they believe they have been told by the authorities in their life. By the middle and end of the primary-school years, largely because they begin to deeply understand the reasons why this is important, most, *but not all*, children become truly concerned about the welfare of others, putting themselves in the other guy's shoes for example. This is because they understand that in making and keeping friends, and to avoid being lonely and isolated, it is important to treat others the same way they want to be treated. They understand this is a good social policy, even if it is not that easy to follow it.

It is not surprising then, that research done over the past 50 years by developmental psychologists indicates that if one looks hard and deep below the surface of observable social behavior, one will find that there is a natural "developmental" pathway, a deep course of a river of growing knowledge, skills, and values, through which important aspects of all young children's fairness reasoning passes and progresses. While the course of this deep river of social development can be very similar for children everywhere, that does not mean that the flow or rate of development is the same for every child. Although these deep developmental aspects of social knowledge, skills and values follow a path largely determined by the biology and cognitive development of our species, it is important to remember that not only might they manifest themselves in different ways in different places, but also that their rate and consistency are malleable. That is, education and socialization practice matter — a lot.

The Importance of Story Telling: How to Choose and to Use

This theoretical framework suggests that moral education programs that are focused on the few basic fairness rules that govern all human societies should be able to use stories that teach these rules, and in the 21st century, this can be done in any type of media that young children can easily access (movies, readings, classroom discussion, plays, and still so very important, being read to). Such stories, when well told, should be able to help children everywhere to develop, through the understanding of these fairness rules as they experience the common social experiences to which these rules are best applied.

During their early years, children's exposure to engaging and personally meaningful stories about what is a fair way for young people, like themselves, to meet their own needs at the same time as they become aware of the needs of other children is at the heart of the development of interpersonal morality, particularly a deeper understanding of the importance of fairness reasoning, for establishing reciprocity in their friendships. Once again, at different times in history in different places around the world, the emphasis on cultivating friendships as compared to an investment in academic growth may vary. But, no matter, just as there are rules of the culture that guide the conduct among young children, there are rules of fairness development as well that are designed to promote their ability to maintain harmonious social relationships.

What then are the fairness topics of importance to preschool, kindergarten, and early primary-grade children? Certainly, they include keeping promises, telling the truth, respecting property rights, sharing, taking turns, and understanding the reasons for rules. Research findings indicate that one effective way to help young children to develop fairness reasoning about how to get along with peers and make friends involves the use of story-telling, story discussion, and story-acting. These types of activities can occur in school, at home, and in other places in the community where young children gather and also interact with their peers. Sometimes these stories are told from one child to another. But our emphasis will be on the stories that caring adults share with the younger generation.

While story telling is very common in the home and at school, we next can ask, what are some good ways to choose stories and use those particular types of stories that seem to invoke what we have identified as basic and fundamental interpersonal fairness rules? Researchers suggest stories with plots that have *open-ended and fairness-oriented dilemmas* to solve or reconcile are very useful for these purposes. In particular, stories that pose solutions to dilemmas that children within a culture may disagree upon are of particular value. Such stories allow valuable opportunities for children to discuss *with others* (*their parents*, *teachers or peers*) the possible solutions to hypothetical fairness situations that do not have an obvious or culturally approved "right answer." They are thus particularly effective at the promotion of many of the forms of social reasoning that will allow children to navigate in their own lives the conflicts that naturally and inevitably arise in their play with peers.

Stories that allow for open-ended discussion and stimulate moral reasoning often do so in the following ways:

- They raise issues, important to children of this age, about what is "right";
- They encourage children to seek their own answers to fairness problems, which can then be shaped and clarified by parents and teachers to help socialize their children and students;
- They promote discussion among children about very important ideas such as "what is good, what is true";
- They offer *within the script or text of the story itself* opportunities for more mature moral reasoning to be expressed by some characters within the stories, and therefore, when considered carefully by their listeners stimulate each child to raise his or her level own of social reasoning. We call such stories, *developmentally structured*.

This approach does not mean to suggest that the child will or should be the authority, or "gets to decide." Rather, we think of these *developmentally structured* stories as themselves a representation of what the characters in the stories say about how to resolve their problems. The discussions are real for the fictional characters. But while their words are fictional for the story's audience, they suggest not only each character's actions and thoughts, but in particular the reasons for their suggested actions. Therefore, the commonplace social situations within the story itself can then be used as the basis for activities that start the child or children who experience the story to move through thinking about the story characters' expressed reasons in the direction of being able to communicate and negotiate with their own peers, especially around interpersonal matters.

We think of these discussions, whether they occur in the classroom or at home, about the (hypothetical) dilemmas as practice for building the important relationships skills of their future. Stories (that allow young children to think about and discuss fairness) are ones that both help children to think on their own, while at the same time help them understand why it is important to be respectful of and listen carefully to the wisdom of their elders and their society. These kinds of stories are also important for parents to read to or with their children. They will allow the parent or teachers to hear what their child's or students' natural social or moral reasoning about a fairness dilemma is like, and to then help the children to be challenged to think in socially more complex ways. That is also why it is important to study and do research in classrooms and even, if possible, in homes to see how this kind of technique is working.

Two Examples:

Many years ago, when I had just finished my doctoral dissertation on the relationship between children's developing ability to take another person's social perspective with their moral reasoning, I worked with Lawrence Kohlberg, a well-known developmental psychologist who was doing research and practice on adolescent development. ① Kohlberg asked me to write stories for young children that had open-ended moral dilemmas embedded in them in a way similar to the open-ended questions he used with adolescents. In the stories my colleagues and I came up with, the conversations within the stories were not just about differing opinions, but about the different levels of perspective taking various characters in the stories used in the justification for the opinions they expressed. Here I share with you two of my favorite stories for preschool and kindergarten age children. ② Below I provide a summary of each of the two stories, and I discuss how they can be used in *story-telling* to implement the ideas I have so far discussed. (A bit later, I will discuss the very important opportunities these developmentally structured stories have for *story acting* by using their scripts for children to act out in class with peers.)

Example 1: "The Wizard's Birthday Party"

This story is about a fantasy land where everything, that is, specifically the traditional social norm of gifts at a birthday party, at least in western culture, "upside down": As we wrote it years ago, two

---

① Kohlberg, L., & Selman, R. L. (1972) Preparing School Personnel Relative to Values: A Look at Moral Education in the School. *ERIC: Clearing-house on Teacher Education*. Washington, D. C. See also, Selman, R. L. and Kohlberg, L. (1972) First things: Values. Guidance Associates, Harcourt, Brace, Jovanovich, Inc., New York, (primary grades.)

② These stories were later turned into scripts by my colleague, and writer, Thomas Glynn so they could be produced relatively inexpensively on a range of digital media (so they could be acted out on film, either by real actors or cartoon characters, and now digital media).

young boys (their English names are Eddie and Andy), about the ages of the children in preschool or kindergarten who would listen to the story, **find a ring on the ground**, (remember this for later on) and when they pick it up they find themselves, magically, in a fantasy forest world, full of strange plants and talking animals. (The story can be written for any demographic group; it could be girls, and they could have Chinese names.) A bear and a deer approach them as all the forest animals are on their way to the Wizard's birthday party. But the bear stumbles over a log and hurts his leg, so the deer goes on alone to get a place in the birthday present line.

It is at the birthday present-getting line it seems, the bear explains, that the Wizard in this fantasy land gives away wonderful presents on his birthday rather than gets them. The bear is afraid the presents will run out by the time he gets to the party, if he can get there at all with his injured leg. Eddie and Andy offer to help, and all three set out for the present line.

When they arrive at the line, they discover that there are only three presents left and two animals ahead of them in line. The bear insists that Eddie go ahead of him, and Andy steps in behind. At least, that way, Eddie is sure of a present.

Or is he? Up comes the deer who earlier had rushed ahead to get in the line. It seems the deer had already been standing in line when his hat blew off. While he was hunting for it, Eddie took his place in line. Will Eddie let the deer steer back in line in front of him or not? Is it fair for Eddie to let the deer back in line, or to keep his place and get the last present for himself?

How Can Teachers and Parents Guide an Open-Ended Discussion Using this kind of Story?

Sustained discussion of carefully constructed stores such as "The Wizard's Birthday Party" may appear to be spontaneous in the children's minds, but that does not mean the discussions should go unmonitored or supported. Discussions on the stories with open-ended social and moral dilemmas need to be well guided by experienced adults who know how to lead children to upward movement along the developmental path of fairness reasoning we described earlier.

The teacher is essential for giving a story such as this one a clear purpose. Without the teacher's help, the stories are merely entertaining and may not be educational, either developmentally or culturally. With the teacher's help the stories will stimulate fruitful discussions that potentially lead to better moral reasoning practice, as viewed from a developmental perspective. Getting a lively discussion going is easiest when there is strong disagreement about what is the "right" moral choice. For instance, if most of the children in the class agree on what action should be taken by the character, the teacher can provide support for the weaker side by asking provocative questions.

For example, in the **Wizard's Birthday Party** story, if most children argue that Eddie *should let* the deer back into line, the teacher may ask:

- Couldn't the deer have waited to get his present before leaving the line to find his hat?
- Who will be around to get a present at the Wizard's *next* birthday,

Eddie or the deer?

To promote social perspective-taking skills, teachers can keep asking:

• When the deer left the line, what should he have done to make sure he kept his place?

• How would you feel if somebody tried to cut in ahead of you in line?

On the other hand, suppose most children think Eddie *should not let* the deer back into line, the teacher can encourage some conflict by asking:

• Was it the deer's fault that his hat blew away? Did he leave the line on purpose?

• How do you think *you* would feel if you lost your place in line even if you did not want to leave it?

Likewise, to promote social perspective-taking skills on this side, teachers can ask:

• How would you feel if you lost your place in line?

• The deer was looking forward to getting skis from the Wizard. Do you think he will be disappointed if Eddie doesn't let him back in line?

Sometimes children try to solve a dilemma like this one by simply avoiding it. For example, in this story, some children will say: "Well, the Wizard has magic powers. He could just make another present so Eddie and the deer could both have one." At this point, it is essential for the teacher to insist on sticking to the "rules of the dilemma". "Remember that the bear worried about the Wizard running out of presents. It has happened before, hasn't it?" the teacher might say, pointing out something in the story the children have overlooked. Or the teacher can make up her own conditions: "The Wizard's magic just can't make another present." In this way, the teacher encourages the class to face the dilemma head on. All of these approaches are designed to promote "social-cognitive" conflict, not only among the listeners, but within the mind of each child.

Example 2: "The Wizard Loses His Glasses"

This story is a sequel, it takes place soon after the first one in the same magical world of wizards and talking animals. This story opens with the Wizard searching for his glasses. His vision is very poor and very blurry without them, so he mistakes the two *boys he invited to his birthday party*, Eddie and Andy, for one *creature*, *a* "*Meeddiemeandy*".

Nevertheless, Eddie and Andy offer to look for the Wizard's glasses, and the Wizard offers to reward them if the glasses are found. With the help of a flying cow, Eddie and Andy cover a lot of territory in their search for the Wizard's glasses. The cow suggests that perhaps the Wizard might have left them at the Peppermint Pool, where he often goes to cool off. Sure enough, Andy spots the glasses in deep water below the pier. With Andy holding his legs, Eddie goes underwater and retrieves the glasses.

The Wizard is happy to have his glasses again. But now he can see his mistake all too clearly — Eddie and Andy are not one "*Meeddiemeandy*", but actually two boys. The Wizard has only *one* reward, a genuine Wizard's watch. Who should have it? Andy found the glasses, but Eddie went underwater to get them. To whom should the

Wizard give the reward? What is the fair thing to do?

Often children will prescribe actions for others that they might find difficult to perform themselves. For example, in the story about the Wizard losing his glasses, some children say that the Wizard should not give the watch to *either* Eddie *or* Andy. In reality, put in that same situation, children would have a great deal of difficulty accepting this solution. The teacher can help the children look at the situation in a more realistic manner by encouraging identification with the characters in the dilemma, and might ask:

• I want you to pretend that I am the Wizard and you are Andy, the boy who first spotted the Wizard's glasses. How would you convince me that I should give *you* the watch?

• Now pretend you are Eddie, the boy who went underwater to get the glasses. What reasons can you give me that *you* should have the watch?

• Now pretend you are the Wizard and have heard these reasons. What is the fair thing for *you* to do?

This second story, about the reward the two boys share for finding the Wizard's glasses, asks for more than a simple choice between alternative solutions to a moral problem. It asks the still more challenging question: What is the fair way to distribute a reward? More important than encouraging a final solution everyone can agree upon about which boy should get the Wizard's watch is encouraging balanced discussion of the various strategies for sharing.

For example:

1. Eddie could have the watch one day, Andy the next.

2. One could have the **ring** they found (at the beginning of the story), the other the watch.

3. They could flip a coin for the watch.

The teacher's role here is less easy to define than in everyday teaching of math, science or even language development which often focuses on the meaning of words (vocabulary). While learning vocabulary words, a student needs to remember that a certain word may have different meanings, and they need to know all the definitions to be a good reader or speaker. But the classroom experience of fairness reasoning — exploring compromise and sharing where both Eddie and Andy have played necessary roles in finding the Wizard's glasses — is an exciting one for young children because the children learn the meaning of words not through the dictionary, but through exchanging ideas among groups and listening to others.

It is quite common for children to go off on what adults might think of as tangents. The teacher must decide how fruitful these diversions will be. For example, after hearing the story read to them, children may begin to discuss the nature of the Wizard's reward. Insofar as such speculation is relevant to the discussion of fairness (the Wizard should find them a second present so both boys would have a reward), this issue should be discussed. However, if the issue appears to be completely unrelated (the Wizard should give them a better watch than that old thing), the teacher should feel free to bring the discussion back within the limits set by the situation.

Children also look for compromises to resolve the dilemma. Valid compromises should be treated as important fairness choices. The teacher should stress reasons why the compromise is a good solution. For instance, in the lost glasses story, here is a compromise solution that children may suggest: Andy could have the watch one day, Eddie the next.

If the children in a discussion group have reached agreement on what should be done, they may be urged to pick the *best reasons* to support their point of view. Throughout, it is important for the teacher to stress that answers to moral questions involve not only a statement of opinion but reasons *why*.

The teacher can best view him or herself as a fairness guide. The primary tasks are helping the child:

1. focus on the conflicts;
2. think about the reasoning he or she uses in solving such conflicts;
3. consider possible moral concerns that may have been overlooked;
4. look for inconsistencies in the ways of thinking that are being discussed; and
5. find means of resolving such inconsistencies.

In these ways the teacher can encourage social thinking and discussion without first taking a position. In fact, the children in the class probably will ask for the teacher's opinion of what is "right". Using stories like the ones we designed, the teacher might answer: "I don't want to influence you now. You should decide for yourself." At an appropriate time, the teacher should feel free to give an opinion but should stress that what she or he thinks is not the only answer, and that it's important for each individual to make his own decision. The teacher should also be prepared to give reasons for her or his opinion. Of course, it is always a good idea to stress the many good reasons given by various members of the class and suggest that maybe, if they think about the story some more and discuss it with family or friends, they may come up with even better reasons ("good reason" refers to reasons that are more socially complex and take in more perspectives).

One principal objective of guided peer-discussion of stories about interpersonal problems in every-day living is to promote the practice of social and moral reasoning in each individual child, and the practice of sharing one's thoughts among the children who are in discussion with one another often lifts the quality of reasoning in the group itself. In these two stories which are designed to focus on interpersonal situations, and ways that the resolution of differences in opinions, or fair distribution of things jointly valued can lead to harmony, the making and maintaining of friendships born out of interpersonal context. The most effective discussion will be one that occurs immediately after the story is told. The following steps will aid fruitful discussion:

A. Review the story with the class.

Before fairness discussions can take place, it is essential that the children know exactly what they are to discuss. Ask a few questions to make sure the children understand the story and are aware of the dilemma. Review the names of the characters in the story and the part each character plays in the unfolding story.

B. Model the discussion for the class.

After telling the story, it is helpful to demonstrate to the class exactly what it means to "discuss". You may need at least three people — older students, teachers, or aides — who should sit in a circle facing one another. To model a discussion of the birthday party, one person should be for the deer getting back his place in line, another for Eddie keeping his place in line, and a third undecided, changing back and forth from one side to the other as the discussion model progresses.

C. Break the class into small groups for discussion.

While the teacher may wish to discuss the dilemma with the class as a whole, small discussion groups of 4 to 6 children probably will be more effective. These groups should include as much diversity in the participants as possible, and should be arranged in small circles around the room — at tables or on the floor so each member of the discussion group can see the other members. The children then should be asked to imitate the model discussion, asking questions, giving reasons, *listening*, and stating opinions *to each other*, not to the teacher. The teacher is free to circulate, listening in on the discussions, keeping them on the track, clearing up problems, and interjecting questions when needed and useful.

D. Keep the discussion balanced with appropriate questions.

The inventive use of questions is the key to a successful small discussion group as an instrument of moral reasoning practice. It is important that each side of the dilemma be fairly represented if a conflict, and consequent moral development, is to occur.

We understand that parents and teachers and counselors may object to the fact that discussion among peers may on occasion allow children to choose lying over telling the truth, bullying over cooperation, or choosing to breaking a promise over keeping it. In life, all children do encounter situations where there are reasons for not keeping promises or for not telling the truth, though usually the reasons they give in situations like the ones we are considering here are either immature reasons, developmentally speaking, or are not good reasons culturally speaking, that is, they go against strong cultural precepts. No matter in what culture or context in which such discussion-oriented stories are held, however, a developmental approach stresses **the importance of having a good reason for taking fair actions**. It encourages children to *think hard* and not blindly accept moral clichés. This emphasis on reasoning and exchanging ideas, under the leadership of an educator who understands when open-ended discussions are valuable educational tools, will lead their students to a stronger and more personal sense of what is "right, fair, and caring".

From story-telling to story-acting: a very worthwhile next step built on an honored tradition.

So far, we have focused mostly on the role discussion and reflection can have on the promotion of moral and social reasoning, and in particular, the reasoning about stories that are both commonly difficult for children most everywhere in the world to figure out, and, at the same time, very compelling for them, as the situations are similar to the ones they confront on a daily basis. Because our emphasis is on the use of these stories for young children, we have not said much about their importance for the promoting or reading and writing skills. We will save that discussion for another day, when the children on whose abilities we are focusing are a little older.

However, I think we can say something about another way our approach might work with young children to facilitate their development.

I am now speaking about story-acting. Mostly, so far, we have imagined an adult reading a story to a group of children, or perhaps having the children watch the story as it is portrayed by actors. But what if the story can be designed to allow the children who first hear it or see it told to them to be themselves the actors in the story.

As it turns out, when we developed these social and moral dilemmas many years ago, we embedded them in actual scripts, that is dialogues among all the actors. We asked a colleague, Tom Glynn, to write a full treatment of a script that could be used as a filmed story, or as a live-action play. I won't include the entire script here, but let's take a close look at the conversation at the end of the first story as it was written in actual script format by Thomas Glynn in the form of a dialogue among the fictional characters in the story. This is how one might bring an otherwise hypothetical fairness dilemma even closer to the everyday life of children who are experiencing it.

Let us enter the ongoing story at the point when the Bear, limping along slowly, and the newcomers to the Wizard's culture, Eddie and Andy arrive at the line of animals patiently waiting to get their own Wizard's Birthday Presents. Eddie starts the conversation by saying, "Hey, I don't see your friend the deer. I wonder what happened to him."

BEAR:

"I don't know. Maybe he got lost. Well, let's get into line before anyone else comes.

You can get in front of me."

EDDIE:

"No, I think you should go first. If it hadn't been for you we wouldn't have even known about the present line."

BEAR:

"No, it's only fair that you go first. You helped me get here."

ANDY:

"Okay, one of us will go before you and one of us will get behind you. Fair enough?"

BEAR:

"Perfect!

Oh my, oh my. Look — there are only three presents left. Oh! I was afraid this would happen. Well, Eddie, you're a lucky fellow. You're third in line so you'll get the last present."

DEER:

"Let me in. I was standing there."

EDDIE:

"No you weren't. We got in at the end of the line — and you weren't here."

DEER:

"I was here before you came. I just got out of line to look for my hat. It blew away and I couldn't find it."

RACCOON:

"Yes, he was right behind me. In fact, I remember him saying that he hoped he would get new skis this year."

ANDY:

"Well, he lost his place when he got out of line. You're

supposed to stay in line. And when you don't, you have to go to the end. That's only being fair."

RACCOON:

"Well, I don't think that's very fair. The deer had that place first, and he waited longer than your friend did. It's only fair that the one who waits longest should get the last present."

BEAR:

"Waiting longer doesn't matter. When the deer got out of the line he gave up his place."

DEER:

"No, I didn't. I planned to come right back. It's still my place. He's got to let me in."

OWL:

"Gentlemen! Gentlemen! Just a minute. Don't be so hasty. Try to look at it from each other's point of view."

RACCOON:

"That's right, think about how the deer feels. It wasn't his fault that he lost his hat. Why should the deer have to go to the end of the line now and miss out on getting a present? Well, I don't think that's very fair. The deer had that place first, and he waited longer than your friend did. It's only fair that the one who waits the longest should get the last present."

ANDY:

"Yes but think about how Eddie feels. He didn't know you were here before. It's not his fault the deer got out of line. Besides, Eddie may never get back to the Wizard's birthday again, so it certainly won't be fair to Eddie if he lets you back in."

DEER:

"Well, what are you going to do? Are you going to let me in or not?"

OWL:

"Yes, Eddie, what are you going to do?"

EDDIE:

"I'm not sure. It's just so hard to know what's fair. The deer was here first and he probably waited longer than I did, but I'm here now.

Should I give up my spot just because he's decided to come back? What is the fair thing to do?"

Notice how we have written this script so each of the different characters in the story takes part in the discussion, and makes an argument for their position, if they have one (the owl here plays the part of one who is trying to get all the parties to use their social and fairness reasoning) based on whose perspective each believes needs to be taken into consideration.

For example, going back to the script we just read, consider the discussion between Andy and Raccoon:

ANDY:

"Well, he lost his place when he got out of line. You're supposed to stay in line. And when you don't, you have to go to the end. That's only being fair."

RACCOON:

"Well, I don't think that's very fair. The deer had that place first, and he waited longer than your friend did. It's only fair that the one who waits longest should get the last present."

So, Andy argues the present should go to Eddie, and Raccoon argues the present should go to Deer. When we wrote these fairness-oriented social and moral dilemmas, we tested the story out on children across the United States whose age ranged from 4 to 8. By looking at changes in students' comments across different ages, we were able to use a developmental lens to see how the responses of the students at different ages differed in their opinions, judgments, and suggested actions. We found that with respect to their opinions as to who should get the present, the deer or Eddie, the responses were divided right down the middle. About half the children thought the deer should get the present, and the other half thought that Eddie should get the present.

We called these aspects of their responses, the "content" of their reasoning, and it was very important for our dilemmas to draw out all the interesting ideas youngsters had. However, in addition, by comparing the responses of the younger and older children in our studies, we were able to extract the developmental variations in their fairness reasoning, and it was these responses we use to write the different perspectives expressed by the various characters in the stories. We went through the same research process with the second story about who should get the reward for finding the Wizard's glasses. Once again about half the children in our study thought it should be Eddie, the other Andy. Sometimes a child would come up with a very clever compromise.

Now, imagine an acting troupe of third graders. They have rehearsed the play in their own classroom, with each actor having a part. The troupe comes to the kindergarten class to put on their rendition of "The Wizard's Birthday Party". They may read their parts or memorize them. Either way, the younger children will now have the opportunity to ask the actors, who not so long ago were the age of the audience members. We think this kind of experience will bring the hypothetical social situation even closer to real life. It is an approach we think would be very worthwhile to implement in practice, and to carefully research, in ways similar to the ways we have studied and considered developmentally structured discussion groups in this essay.

Some final thoughts on how to understand the promotion of fairness reasoning within and across cultures

To review the connection between developmental and cultural ways of interpreting the way children understand, think about and discuss these stories, a final word is now necessary. We have mainly focused on developmental ways of understanding young children's moral, fairness, and social reasoning. However, have we done justice to what could be called a cultural analysis, one that would explore whether opinions differed depending upon where the students lived in the world, with whom and under what differing circumstances? Importantly, it is most often a society's cultural values that are often seen as most important to that society's leadership. If opinions about norms of fairness, etc., differ across as well as within cultures, as they most likely do, it would be valuable to know how these differing values play a part in the opinions were justified. This suggests it is very important to compare not only across "macro" cultures, but also within cultures, for example students from different backgrounds within a nation, especially nations that are large in area, and diverse in many ways. How might opinions differ when within any cultural lens, the focus, for example, is between girls versus boys, or students from different regions, schools, or from students growing up with parents with different sources and levels of income.

Consider the case of a youngster who allows a friend to always cut in line in front of him. This youngster, according to his mother, is always the last one in the crowd of children to take a photo with and receive Santa's present. "He didn't see the need to push forward, believing his turn would come sooner or later, and it doesn't matter whether he gets it." In his gym class, his friend always stands in front of this young boy even though his friend arrives later. And the boy always lets him. When his mother asked him what he thinks about his friend doing that, her son says: "It is his problem; not mine".

Now, how can we understand this young person's social behavior? What theoretical framework can help us? In reality, one can understand the comment, "It is his problem, not mine" from the perspective of any number of theoretical lenses. For example, evolutionary theory talks about how alpha males will produce the most offspring which may account for the behavior of the friend of this young boy. A personality theory will speak to traits such as inhibited and uninhibited individuals, relating back to biological templates, or even simply the social psychology of knowing the context of their friendship (who is bigger, who is richer, who is more aggressive, who is more caring, etc.). However, when it comes to socializing our youth, our children, our students, our citizens, most adults in authority primarily look at what needs to be done through the lens of culture, that is our own socio-political culture and our own personal relationship to it. A theory of culture might look at the importance of hierarchy in the context of keeping order and harmony. If the culture says, no breaking back into line, that is what the educator will want the young child to learn.

We see cultural lenses and developmental lenses as operating at different levels of human social behavior. Consider an analogy to "eating behavior". One can see how someone eats, but we cannot see how the stomach looks or works without good research tools. Just like an analysis of digestion might be better understood by looking at the level of the body organ, it also needs to look at an even harder level to see, the cellular level, the level of the chemistry within the stomach. Seeing the stomach is like seeing cultural forces and dynamics. Understanding cultural forces is like understanding the structure and function of the stomach. Seeing the cells within the stomach, and its chemistry requires a deeper look. Seeing developmental forces is like seeing the functioning of the cells and chemistry within the stomach. Both need to be understood to understand eating behavior. These multi-level studies are what we call organismic.

Both cultural and developmental analyses are also organismic. Both cultural and developmental aspects of social behavior are not easily seen at first glance. But, like a body's organ, a cultural view is still more accessible to see than, like a cellular view, a developmental view. We think that is one reason why, when there is a clash between what the cultural view proposes and what the developmental view proposes, the developmental view will tend to be second in line, will give way, will be less obvious to parents, to educators, etc.

For instance, in our first story, the social actions of the deer in the birthday party story, insisting on being let back into line, may not be the voice of the most developmentally advanced social perspective expressed, but the deer is obviously bigger than the boys, and certainly sounds louder. Sometimes, in a certain culture, perhaps often, the loudest voice can trump the voice of fairness. In some contexts, if a firm authority is in place, the choices available to the deer and the two boys might be very different than if only the rules of the peer culture are in play.

However, the developmental analysis allows us to look at underlying social understanding, skills, and values each child has practiced. These skills are important no matter in which culture they are being utilized. One can argue pro or con the Deer's perspective, at the full range of developmental levels. That is why, under the conditions we have established for dilemma/story discussion, in the hands of a practiced educator. I think it is a good idea to let the child exercise her best developmental skills in hypothetical situations as the child listens to the ideas of the other children. In this way, paradoxically perhaps, young children can more safely come to understand the social rules of their own culture, both explicit and implicit, while they develop their own sense of what is right and what is fair. They can think for themselves in certain contexts. They can be sensitive to their cultural norms in other. They need to be able to do both, and both at the same time.

Our research group[1] feels that a story with a dilemma that divides the readers, listeners, or watchers of the story on what to propose to do, and why, is a good one for use in the development of not only fairness reasoning but the promotion of the discussion skills that are important energy for such development. When the culture does not provide a clear rule, then young people will come up with their own. For instance, when we wrote this story which involves both culturally specific and developmentally general aspects of social experience, we purposefully presented these different sides to the dilemma into the story. And for each side, we had the actors express a range of levels of reasoning. Returning to the story, let's revisit what, after providing an initial opinion the Raccoon goes on to say:

> "That's right! Think about how the deer feels. It wasn't his fault that he lost his hat. Why should the deer have to go to the end of the line now and miss out on getting a birthday-present? Well, I don't think that's very fair! The deer had that place first, **and he waited longer than your friend did.** It's only fair that the one who waits the longest should get the last present."

You may or may not agree with Raccoon, but I think you will agree that Raccoon's second attempt at a justification is a better argument than Raccoon's first, not because it is longer, but because it provides a more socially complex set of justifications that take in the perspectives of more

---

① https://xmedia.gse.harvard.edu/

parties to the disagreement.

Considering and/or coordinating social perspective is another basis upon which I also think stories like these are a good way to promote children's reasoning about fairness across all cultures, as long as the design of the educational opportunities seriously takes account of the cultural contexts in which discussions are taking place. One thing this means is that stories with open-ended endings need to be designed and written "locally", that is, by those people, those professionals, who deeply understand the culture of the children and teachers and parents who will be discussing these stories. However, if I am correct, it is also the universal aspects of social awareness, the deep social awareness structures that follow the laws of social-cognitive development I have sketched out much earlier in this essay, that must not be ignored or forgotten. For these are important foundations upon which we can build the science and practice of inter-group relations, from the bottom up as well as top down. What do you think? We think further research on these questions is very important to undertake.

5. Appropriate Curricular Topics in Early Childhood Classrooms

Catherine E. Snow

Harvard University

One of the secrets about young children that early childhood educators rarely share with others is how incredibly sophisticated young children's thinking is. We too often underestimate 2 - 5 year-olds, thinking that our role as educators is just to be sure they learn a lot of the basics — reciting the alphabet, writing a few dozen characters, reading and writing their names, labeling colors and shapes, counting to 50 — so they emerge from preschool ready for school. But the most gifted teachers of young children concentrate as well on what adults can learn from young children, not just what we can teach them. The thesis of this chapter is that the first thing we can learn from children is what to teach them.

Learning from children

Learning from children starts, of course, with listening to them.

When they feel comfortable with adults they trust, children talk a lot, and ask an overwhelming number of questions. One longitudinal study of four children aged 18 to 65 months who were growing up in the U. S. found that they asked 75 – 150 questions an hour (Chouinard, 2007). Although some of the questions were requests (*Can I watch TV? Will you tie my shoes?*), the majority were efforts to seek information from adults, and it became clear that the children were truly interested in the answers, because they persisted if the adults failed to respond or responded in an unsatisfactory way.

What can we conclude from the fact that children ask so many questions? First of all, of course, it means that they are very curious. Second, that they know what they don't know. Third, that they assume adults are willing and able to help them learn. As educators, we couldn't ask for a more desirable learner profile! Multiply out the learning opportunities children are creating for themselves:

100 questions per hour
× 3 hours per day of interaction
× 365 days per year
× 4 years
= 390,000 opportunities to learn, before kindergarten

Of course, not all children experience these multiple opportunities to learn. In some settings, children are discouraged from asking questions. In some settings the adults can't or won't answer, perhaps because they see talkative children as cheeky or out of control, or perhaps because they value quiet children more highly than curious children, or perhaps because they are convinced that what they want to teach is more important than what children want to learn. Such an attitude might work for older students — high-school students intent on passing entrance exams to university are often willing to work on learning material they do not find intrinsically interesting. But 2 – 5 year-olds are not so malleable. Their learning is much more efficient and much more effective when it responds to their own curiosity-fueled questions.

Debates about early childhood programs

Does this mean that a good early childhood curriculum could just be a series of conversations with children about their interests? In fact, there has been a long-standing debate in the early childhood world about this question — to what degree early childhood curricula should be teacher-directed vs. child-responsive. The strongly child-responsive approach was considered appropriate, indeed optimal, under the former NAEYC (National Association for the Education of Young Children) standards, which emphasized developmental appropriateness as the key criterion determining quality and social learning as a primary purpose of early childhood education. Perhaps the best known and most high-quality implementation of the responsive-curriculum model, Reggio Emilia, in fact does operate with richly structured curricula, but ones that are invented on the spot in response to emergent interests and activities in the classroom (http://www.aneverydaystory.com/beginners-guide-to-reggio-emilia/main-principles/). Other examples of this approach include the High/Scope model developed in the 1960s by the High/Scope

Institute in Ypsilanti, Michigan (Frede & Barnett, 1992), and subsequently adopted by many early-childhood centers in the U. S., including Head Start, as well as in Europe (e. g., Kaleidoscope, the Dutch version).

But the High/Scope version of child-responsive programs has been criticized as not very rigorous and unable to ensure that all children enjoy equal opportunities to learn. Meanwhile, rich responsive curricula like Reggio Emilia require optimal conditions to work well — a low adult to child ratio, lots of resources for responding to child interests, highly qualified teachers, and (some would argue) a larger cultural context that is aligned with the practices and relationships on which such an approach relies. Thus, though many U. S. early childhood programs profess to be inspired by the Reggio Emilia model, none has managed actually to replicate it.

The alternative, and indeed a common response to the perceived flabbiness of the poorly implemented child-responsive curriculum approach was to propose tightly scripted EC curricula, replete with specific learning goals and standards, and a promise to graduate children ready for school. For example, the Pyramide approach was introduced in the Netherlands in an effort to speed up learning for the many immigrant second language speakers of Dutch flooding urban EC classrooms; classroom practices consisted mostly of scripted direct instruction, memorization and repetition of dialogues, and practice reading and writing simple words. Direct instruction (DI) is an approach made popular in the U. S. by Siegfried Engelmann, who argued that it promoted equity by designing learnable tasks for all children.① Implementation of such models in early childhood contexts has been rare, especially after the results of a comparison of DI to the High/Scope and a business-as-usual nursery school model showed negative effects on every measure from the DI experience (Schweinhart & Weikart, 1998).

So how do we find a golden mean between the highly prescriptive DI programs that lack developmental appropriateness, and the open-ended responsive programs that demand high levels of experience, knowledge, and skill from teachers as well as rich and wide-ranging materials and resources? What is the right mix of preplanned activities and responsiveness to children's curiosity? Is there a way to make DI more engaging, or to make child-responsive curricula easier to implement and more even in quality across sites? Is there a way to embed children's questions into more scripted, teacher-led programs, or to enrich the answers to those questions in the open-ended programs? Addressing those dilemmas might show the way to higher quality and greater replicability in EC classrooms.

I argue that seriously considering children's questions could give us insights about how to do this — insights into what they know and what they need to know. Because the fact of the matter is that there is a list of topics that many young children are interested in, and a way to make any of those topics a source of deep and broad learning. The solution, then, is to have the resources for following up on the questions available so that EC teachers can easily access them when needed.

---

① https://www.nifdi.org/15/index.php? option=com_content&view=article&id=52&Itemid=27

Let me provide an example of how this might work. In a child-responsive classroom serving 3 – 4-year-olds, the first organized activity of the day is typically a morning meeting, and such a morning meeting often includes reading one or more books aloud. The book-reading interaction typically (if teachers are decently trained, at least) creates an opportunity for questions from the children. The questions might focus narrowly on the topic of the book, or more broadly on topics related to the book. Consider, for example, what might happen after reading the book *Hug* (see Chapter One for a summary of *Hug* and some pictures from it). This book could lead to questions about many different specific topics: a set of factual topics related to biology (animals that live in jungles, names for baby animals of different species, the sounds animals of different sorts make, what the animals eat, how they sleep), to geography and biomes (What are jungles exactly? How do they differ from deserts, mountains, savannahs, and zoos? What kinds of animals and plants inhabit those different spaces?), or to different emotions (the chimp is first curious, then sad, then distressed, then relieved and overjoyed) and different social relationships (friends, enemies, siblings, parent-child).

Of course, the normal teacher is unlikely to be able to follow up on all those possible topics, nor would responding to all of them necessarily be a good idea. But if the teacher is prepared to listen carefully and to recognize the children's questions as reflecting curiosity about one or several of those topics, s/he could then lead a discussion designed to help the class decide whether they would like to pick one for further study. In a well-equipped classroom, s/he would then have access to curriculum packets useful for supporting any of those topics. S/he might have available, for example, a crate with books about jungle animals in groups and individually (see Appendix), as well as a few lesson plans with ideas for related multi-day activities: working in small groups to model different animals or animal masks in papier-mâché, researching and building a jungle habitat, researching the foods preferred by different animals and drawing or pasting pictures of those foods onto posters, and so on. ① The crate might include poems or songs that relate to the topic, and some suggestions for YouTube videos showing animals in their natural habitats. A rich array of resources could help children learn a lot about animals and animal life, while embedding math, music, art, and science into the activities. The read-aloud books for the next few days could all focus on related topics, and by the time children have satisfied their curiosity and are getting bored with the topic, they will have acquired a lot of useful information.

What if the children don't display curiosity about animals after hearing *HUG* read aloud? There should be another crate with books, suggested activities, and lesson plans for learning about emotions, and another for friendship, and another for the topic of mothers and babies, and so on. Thus the curriculum can be responsive to child interests by virtue of strategic deployment of the resources, and all the good thinking that goes into designing rich curricula can be exploited but in a way that recognizes that children learn better and faster when they are deeply

① See the resources and materials in the 7-week long *Let's Know* preK curricular unit on animals for ideas and materials; http://static.ehe.osu.edu/downloads//projects/larrc/1_Animals_PreK_Teacher%20Manual_cohort%202_digital_r.pdf engaged in the topic.

Conclusion

The field of early childhood has now developed dozens of different curricula, commercial and not-for-profit, many of which have some grounding in research principles and most of which offer excellent suggestions of books to read aloud, clever ideas for small group activities, and guidance to teachers about how best to use those resources. Unfortunately, these resources have not in general been proven to greatly improve child outcomes. I think it is worth considering whether the disappointing findings about their impacts on child performance reflect, not poor curricular design or low fidelity of implementation, but lack of attention to the children's interests. Having documented briefly in this chapter ideas for how to organize a curriculum on jungle animals, I clearly am committed to the idea that jungle animals, their habitats, and their habits could constitute a good EC curriculum topic. But however charming the books included, however clever the songs and rhymes, however integrated the various activities, nothing will be learned if the children are not interested. The challenge is to marry the excellent curricular design with child engagement, and the best mechanism for doing that is to listen to children's questions. They tell us what topics are of interest and what information the children are ready and eager to learn.

This chapter is, in effect, a plea to the field of early childhood to develop an array of well-designed, carefully curated, modular curricular resources, that would offer teachers the luxury of attending to what children want to know and the assurance that they can find the resources they need in order to respond. Rather than being limited to either prepackaged curricula or open-ended exploration, we could make early childhood classrooms more like natural history museums, offering the freedom to go spend time with the dinosaur exhibit or the flowering plants or the sea animals, in order that children can learn about what they find most interesting at the time that they are interested. But natural history or science museums are too limited a metaphor, because children's curiosity might lead them to questions about history, about art, about human relationships, or myriad other topics not represented in science or natural history museums. So a better metaphor might be the Wikipedia—accumulating information about a topic in response to readers' and editors' curiosity about it, and sharing that information widely. The Wikipedia, though, is a relatively inert storage device for knowledge, whereas good EC curricula have components that can be paged through, listened to, manipulated, and interacted with, even while they are being expanded by their users. If we put our design resources together, we could offer children their own version of Wikipedia — a place to get their questions answered.

Appendix: resources for a curricular unit on jungle animals

Some of the many possible books to include for Readalouds

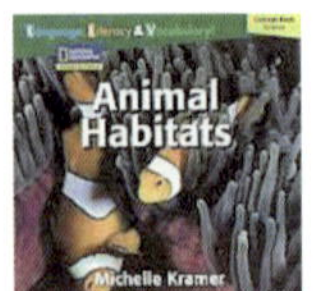

Animal Habitats by Michelle Kramer

The Monkey and the Crocodile by Paul Galdone

Living Things Series by Bobbie Kalman

If I Were a Jungle Animal (Hardcover) by Amanda Ellery

If You're Happy And You Know It: Jungle Edition (Hardcover) by James Warhola (Editor)

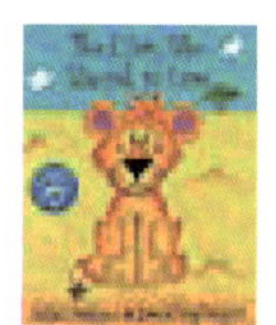

The Lion Who Wanted To Love (Orchard Picturebooks) by Giles Andreae

Hot Hippo (Paperback) by Mwenye Hadithi

Ideas for literacy-support activities:

Start with an existing poem/song, then work with the class to write variants for other animals, e. g. the Zebra song from https://www.pinterest.com/pin/277956608224083593

I'm a little zebra
White and black
With a busy mane
Going down my back
I like to gallop
Run and play
Out on the African plains
All day.

Sources of ideas for crafts and art activities (not all these are equally good, but they offer an array of ideas for children of different ages):

https://www.kidssoup.com/craft-and-resource/deep-in-the-jungle-preschool-lesson-plans-and-activities

http://www.preschoolexpress.com/theme-station12/jungle.shtml

https://www.educatall.com/page/447/Jungle.html

Songs and rhymes:

https://www.youtube.com/watch?v=NNELmTbw9yM

Movement activities:

https://www.youtube.com/watch?v=GoSq-yZcJ-4

References

Chouinard, M. (2007). Children's questions: A mechanism for cognitive development. Monographs of the Society for Research in Child Development, Serial No. 286, Vol. 72, No. 1

Frede, E. & Barnett, S. (1992). Developmentally appropriate public school preschool: A study of implementation of the high/scope curriculum and its effects on disadvantaged children's skills at first grade. Early Childhood Research Quarterly, 7, 483 - 499.

https: //www. researchgate. net/profile/Lawrence _ Schweinhart/publication/234577267_Why_Curriculum_Matters_in_Early_Childhood_Education/links/00b7d539f27f8d25cf000000. pdf

Schweinhart, L. & Weikart, D. (1998). Why curriculum matters in early childhood education. Educational Leadership, 57 - 60.

6. Selecting Books to Read with Young Children: Different Formats, Different Interactions

Catherine E. Snow

Harvard University

Advice that every parent and every early childhood educator hears recurrently is to spend lots of time reading books with children. Reading books aloud is promoted for its proven capacity to contribute to several aspects of child development (see Mol, Bus, de Jong & Smeets, 2006, for a review), as well as for the exposure it offers to stories central to the culture, for the capacity of those stories to get children thinking about moral and interpersonal conflicts and dilemmas (Dowdall, Melendez-Torres, Murray, Gardner, Hartford & Cooper, 2019), and of course for the social value of sharing enjoyable narratives and the cognitive value of discussing them.

But the generalized advice to share picture books with young children fails to attend sufficiently to a number of issues that need serious consideration: a) what the adult's role should be when presenting books to children; b) whether the positive effects of shared book reading are the same for all sorts of books; and c) how the adult's role might differ as a function of the type of books being read.

Adult role

First, it must be acknowledged that the definition of what adults should be doing when reading or playing with children varies across cultures and social classes. In Japan, for example, parents are advised to sit back and just let children enjoy the books on their own. The belief is that reading the text or imposing a conversation on the books limits imagination. Such a view is, of course, not based in hard evidence, but it springs from an important cultural commitment to leaving children free and to valuing creativity and fantasy.

It is clear, though, that if we want to reap the linguistic, cognitive, and social benefits available from book reading, adults need to take a more active and interactive role (Wasik, Bond & Hindman, 2006). The approach often recommended in U. S. early childhood contexts is 'dialogic reading', first introduced by Russ Whitehurst (Whitehurst, 2002; see also Lonigan & Whitehurst, 1998), proven to be a set of techniques that parents, librarians, and early childhood personnel can easily learn, and proven to generate improved language abilities in children. Dialogic reading involves going through the book the first time telling or reading the story while pointing out the pictures, but over successive readings involving the child (ren) increasingly actively in describing the pictures, in telling the story independently, and responding to questions that require inference and evaluation (why do you think the big bad wolf wanted to blow the piggy's housc down? What would you do for protection against a big bad wolf?). This is the approach early childhood educators in most U. S. classrooms approximate, so we will take it as the default "good practice".

Different kinds of books

The dialogic reading approach is not, however, equally applicable to all sorts of books. Consider the books we share with the youngest children — alphabet books and counting books. While active involvement of the child in naming letters or recognizing numbers is certainly the goal, it makes little sense to expect inferences or evaluation with such books. 'Why does A stand for apple?' is not a question a 3-year-old should be expected to answer!

Similarly, books that mostly play with rhymes and nonsense do not lend themselves to inference or evaluation. Dr. Seuss' *Hop on Pop* and *Green eggs and ham*, for example, can be read for fun, but there is not much narrative arc to explore nor character motivation to probe. A standard way to read such books is to increasingly let the child fill in the rhymes, and many do ultimately memorize the entire text, but not as a result of standard dialogic reading techniques, which model comprehension processes rather than word recognition.

We often think of narratives as the default when considering picture books for young children. While the majority of books appropriate for young children are narrative, some researchers (e. g., Duke, 2004) are recommending providing an array of nonfiction books as well, in part because they may be more effective in building children's background knowledge, and because some children may prefer them to narratives. Obviously the way one reads nonfiction will also differ from the way one reads stories in which characters' actions and emotions can be explained. Some of the features of dialogic reading are relevant — most importantly the central idea that the child should be an active participant in the processing of the information — but some may not be applicable at all.

Selecting books for discussability

The central notion of dialogic reading is, simply, that children should be talking and not just listening during book-reading sessions. Dialogic reading is one instantiation of the important claim that children learn to talk by talking, and it offers techniques to ensure that children have opportunities to talk during an activity that some adults might think of as primarily opportunities for children to listen.

If promoting talk is a primary purpose for book reading, then it makes sense to think about selecting books (at least for children aged 3 and up) for their degree of discussability. Some books are wonderful just to listen to — but others need to be taken in small chunks, and talked about at length. Such highly discussable books deserve more time in early childhood classrooms, where the group discussion can lead to important insights for all the participants, adult as well as child.

One model of a highly discussable picture book for young children, is Todd Parr's *The Peace Book.* This book features illustrations that could well have been produced by children — thus lending themselves as models for reproduction or extension. Each page of *The Peace Book* makes a discussable claim about a single instantiation of peacefulness, and over the course of the book multiple dimensions of peace are posited. Peace is seen as exemplified in self-care (*peace is taking a nap*, *peace is thinking about someone you love*). Connections with others are a definition or a source of peace (*peace is making a new friend*, *peace is helping your neighbor*, *peace is learning a new language*). Concern for the state of the natural world is proposed as an aspect of peace (*peace is keeping the water blue for the fish*, *peace is planting a tree*). The acceptance of various forms of diversity is noted as equivalent to peace (*peace is listening to different kinds of music*, *peace is reading all different kinds of books*, *peace is wearing different clothes*). Most powerfully, perhaps, social justice is equated to peace (*peace is enough pizza for everyone*, *peace is everyone having a home*). These are just a few of the many provocative claims about the definition of peace presented by Parr in his book.

The wonderful thing about this book is that each of these claims is discussable (Why is giving someone a hug equivalent to peace? What does listening to others' music have to do with peace?). Many of the claims are discussable, not just with 3 or 4 year olds, but also with adults. For example, one perhaps slightly surprising claim is "Peace is keeping the streets clean". This proposition raises multiple possibilities: Do dirty streets generate disorder and discord? Or are dirty streets the product of a society in which individuals do not value peaceful relations with one another? Or are dirty streets just another symptom of a society that can't attend to keeping the peace? If one agrees that accepting civic responsibility contributes to peace, that has enormous implications for what we teach children all through school, and for how we make laws and engage in social policy. That is a topic for discussion in kindergarten as well as in graduate programs in political science. More attention to the conditions for peace in both those settings would be of great value to us all.

Conclusion

The right choice of a book to read with a young child depends on many factors — the age of the child, the child's interests, but also importantly the short-and long-term goals of the activity. Alphabet books can help children master the early stage of conventional literacy. Nonsense rhyming books can help build children's phonological awareness and provide them fun with language. Narratives give them a chance to consider others' thoughts and feelings. Nonfiction gives them access to information about topics of interest to them. Books that take an innovative look at important topics and that make controversial claims give them a chance to grapple with big issues and think deep thoughts.

All of these goals are achieved, of course, only if the adult participants in the book-reading activity ensure that the children are actively engaged, thinking and talking rather than just listening. Thus the discussability dimension should be one important consideration as we select books for reading aloud. Book-sharing can be an opportunity for children to develop language, including narrative skills (Lever & Senechal, 2011), to build their theory of mind understanding (Dowdall et al., 2019), and to acquire vocabulary and important content knowledge (Smith & Dickinson, 1994; Snow, 2017). The child's active participation in the shared reading is crucial to these positive outcomes

(Kang, Kim & Pan, 2004), and the stimulating effect of books on the quality and complexity of adult speech is one of the key mechanisms (Massey, Pence, Justice & Bowles, 2008). The potential for positive effects from shared book-reading is enormous, but only with an optimal convergence of the child, the activity, the text, and the interaction style.

References

Dickinson, D., & Smith, M. (1994). Long-term effects of preschool teachers' book readings on low-income children's vocabulary and story comprehension. Reading Research Quarterly, 29, 104 - 122. doi: 10.2307/747807

Dowdall, N., Melendez-Torres, G. J., Murray, L., Gardner, F., Hartford, L. & Cooper, P. J. (2019). Shared picture book reading interventions for child language development: A systematic review and meta-analysis. Child Development, xxx 2019, Volume 00, pages 1 - 17. https://doi.org/10.1111/cdev.13225

Duke, N. K. (2004). The case for informational text. Educational Leadership, 61, 40 - 44.

Kang, J., Kim, Y.-S., & Pan, B. (2009). Five-year-olds' book talk and story telling: contributions of mother-child joint bookreading. First Language, 29, 243 - 265. https://doi.org/10.1177/0142723708101680

Lever, R. & Senechal, M. (2011). Discussing stories: On how a dialogic reading intervention improve kindergartners' oral narrative construction. Journal of Experimental Psychology, 108, 1 - 24. https://doi-org.ezproxy-test.uio.no/10.1016/j.jecp.2010.07.002

Lonigan, C. & Whitehurst, G. (1998). Relative efficacy of parent and teacher involvement in a shared-reading intervention for preschool children from low-income backgrounds. Early Childhood Research Quarterly, 2, 263 - 290. https://doi-org.ezproxy-test.uio.no/10.1016/S0885-2006(99)80038-6

Massey, S., Pence, K., Justice, L. & Bowles, R. (2008). Educators' Use of Cognitively Challenging Questions in Economically Disadvantaged Preschool Classroom Contexts. Early Education and Development, 19. https://doi.org/10.1080/10409280801964119

Mol, S. E., Bus, A., De Jong, M., & Smeets, D. (2008). Added value of dialogic parent-child book readings: A meta-analysis. Early Education and Development, 19, 7 – 26.

Parr, T. The Peace Book.

Snow, C. (2017). The role of vocabulary in children's language learning: A fifty-year perspective. Infancia y Aprendizaje. http://dx.doi.org/10.1080/02103702.2016.1263449

Wasik, B., Bond, M., & Hindman, A. (2006). The effects of a language and literacy intervention on Head Start children and teachers. Journal of Educational Psychology, 98, 63 – 74. doi: 10.1037/0022 – 0663.98.1.63

Whitehurst, G. R. (2002). Dialogic reading: An effective way to read aloud with young children. https://www.readingrockets.org/article/dialogic-reading-effective-way-read-aloud-young-Mol, S. E., Bus, A., De Jong, M., & Smeets, D. (2008). Added value of dialogic parent-child book readings: A meta-analysis. Early Education and Development, 19, 7 – 26.

Xu Zhao

Xu Zhao is Associate Professor and Director of Research in Chinese Youth Mental health and Wellbeing at the Werklund School of Education, University of Calgary, Canada. Her research in North America and China explores one broad question: *Facing rampant achievement anxiety and social stress, how can educators and parents promote children's academic learning and at the same time protect their mental health and socioemotional well-being*? She is the author of *Competition and Compassion in Chinese Secondary Education* (New York: Palgrave MacMillan, 2015). She earned her doctorate in Human Development & Psychology from Harvard University.

7. Bicultural Issues in Bilingual Education

Xu Zhao

University of Calgary

In China, bilingual (English and Chinese) early childhood education has become part of the everyday vocabulary of educators and parents (Feng, 2005). It is often touted as a new form of education that has great potential for integrating the best ideas from the long Chinese tradition of education and modern Western developmental and educational sciences. However, similar to the contentiousness of bilingual education (often English and Spanish) in the United States, there is no consensus among Chinese educationalists about what a bilingual education means; the benefits and costs of bilingual education, the pedagogical theories and approaches, and the long-term cultural and political implications are all being debated (Gao & Wang, 2017; Gao & Ren, 2019). The discussion among Chinese scholars largely focuses on questions such as whether new brain research provides evidence for the introduction of a second language in a critical developmental period, how to adopt the various Western bilingual education models, and what teaching materials and learning activities best promote young children's interest in learning English. Bilingual education is framed mostly as a "scientific" issue, as if children are growing up and learning linguistic codes in a cultureless, classless, and genderless scientific laboratory, following universal principles of development and learning. This approach to early childhood education has been criticized by anthropologists and cultural psychologists from within Western scholarship itself, for failing to take into consideration of the sociocultural contexts of child development and individual variation in learning (e.g., Mallory & New, 1994; Rogoff, 2003).

What is often left out of the literature on bilingual education is that the idea that bilingual education involves not only two linguistic systems, but also bringing together two cultural worlds with different and even conflicting pedagogical traditions and communication styles, interpersonal norms, societal values, and beliefs about learning. In practice, as our research shows, bilingual early childhood education (ECE) programs in China often adopt Western ECE theories and curriculum models as exemplars, but neglect the disjunctions between theory and practice, and pay little attention to the cultural disconnect between the agenda of their curriculum and the educational goals of Chinese parents. That is, until conflicts occur. The same problem of uncritically adopting Western ECE theories and models also occurs in other Asian societies, such as Taiwan (Lee & Tseng, 2010). Yet, with a few exceptions (e.g., Cheng, 2012; Johnston & Wong, 2002; Lee & Tseng, 2008), there is a lack of empirical research on how culturally different educational beliefs, practices and values manifest themselves in the teaching and learning activities of bilingual ECE programs in China and other Asian societies.

Bilingual education is by nature a process of bicultural interaction and intercultural communication. Taking a sociocultural approach, Western scholars of language development have argued that the process and outcomes of language learning should not be considered from the perspective of language proficiency but in terms of communicative effectiveness and social appropriateness (Snow, 1992). For English language learners, the emphasis is not on whether children are learning "standard" English, but on their ability to effectively and appropriately function when interacting with native English speakers and use the new language to complete various tasks. To help children develop the skills of effectively communicating in two languages and between two cultural worlds, bilingual education needs to provide children with the opportunity to interact with native English-speakers. Bilingual education also needs to support children in understanding and appreciating meaningful cultural differences, including the ways people in different societies communicate and interact with each other, so that they develop the critical capacity to take cultural perspectives into consideration and switch communication styles based on their audience and situation.

Young children in bilingual ECE programs interact with educators who are native speakers of different languages; the children also negotiate between cultures, including the two cultural worlds of school and family. For these reasons, bilingual ECE education in China and other Asian societies will benefit from a systematic body of knowledge about how East meets West in the specific context of bilingual ECE programs. This body of knowledge also needs to take into consideration the relationship between school and family as well as the social, economic, and political contexts of the broader society in which they function. Currently, there is no such synthesis of the cross-cultural and intercultural issues that educators, parents, and children in China need to negotiate in developing, implementing, and experiencing a bilingual education curriculum. In this article, I aim to identify a few key areas of culturally different values, beliefs, and practices related to child development and education that I believe have important implications for bilingual education in China and may also inform related research and practices in other Asian societies.

Due to the lack of empirical studies that could directly inform a synthesis report, my analysis is based on research from related areas, including language socialization, bilingual education, cross-cultural psychological research on children, and parental educational beliefs in China and other countries. A key message from cross-cultural research on child development is the idea that cultures differ in their assumptions about children, including the desirable outcomes of child development, the status of children, and appropriate adult-children interaction and communication styles (Ochs & Schieffelin, 1984; Rogoff, 2003; van Kleeck, 1994). Researchers such as van Kleeck (1994) and Crago and Cole (1991) highlighted five areas of cultural differences in language socialization: (1) aspects of social organization related to interaction, (2) the value of talk, (3) how status is handled in interaction, (4) beliefs about intentionality, and (5) beliefs about teaching language to children. Accordingly, in different cultures, different communication skills are considered important and different approaches for teaching are valued (Crago, 1992; Schiffelin and Ochs 1986). These differences not only influence the process of bilingual education, but also impact children's long-term construction of self- and social identity. Therefore, scholars have argued that language teaching strategies must be adjusted to match cultural values, language socialization practices, and developmental goals for children (Ball, 2010; van Kleek, 1994).

Informed by the above literature, in this article I highlight four key areas of cultural differences in language socialization and early learning that I believe are salient for bilingual early childhood education in China. They include: (1) self-construal and adult-child interaction styles; (2) The value of talk; (3) assumptions about learning; and (4) beliefs about intentionality, expressions of emotion, and desirable moral characteristics. I unpack each of the four areas by introducing relevant cross-cultural research findings and then contextualizing the cultural differences in the Chinese context. I focus on these issues in the context of early childhood education in China and bilingual programs for children aged 3 – 6 who are taught by teachers that are either Chinese or English native speakers. However, to take children's long-term development into consideration, I also draw on research about older children and adolescents; the bicultural issues highlighted in my analysis are certainly relevant for bilingual education at the elementary and secondary levels. In the following sections, I first introduce these bicultural issues through providing examples from the literature. I then discuss the implications of including a cultural understanding component in bilingual education and addressing cultural disconnects between families and ECE programs.

The Ideal Self and Styles of Communication

The first important area of cultural difference is differences in the self, or self-construal. Specifically, it is the extent to which one defines the self independently or interdependently. Cross-cultural psychologists have typically characterized Western culture as emphasizing individuals' independence and autonomy and Eastern culture as emphasizing individuals' sense of self being embedded in social relationships (Markus & Kitayama, 1991). In adult-child interactions, children in East Asian societies are often expected to develop and demonstrate qualities such as obedience, respect, and compliance; whereas children in Western societies are encouraged to show self-awareness, initiation, and assertiveness from a young age (Chao, 1994, 2001; Johnston & Wong, 2002).

Cultural differences in self-construal have a profound influence on how individuals communicate and interact with others. Specific to bilingual ECE programs in China are the different ways in which native Chinese and English adult speakers provide care and give instructions to children. For example, Chinese parents are found to use more "directive" speech acts when interacting with their toddler children; within a Chinese context, this pattern of behavior is not associated with negative parenting styles such as being authoritarian and controlling, as is the case in North America (Helle & Mariner, 2001). In contrast, in dominant North American culture, instruction and discipline are often expressed in a language of choice, even though children are also expected to respect teachers as authority figures (Hoffman, 2001).

Understandably, these cultural differences in speech acts influence the ways children learn to communicate with adults and with each other. A child who has been socialized to accept Chinese adults' directive style of communication may be confused by an English-speaking teacher who gives instructions in the form of a question about the child's own intention, such as, "do you want to put your shoes on the shelf?" The confused child's unspoken response may be something like, "I don't know. What do *you* want me to do?" In contrast, when children have become used to a Western style of instruction and interaction but have not developed an understanding of cultural variations in communication styles, they may interpret the ways their Chinese teachers and parents speak to them as harsh and lacking respect for their independence.

How children interpret adults' communication styles depends on the perceived power relationship between the two languages and their relative social status in Chinese society. Despite China's recent rising as an economic superpower in the world, the assumption held by many individuals in China is that Western approaches to family and school education are more "scientific" and should be readily adopted in China to make Chinese society more "modern." This attitude influences children's interpretations of adults' communication and interaction styles and risks undermining their relationships with their Chinese-speaking teachers and parents. The accumulation of such cultural differences within Chinese society may further widen the cultural gaps that already exist in families, between generations, and in broader society due to rapid social and cultural changes. How to help children understand the cultural issues associated with bilingual education is an important question for children's long-term psychosocial development and the development of healthy family relationships in China.

The Value of Talk

A second area of cultural difference considered here is the extent to which verbal expression is valued in education and in social life in general. Researchers have argued that cultures differ in their attitudes toward (a) the amount of talk that is valued, (b) the role of talk in teaching children skills, and (c) the role of verbal skills in children's display of knowledge (Van Kleeck, 1994). In mainstream North American culture, children's vocalization and verbalization are strongly encouraged from birth through the school years. In general, there is a negative perception of quiet and shy children (Chen et. al., 2009). In dominant North American culture, children are socialized to interact freely and frequently with adults, and to show off their communication skills. This is not the case in East Asian societies such as China and Japan, or among non-dominant cultural groups in North America. For example, Indigenous children in North America are encouraged to listen rather than talk (Crago, 1990). Japanese immigrant parents often view a quiet child as a good child (Coles, 2003).

Similarly, in traditional Chinese families, children are often considered too young to be partners in conversation (Johnston & Wong, 2002) and are discouraged from giving opinions when adults are talking. A common response to children who try to jump in on a conversation between adults is, "children should not talk when adults are having a conversation" (小孩子别插话), which is expressed in tones ranging from a gentle reminder to a harsh reprimand. Despite the influence of Western educational ideas in Chinese cities, many Chinese parents still consider it a problem when children habitually make remarks during adults' conversations. Chinese parents frequently ask about how to stop this behavior in Chinese online educational forums. In recent years, online responses to this question have become diverse, clearly influenced by Western notions of child development and education. Discussions have begun to incorporate "modern" childrearing theories and beliefs, including that children should be respected as independent humans and that their self-esteem needs to be protected (e. g., Zhihu, 2015). Instead of interpreting children's talkativeness as discourteous, some discussion participants argue that it shows children's curiosity, need for attention, and eagerness to express their ideas. These participants' suggestions for parents include encouraging their children to participate in adults' conversations, paying close attention to what they say, and acknowledging the value of their ideas. However, other discussion participants argue that, except for in situations that require immediate attention from adults (e. g., the child is vomiting or has a bleeding nose), children should learn to control their impulses, practice patience, and not interrupt adults' conversations. Corresponding suggestions for parents include raising a hand to show an approaching child that he/she should not interrupt or apologizing to one's adult company first, and then briefly responding to one's child, reminding the child of the importance of not interrupting adult conversations.

The traditional Chinese practice of discouraging children from participating in adults' conversations is not a uniquely Chinese practice. Parents in all modern societies, Eastern or Western, ask questions about why children interrupt adults' conversations and how to teach children not to interrupt. As suggested in the old English proverb, "children should be seen and not heard," the same practice once prevailed in Western societies and still exists in some traditional families. The challenging question facing bilingual educators in China is whether teachers and parents should adopt the modern Western value of children's verbalization, and frequently elicit their talk during adult-child interactions, or whether they should respect the traditional Chinese value of children being quiet and listening.

Research has shown shifting values among urban Chinese parents in the last 20 years, including a change from favoring shy and quiet children to valuing outspoken and outgoing children (Chen et al., 2009). My own research shows that middle-class parents in Shanghai stress the importance of socializing their children to overcome shyness and become more sociable (Zhao & Gao, 2014). I have also observed young urban middle-class Chinese children's eagerness to demonstrate their verbal abilities in front of adults in a similar way to Western middle-class children's readiness to show off their verbal capacity. This observation indicates that middle-class Chinese parents are encouraging their children to freely express their opinions and compete with peers to demonstrate their verbal skills. This demonstration of verbal capability is a phenomenon arguably related to the introduction of the market economy in China and the emergence of values associated with competition and self-promotion (Zhao, 2015; Zhao, Selman & Luke, 2018). Nevertheless, our research also shows Chinese parents' contradictory beliefs about desirable qualities in children (Zhao & Gao, 2014). Both empirical research and philosophical discussions are needed to address questions around how teachers should support bilingual children who may be confused about culturally different social norms and practices around when to speak, when not to, and how to participate in conversations with adults and peers. These are important questions for bilingual education in China due to the historically wide cultural gaps between English-speaking Western countries and Chinese society. These questions are also important because of the diverse and contradictory beliefs and practices about childrearing and education that co-exist in China today and the need for information and guidance among anxious parents and teachers.

Assumptions about Learning

There is a rich body of literature on how cultures differ in their beliefs about learning and the ways the learning environment is organized for children (e. g., Li, 2013). Researchers often contrast the Western play-based and child-centered approach to early childhood education with the Eastern academic-oriented, teacher-directed approach relying on writing, drill, and practice (Zhang & Pelletier, 2012). Whereas the Western curriculum model often requires movement, play, human connection, and a caring environment for learning (Epstein & Hohmann, 2012), the Eastern curriculum model is based on the idea of cultivating in the young child the habits of hard work and discipline and a respect for learning (Li, 2013). Specific to language acquisition, in North American middle-class culture, parents consciously engage their young children in "child-directed talk" (van Kleech & Garpenter, 1980) or "child-directed speech" (Snow, 1977). When talking to a child, adults adapt their language to the level of the child, speaking in a simplified and clear way and talking about concrete issues that the child can understand. In activities that involve parents and children, parents using child-directed talk constantly explain to their children what is going on and invite children to narrate their tasks (Health, 1989). From this perspective, the roles of educators (both teachers and parents) include: getting children to communicate frequently; encouraging children's equal participation in a conversation; being aware of language ability and simplifying language when talking to children; asking children questions to elicit verbal displays of knowledge; offering verbal explanations of activities; and being responsive to children's initiations (Van Kleech, 1994). Direct instruction is restricted to teaching children how to use politeness routines such as "please" and "thank you."

This Western approach to language socialization has influenced the curriculum models of bilingual ECE programs in large Chinese cities such as Beijing and Shanghai, as well as the parenting practices of upper-middle-class adults who have studied or worked overseas (Zhao, Selman & Luke, 2018). Yet traditional briefs are still strong among Chinese parents within China and immigrant Chinese families in Western countries. For example, compared to Canadian-or European-born mothers, Chinese Canadian mothers are more likely to strongly believe that children learn best with instruction and not to believe that children learn while playing; they are also more likely to report using picture books and flash cards to teach new words (Johnston & Wong, 2002).

Important questions remain as to how the Western approach to language acquisition and the notions of child-centeredness and play-based learning relate to traditional Chinese ideas of education, particularly the heavy reliance on direct instruction and recitation of classical texts when introducing children to the Chinese orthography and character-based writing system. More specifically, considering the different skills required for children to learn English and Chinese (e. g., memorization of Chinese characters is required for learning how to read and write in Chinese), how would the Western approach to language development and ECE curriculum models prepare bilingual Chinese children for making the transition from spoken to written Chinese, if traditional teaching techniques are abandoned? If the Chinese techniques continue to be used, how could the two approaches be reconciled, in theory and in practice, to address parents' questions about their children's English *and* Chinese language development and their school readiness compared with their peers attending English-or Chinese-only ECE programs?

Answering the above questions requires more empirical research to better understand the specific conditions of bilingual ECE programs in China. In North American Chinese language programs, when and how to start teaching pinyin and Chinese characters to young children (e. g., in kindergarten and first grade) has been controversial (Everson, Chang, & Ross, 2016). However, researchers do agree that the Chinese tradition of helping young children repeatedly recite and read texts aloud and repeatedly handwrite characters has significant pedagogical meaning, in addition to being a cultural tradition. Repeated recitation and writing aid in the early development of literacy skills, help children gain a strong sense of the Chinese language, and support their future comprehension (Leung & Ruan, 2012). Through handwriting practice, children learn to deconstruct characters into a unique pattern of strokes and components and then regroup these sub-characters into a well-formed character. This ability is believed to facilitate children's awareness of a character's internal structure, which supports their understanding of the connections between the form, meaning, and phonological elements of the Chinese writing system. This skill may also be associated with the quality of lexical entries in long-term memory (Flores d'Arcais, 1994; Guan, Liu, Chan, Ye, & Perfetti, 2011). Therefore, researchers have argued that the practice of text memorization and writing Chinese characters by hand needs to be an integral part of any Chinese curriculum, as long as it is embedded in meaningful communicative activities (Everson, Chang, & Ross, 2016).

Intentionality, Emotion Expression, and Desirable Moral Characteristics

Another important yet often neglected cultural issue is how language socialization and child development are influenced by culturally different assumptions about intentionality, emotion expression, and desirable social and moral characteristics. In North American middle-class culture, for example, adults often help children verbally interpret their intentions and emotions and consciously expand their vocabulary in this area (Van Kleeck, 1994; Snow, 1977). The assumption is that children are intentional from birth and it is important for adults to help interpret the internal states of young children. Accordingly, socialization in dominant

North American culture often involves encouraging children to clarify their needs and make decisions based on their own needs and desires; ECE curricula are designed to be "child-centered" to follow children's interests and foster qualities such as independence, self-governance, and creativity.

In China, adults traditionally do not pay the same attention to children's intentions and their expression as their Western counterparts do. Similar to early research findings from Japan (Caudill & Weinstein, 1969), Chinese caregivers often anticipate and address a child's needs (e. g., needs for food or water) without much verbal exchange. To date, no empirical research has systematically documented how new generations of Chinese teachers and parents socialize young children in expressing their desires and emotions. There is also a lack of empirical research documenting the extent to which adults offer children opportunities to make their own choices in different domains of life (e. g. food, clothes, use of digital devices, and education-related issues), and what repertoires of expression related to individuals' internal states are used by Chinese adults when talking to children. Yet, it is for sure that children living between two cultural worlds will observe adults' speech acts and behavioral patterns and will have value judgments about what they will consider normal within one cultural world.

From psychosocial and moral perspectives, traditional Chinese adults see the primary task of socialization as helping children develop the capacities for controlling their personal desires and emotions (Desjarlais, Eisenberg, Good, & Kleinman, 1995). Chinese children are often encouraged to be aware of other people's needs and "yield out of courtesy” （礼让） when there is a conflict between one’s own desire and that of others. This is shown in the famous Chinese idiom story *Kong Rong Rang Li* (孔融让梨). In this story, which has been used for moral education by Chinese adults for two thousand years, Kong Rong, a four-year-old child living in the period of Dong Han (AD 25 – 220), demonstrated the desirable virtue of yielding by giving his older and younger brothers the bigger pears his father brought home and keeping the smallest for himself. This story reflects the Confucian emphasis on the achievement of moral characteristics, specifically the development of humanism, in early childhood education, with the central goal of helping children learn to get along with others. Yet, this tradition is in sharp contrast with the Western approach of encouraging children to express their desires and insist on their interests being protected. How to reconcile the gaps between the two cultures is a very challenging question facing bilingual educators and parents.

Learning to speak two languages can mean living in two different emotional worlds, travelling back and forth between those two worlds, and even living suspended between the two worlds (Matsumoto, 1994; Ożańska-Ponikwia, 2019; Wierzbicka, 1999; 2004; 2009). How people perceive themselves and the world around them depends on the vocabulary provided by their native or non-native language (Wierzbicka, 2009). Even for younger generations of urban Chinese parents, many cannot comfortably tell their children “I love you” in Chinese, and it is even harder for grandparents. Another example is individuals’ affective orientation toward the self. Cross-cultural researchers have observed a self-critical focus among Japanese individuals, contrary to Americans’ focus on maintaining a positive self-view (Kitayama, Markus, Matsumoto, & Norasakkunkit, 1997). This belief in self-criticism as the path to self-improvement is shared by many Chinese adults and is still reflected in Chinese parents' common practice of pointing out their children's weaknesses in comparison to their peers' strengths as a way to motivate their children to work harder and improve themselves (Zhao, Selman & Luke, 2018). Even though these educational beliefs and practices have changed in China to various extents, they still have a strong hold in Chinese adults' expectations for children and their ways of parenting, which can be at odds with Western ECE theories and curriculum models.

Here, it is important to note that these cultural differences should not be essentialized or treated as if they characterize all Chinese and Western individuals, regardless of place and time. Cultural differences need to be placed in historical context and empirically examined. For example, on the surface, the Confucian emphasis on self-discipline and yielding out of courtesy seems to be contrary to Western ECE emphasis on values of individual achievement, potential, and needs. In reality, these values can co-exist in both systems. The fostering of social awareness among children, particularly their capacity to take social perspectives, is a major field of research in Western developmental psychology (e.g., Selman, 2007), and a critical component of school curriculum in North American and European countries. In fact, compared with Chinese children who are pressured by parents and teachers to focus on academic achievement, North American children are more concerned about whether they can make and keep friends. North American children may not be taught to "yield out of courtesy," but they are encouraged to be kind and helpful, to collaborate with other children, control one's own desires when necessary, and make compromises when conflicts arise between friends. The fostering of these social values and skills is the most important goal of ECE in North American societies.

In China, social and economic changes in the last 40 years have been accompanied by a promotion of individualistic values in education (Zhao, 2016). As mentioned above, traditional teachings on being modest, yielding out of courtesy, and sacrificing one's own interests to serve others have to some extent been replaced by the encouragement of competition-based achievement, demonstration of talents, and the expression of individuality (Zhao, 2015). Well-educated middle-and upper-middle-class urban parents all attach importance to respecting children's right to make autonomous decisions and protecting children's self-esteem and emotional wellbeing (e. g., Zhao & Gao, 2014; Zhao, Selman & Luke, 2018). However, gaps and contradictions exist between what parents believe they should do and what they actually do, especially when their children's academic performance is not up to their expectations.

The gaps and tension between what is explicitly emphasized and what is actually practiced exist in all societies, only manifesting themselves in different ways. For example, even though self-expression, choice, and autonomy are strongly valued in American education, cross-cultural researchers have argued that, compared to Japanese schools, American educators exercise more much control over what children do and say in the classroom (Hoffman, 2000). Further, the valuing of self-expression in

American schools and society is also a coercive force. Children do not have the real freedom of *not* expressing themselves, and they must learn what to leave out in self-expression (Tobin et. al. 1989). When bilingual ECE programs in China adopt Western ECE theories and curriculum models, what levels of control should teachers exercise? Can they organize adult-directed activities, provide direct instruction, and instill the traditional Chinese values of self-discipline and hard work into children? These are not "scientific" questions that have ready answers; they are cultural and educational questions to be addressed by Chinese educators and parents together. Again, how the gaps between theory and practice play out in bilingual ECE programs in China requires close empirical examination.

How to Educate Bilingual and Bicultural Children?

In this section, I make the argument that it is important for bilingual ECE programs in China to include a component of culture education and engage teachers and parents in conversations about important cultural issues. As mentioned at the beginning of this article, the educational goals of bilingual programs in China should not be limited to the teaching of linguistic and literacy skills in Chinese and English. Bilingual ECE programs need to foster children's ability to understand and appreciate the differences between the two cultures and to take different perspectives and integrate opposing values, so that they learn to cope with tensions between the cultures and develop a coherent bicultural identity. In fact, culture education, or cultural and heritage education, has become an important part of school curricula in Western European countries where leaders and regular people are increasingly concerned about the protection and promotion of cultural heritage being threatened by globalization (DICHE, 2016). Even though China has a large culturally homogenous Chinese-speaking population, it faces the same threat to its cultural heritage from globalization, as younger generations of Chinese look up to Western culture and avoid the old (Wong, 2002).

What is culture education? Barend van Heusden of the Groningen University in the Netherlands has argued that culture education mainly consists of the capacity for reflection. Through culture education, children learn to reflect upon their own culture, others' cultures, and culture in general. According to van Heusden, this capacity for self-reflection first requires knowledge of different cultural traditions. Second, it requires an understanding of a culture's unique characteristics and how these characteristics contribute to and connect with universal, human struggles. Culture education can be taught through different subjects, including current events, history, arts, philosophy, science, and lessons about citizenship. The goal is to help children develop self-consciousness and cultural self-consciousness, as these are critical abilities for living in a multicultural world. For young children in ECE programs, arts and storytelling are developmentally appropriate tools for stimulating children's imagination and fostering their capacity for self-reflection.

To the above ideas about culture education, I would add the argument that culture education should also aim at reducing cultural, racial, and gender biases and cultivating in children an interest in, a respect for, and an appreciation of the values of different cultural traditions, both their own and others. Most importantly, the respect for and appreciation of all cultural traditions need to be reflected in the curricula of bilingual ECE programs through the introduction of stories, arts, and rituals from both China and Western countries. Secondly, the teaching materials need to be carefully selected to eliminate culturally biased messages. Thirdly, ECE program staff need to examine their own perceptions of Chinese and Western culture to avoid essentializing views of cultural differences and to develop a historical perspective of Chinese and Western societies. Teachers also need to be conscious about the hidden messages about culture, gender, and race that are conveyed in how they interact with children and with one another.

Finally, I emphasize that culture education plays a critical role in supporting bilingual Chinese children to grow up into responsible and capable global citizens, especially the aspect of culture education related to connections between Chinese and Western values. Our research with newly arrived Chinese students in Canadian high schools suggests that a major challenge facing their social integration is their perceived lack of knowledge about North American values-social, moral, and political (Zhao & Arthur, 2017). For example, a Chinese girl in 10th grade, who had arrived in Canada a year earlier, told us that she was always too nervous to talk to the local students, and it was not because she did not know enough English words or grammar to express herself, but because she did not know *what* to say to her Canadian peers. She articulated the problem as, "I don't know what to say to the Canadian students. I don't know what they value." Without knowing what Canadian students value and how the Canadian values relate to her own, she constantly worried about saying something boring or offensive and suffered from anxiety and self-doubt. Our research suggests that the experience of culture shock due to different social, moral and political values is common in Chinese students at both North American schools and universities (Zhao, Yu & Zhang, 2019).

The psychological struggle of Chinese students in North America, especially their feelings of anxiety and self-doubt, may be related to the Asian focus of self-criticism mentioned earlier. However, we also find that the young newcomers in our study who are from other countries, including Japan, the Middle East and Latin American countries, are generally more confident than newcomers from China in communicating with their Canadian peers, despite their limited knowledge of English. Through in-depth interviews, we find that the basis of their social confidence as newcomers to a country lies in their perceived knowledge of the fundamental social and moral values shared by people from all cultures, including respect, friendliness, kindness, and being helpful (Zhao & Arthur, 2018). "We are all human beings" is a common refrain when talking about what they know about their Canadian peers. In contrast, despite the Confucian humanistic tradition that emphasizes the same values, the Chinese participants in our study did not have the same confidence in the universality and cross-cultural transferability of their life experience in China and the values they have learned there. This raises questions about what is missing in Chinese children's educational experience starting from a young age, particularly their exposure to discussions about cultural values and how they guide what people say and do in different societies.

Reducing Cultural Disconnect between Home and School

In addition to providing age-appropriate culture education in ways appropriate to their age, it is equally if not more important to engage teachers and parents in conversations about culture. Western ECE scholars strongly advocate parents' active involvement in ECE programs and home literacy activities to promote early learning and development (Arnold, Zeljo, Doctoroff, & Ortiff, 2008; Powell, Son, File, & San Juan, 2010). Parents' active involvement in their children's learning is considered to improve children's academic, behavioral, and social outcomes (Marcon, 1999; Senechal, 2006). However, related to the bicultural issues discussed above, major areas of cultural disconnect exist between bilingual ECE programs and Chinese families that challenge the building of a trusting and collaborative relationship. These areas of cultural disconnect often converge to create conflicts around the question of whether children are being taught "serious" things such as words, math, piano, and drawing in ECE programs taking the Western play-based and child-centered approach. In our research in Beijing, a common complaint from parents is: "Kids in the programs play all the time and learn nothing." This concern is shared by immigrant Chinese parents in Western countries whose children are enrolled in local schools (Guo, 2012). Interestingly, the major concern of the staff of those ECE programs is often the levels of stress on all parties: "Chinese parents give too much pressure on their children and on us [for academic-oriented learning and achievement]."

Chinese parents' education-related anxiety has social, cultural, economic, and historical origins (Zhao, Selman & Luke, 2018); it is beyond the capacity of ECE programs to bring major shifts in parents' educational beliefs and practices. Yet, educators can improve the situation by engaging parents in curriculum decisions and involving them in conversations about the major areas of cultural differences that influence the process and outcomes of bilingual education. Parents' active engagement supports the development of collaborative relationships between families and ECE programs, which is critical for addressing potential cultural disconnects between families and bilingual ECE programs. Ideally, teachers and parents work together to reflect upon their own beliefs and practices about child development and learning, the Chinese tradition of education and its comparisons with Western ECE theories, and the linguistic and cultural differences between Chinese and Western societies. This collaboration between parents and educators will contribute cultural and linguistic resources to curriculum development and implementation. Parents' direct participation will also amplify opportunities for early learning in the home environment.

How can ECE programs engage parents in the above activities? Here I provide a list of practical strategies for strengthening the line of communication between ECE programs and parents and connecting learning activities in ECE programs and at home. This list is adapted from research-tested strategies recommended for bilingual ECE programs in North America (Baker, 2019). Chinese educators can explore new ways of engaging parents based on the local conditions of their programs.

1) *Providing information on ECE Programs*

It is recommended that at the beginning of the year, teachers send home a large amount of information about the ECE program and about teachers and their backgrounds. This helps parents feel welcome and build confidence in the program. Further, with families' permission, teachers can prepare a class contact sheet with family names, photographs, and contact information to be distributed to parents through a WeChat group. This facilitates connections among families and supports the building of a sense of community among parents.

2) *Inviting families to provide culturally and linguistically relevant materials*

Teachers encourage families to provide materials for classroom use. Materials may include: lists of Chinese words often used at home; children's favorite books at home; and household objects for use in dramatic play (such as empty food containers, dress up clothes, dolls, etc.).

3) *Organizing regular teacher-parent meetings and welcoming spontaneous conversations*

Program staff (teachers and directors) can regularly invite parents for teacher-parent meetings, either individually or in a group. This provides opportunities for teachers and parents to have discussions about the curriculum and exchange ideas about children. It can also include in-depth discussions about the cultural issues mentioned above. In addition, program staff can keep their doors open and welcome informal conversations with parents whenever possible. During the conversations, staff can strive to offer a relaxed environment and encourage a high comfort level for parents.

4) *Writing newsletters*

Teachers can write regular (e.g., weekly) newsletters to share information with families about class curriculum, events, and happenings. These newsletters can include photographs of children engaged in classroom activities or play. Parents and teachers can communicate on WeChat about questions and events. It is also recommended that teachers reach out to parents after the first few weeks of the program to see if they have any questions or concerns.

5) *Sending books and stories home*

A common practice in North American ECE programs is for teachers to send books home for parents to read aloud with children. Teachers can also include suggestions on how to read aloud to children and how to engage children in conversations about the books. For bilingual programs, the books may be in English or Chinese. To engage parents further, teachers can also send home pictures or books made by students and encourage parents to read books with their children in Chinese (and English if the parents know English). .

Conclusion

Bilingual early childhood education is still very new to China. Even though it seems to be an easy solution to turn to Western developmental sciences and educational theories for help and guidance, it is desirable and also necessary to consider how to integrate Western theories with Eastern beliefs, values, and wisdom. Asian-style kindness, gratitude, humility, reciprocity, and cooperativeness are valued in Western countries as much as in Asia. It is my view that the provision of bilingual education in China needs to be based on a good understanding of the different assumptions underlying the linguistic, cultural, and educational practices of both East and West. Ideally, Chinese educators and parents need to make decisions on curriculum design themselves through a process of learning, discussion, and experimentation that is facilitated, documented, and evaluated by educational scholars and empirical researchers from both within and outside China. In this process, the stakeholders (educators and parents) need to clarify their own beliefs about the fundamental values of Chinese society and the goals and roles of education in shaping the future generations of Chinese youth. This process is also an opportunity to re-examine the question facing Chinese education and society since at least the end of the 19th century: what does it mean to be Chinese, nationally and internationally?

References

Arnold, D. H., Zeljo, A., Doctoroff, G. L., & Ortiz, C. (2008). Parent involvement in preschool: Predictors and the relation of involvement to pre-literacy development. The School Psychology Review, 37(1), 74 - 90.

Ball, J. (2010). Enhancing learning of children from diverse language backgrounds: Mother tongue-based bilingual or multilingual education in early childhood and early primary school years. UNESCO: http://www.ecdip.org/docs/pdf/UNESCO%20Mother-tongue%20based%20EY%202010.pdf.

Caudill, W., & Weinstein, H. (1969). Maternal care and infant behavior in Japan and America. Psychiatry, 32, 12 - 43.

Chao, R. K. (1994). Beyond parental control and authoritarian parenting style: Understanding Chinese parenting through the cultural notion of training. Child Development, 65, 1111 - 1119.

Chao, R. K. (2001). Extending the research on the consequences of parenting style for Chinese Americans and European Americans. Child Development, 72, 1832 - 1843.

Chen, X., Wang, L., & Wang, Z. (2009). Shyness-sensitivity and social, school, and psychological adjustment in rural migrant and urban children in China. Child Development, 80, 1499 – 1513.

Cheng, L. (2012). English immersion schools in China: Evidence from students and teachers. Journal of Multilingual and Multicultural Development, 33 (4), 379 – 391.

Coles, R. (2003). Children of crisis: Eskimos, Chicanos, Indians. New York: Hachette Book Group.

Crago, M. (1990a). Development of communicative competence in Inuit children: Implications for speech-language pathology. Journal of Childhood Communication Disorders, 13, 73 – 83.

Crago, M., & Cole, E. (1991). Using ethnography to bring children's communicative and cultural worlds into focus. In T. Gallagher (Ed.), Pragmatics of language: Clinical practice issues (pp. 99 – 131). San Diego: Singular.

Crago, M. (1992). Ethnography and language socialization: A cross-cultural perspective. Topics in Language Disorders, 12(3), 28 – 39.

DICHE (2016). Research agenda. http://www.diche-project.eu/documents/DICHE_research-agenda_v2016-03.05.pdf.

Epstein, A. S., & Hohmann, M. (2012). The High scope preschool curriculum. Ypsilanti, MI: High Scope Press.

Everson, M. E., Chang, K., & Ross, C. (2016). Developing initial literacy in Chinese. In S. C. Wang & J. K. Peyton (Eds.), CELIN Briefs Series. New York, NY: Asia Society.

Feng, A. (2005). Bilingualism for the minor or the major? An evaluative analysis of parallel conceptions in China. International Journal of Bilingual Education and Bilingualism 8 (6), 529 – 551. doi: 10.1080/13670050508669067.

Flores d'Arcais, G. B. (1994). Order of strokes writing as a cue for retrieval in reading Chinese characters. European Journal of Cognitive Psychology, 6 (4), 337 – 355.

Gao, X. & Wang, X. (2017). Bilingual education in the People's Republic of China. In O. García, A. M. Y. Lin & S. May (Eds.), Bilingual and multilingual education (pp. 219 – 231). New York: Springer.

Gao, X. & Ren, W. (2019) Controversies of bilingual education in China. International Journal of Bilingual Education and Bilingualism, 22(3), 267 – 273, DOI: 10.1080/13670050.2018.1550049.

Guan C. Q., Liu Y., Chan D. H. L., Ye F., & Perfetti, C. A. (2011). Writing strengthens orthography and alphabetic-coding strengthens phonology in learning to read Chinese. Journal of Educational Psychology, 103, 509 - 522.

Guo, Karen. (2012). Chinese immigrants in New Zealand early childhood settings: Perspectives and experiences. Early Childhood Folio, 16(1), 5 - 9.

Halle, T., & Mariner, C. (2001, April). Examining survey measures of the mother-child relationship across three racial/ethnic groups. Paper presented to the Society for Research in Child Development, Minneapolis, MN.

Heath, S. B. (1989). The learner as cultural member. In M. Rice & R. Schiefelbusch (Eds.), The teachability of language (pp. 333 - 350). Baltimore: Paul Brookes.

Johnston, J. R., & Wong, M. A. (2002). Cultural differences in beliefs and practices concerning talk to children. Journal of Speech, Language, and Hearing Research, 45(5), 916 - 26.

Lee, I. F. & Tseng, C. L. (2008) Cultural conflicts of the child - centered approach to early childhood education in Taiwan. Early Years, 28(2), 183 - 196, DOI: 10.1080/09575140802163600.

Li, J. (2013). Cultural foundations of learning: East and West. New York: Cambridge University Press.

Mallory, B. L. & New, R. S. (Eds.) (1994). Diversity and Developmentally Appropriate Practices: Challenges for Early Childhood Education. New York, NY: Teachers College Press.

Marcon, R. A. (1999). Positive relationships between parent school involvement and public school inner-city preschoolers' development and academic performance. School Psychology Review, 28, 395 - 412.

Markus, H. R. & Kitayama, S. (1991). Culture and the self: Implications for cognition, emotion, and motivation. Psychological Review, 98(2), 224 - 253.

Matsumoto, D. (1994). Culture and Emotion. In L. Adler & U. Gielen (Eds.), Current perspectives in cross-cultural psychology, New York: Praeger.

Kitayama, S., Markus, H. R., Matsumoto, H., & Norasakkunkit, V. (1997). Individual and collective processes in the construction of the self: Self-enhancement in the United States and self-criticism in Japan. Journal of Personality and Social Psychology, 72(6), 1245 - 1267. http://dx.doi.org/10.1037/0022-3514.72.6.1245

Katarzyna Ożańska-Ponikwia (2019). Expression and perception of emotions by Polish — English bilinguals I love you vs. Kocham Cię. International

Journal of Bilingual Education and Bilingualism, 22 (4), 493 - 504. https://doi.org/10.1080/13670050.2016.1270893.

Ochs, E. & Schieffelin, B. (1984). Language acquisition and socialization: Three developmental stories and their implications. In R. Shweder & R. LeVine (Eds.), Culture theory: Essays on mind, self, and emotion (pp. 276 - 320). Cambridge: Cambridge University Press.

Powell, D. R., Son, S., File, N., & San Juan, R. R. (2010). Parent-school relationships and children's academic and social outcomes in public school pre-kindergarten. Journal of School Psychology, 48(4), 269 - 292.

Rogoff, B. (2003). The cultural nation of human development. New York: Oxford University Press.

Ruan, J. & Leung, C. B. (Eds.) (2012). Perspectives on teaching and learning English Literacy in China. New York: Springer.

Schieffelin, B., & Ochs, E. (1986). Language socialization. Annual Review of Anthropology, 15, 163 - 191.

Selman, R. L. (2007). The promotion of social awareness: Powerful lessons from the partnership of developmental theory and classroom practice. New York: Russell Sage.

Senechal, M. (2006). The effect of family literacy interventions on children's acquisition of reading. From kindergarten to grade 3. A meta-analytic review. Washington DC National Institute for Literacy.

Snow, C. (1977). The development of conversation between mothers and babies. Journal of Child Language, 4, 1 - 22.

Snow, C. (1992). Perspectives on second-language development: Implications for bilingual education. Educational Researcher, 21(2), 16 - 19.

Tobin, J. J., Wu, D. Y. H. & Davidson, D. H. (1989). Preschool in Three Cultures: Japan, China and the United States. New Haven, Conn.: Yale University Press.

van Kleeck, A., & Carpenter, R. (1980). Effects of children's language comprehension level on adults' child directed talk. Journal of Speech and Hearing Research, 23, 546 - 569.

van Kleeck, A. (1994). Potential cultural bias in training parents as conversational partners with their children who have delays in language development. American Journal of Speech-Language Pathology, 3, 67 - 78.

Wierzbicka, A. (1999). Emotions across languages and cultures: Diversity and universals. Cambridge: Cambridge University Press.

Wierzbicka, A. (2004). Bilingual lives, bilingual experience. Journal of Multilingual and Multicultural Development 25(2&3), 94 - 104.

Wierzbicka, A. (2009). Language and metalanguage: Key issues in emotion research. Emotion Review 1(1), 3-14.

Wong, Q. E. (2002). China's search for a national history. In Q. Edward Wong & George G. Iggers (Eds.), Turning points in historiography: Cross-cultural perspective. Rochester, NY: The University of Rochester Press.

Zhao, X., & Gao, M. (2014). "No time for friendship": Shanghai mothers' views of adult and adolescent friendships. Journal of Adolescent Research, 29(5), 587-615. DOI: 10.1177/0743558413520225.

Zhao, X. (2015). Competition and compassion in Chinese secondary education. New York: Palgrave MacMillan.

Zhao, X. (2016). Educating competitive students for a competitive nation: How and why the Chinese discourse of competition in education has rapidly changed within three decades? Berkeley Review of Education, 6(1), 5-28.

Zhao, X. & Arthur, N. (March, 2017). Social anxiety in adolescent newcomers in Canadian schools: A research-based intercultural relationship intervention. Poster presentation at the 49th Banff International Conference on Behavioral Science, Banff, AB

Zhao, X. & Arthur, N. (2018, October). Intercultural Relationships between Adolescent International Students and Local Students in High Schools. Paper presentation at the International Metropolis Conference, Sydney, Australia.

Zhao, X., Selman, R. L., & Luke, A. (2018). Academic competition and parental practice: Habitus and change. In M. Mu, K. Dooley, & A. Luke (Eds.), Bourdieu and Chinese Education (pp. 144 - 174). NY: Routledge.

Zhao, X., Yu, E., & Zhang, S. (2019). Intercultural competence in higher education: A normative anchor, a developmental perspective, and a discursive approach. Journal of Educational Thought, 51(3). 261-280.

Zhang, J., & Pelletier, J. (2012). Cultural differences: An international perspective on early childhood education. Frontiers of Education in China, 7(1), 1-4.

Zhihu (2015). Is it correct to say, "Adults are talking. Kids should not jump in"? https://www.zhihu.com/question/31384603.

8. How to Raise Good, Happy and Successful Children?

Xu Zhao

University of Calgary

Through thousands of years in China, guided by the Confucian tradition, education has aimed to teach children how to *be* human (做人), or how to become a person who is socially capable, morally principled, and aesthetically cultivated. In China today, parents and educators debate with each other and with themselves about what qualities should be fostered in Chinese children so that they are good and happy, but also develop the skills to be successful in an increasingly competitive and demanding global job market (Zhao, Selman & Luke, 2018). This question is even harder for parents and teachers of children attending bilingual (Chinese and English) education programs, as languages forge how people think, and bilingualism involves not only different linguistic systems but also different ways of thinking, doing, and being. Thus, the tasks facing parents and educators of bilingual children involve not only supporting children's language development, but also fostering in them the qualities that will make them the successful global citizens, as many of these children will study and work in international settings.

To achieve this goal, Chinese adults can no longer rely on traditional beliefs and practices *alone* for guidance. Often the challenges they encounter are not scientific ones which answers can be found in research conducted elsewhere. More often, their questions are new and specific to the complicated social and cultural contexts of contemporary Chinese society. To raise children who are good, happy, and successful global citizens, educators and parents need to be self-motivated and self-directed learners who seek guidance from the Chinese tradition and to learn from Western developmental and educational theories. They also need to be thoughtful and creative in adapting theories and ideas to their own educational practice. In other words, it is particularly true in China today that a good education is a learning journey for both children and educators.

To inform and support this learning journey for Chinese educators, particularly in the emerging field of bilingual education, in this article I reconsider the primary goals of education for Chinese children from the perspective of a developmental and cultural psychologist. Specifically, I focus on the question of what qualities and skills Chinese children need to develop to be socially, morally, and professionally competent and lead a fulfilling life within and outside China. To achieve this goal, I first introduce how the image of Chinese children in Western media coverage has changed since the late 1970s. Through this example, I aim to make an argument about why the Confucian emphasis of moral education should continue to be the primary goal of education in the 21st century. I then present two major theories which explain how children, at least those growing up in Western society, develop their social competence and moral reasoning. I briefly discuss the implications of these theories for educational practice in China. Next, I consider the important skills that individuals need to achieve professional success in a globalized and technology-driven world. Finally, I share some insights I have gained from my own research about the important qualities in children that educators and parents should strive to protect and promote to ensure their long-term positive development and success.

The Education of Chinese Children: From "Well-Behaved" to "Lord of the Flies"

The image of Chinese children portrayed in North American media and academic research has dramatically changed since the late 1970s. In 1981, a New York Times article titled "How China raises its well behaved children" described Chinese children in nursery schools as "poised, quiet, obedient, and quick to follow their teachers' instructions" (Butterfield, 1981). In the eyes of the American observers, Chinese children at the time seldom exhibited the "boisterous aggressiveness or selfishness" of their American counterparts, nor did they show the typical signs of anxiety and tension that were common among American children. The report attributed these good qualities of Chinese children to the Chinese tradition of childrearing, including parental practices such as fostering an intimate and close relationship between children and care-givers, carrying babies around instead of pushing them in a stroller, swaddling young babies, and co-sleeping with children until they are at least two or three years old. They also observed that the activities in Chinese nursery schools were highly structured, and Chinese parents and the nursery school teachers were all warm, kind and attentive. But the same report also raised questions about the approach of the Chinese nursery schools. It noted that the Chinese children who were raised at home tended to be "more spoiled and livelier" than those in the nursery schools, and some Chinese parents worried that the tough regimentation of the nursery school and kindergarten might make their children too placid and uncreative. The report suggested that "the careful docility that Chinese inculcate in their young may result in less individuality and a greater tendency toward conformity and acceptance of authority when they become adults."

Ironically, while the traditional Chinese child-rearing practices to foster attachment between children and parents are increasingly adopted by middle-and upper-middle-class parents in North America, Chinese parents and teachers have tried to learn from Western "scientific" childrearing practices to reduce dependency in young children through practices such as sleep training and letting infants as young as four months old sleep in their own room. Further, economic reform and social change in China has led to a shift in values among urban parents from favoring quiet, shy, and compliant children to valuing those who are outspoken and outgoing (Chen, Wang & Wang, 2009). The change in family structure has also had profound impact on child-rearing practices in China and children's developmental outcomes. In 2013, a study conducted by researchers at Monash University in Australia and published by the journal *Science* reported that Chinese children who are the only child in the family are "significantly less trusting, less trustworthy, more risk-averse, less competitive, more pessimistic, and less conscientious" than those who were born in the same period but had siblings (Cameron, Erkal, Gangadharan & Meng, 2013). This study was based on measures completed by 421 Beijing men and women who were born within an eight-year period that included dates just before and just after the one-child policy took effect in 1979. Our own research in Shanghai, based on qualitative interview data from adolescents aged 13 - 16, also suggests the prevalence of interpersonal mistrust and a feeling of powerlessness among urban Chinese youth (Zhao, 2015).

Loneliness is a major challenge for the Chinese children who come to study in North American schools and universities. My research with Chinese students enrolled in Canadian high schools suggests that many of them feel isolated and have difficulties in connecting with their host families and making friends in school. After school, they typically stay in their own room, doing homework, chatting online with their friends in China, or playing online games. As an academic researcher focusing on the social integration of young newcomers, I have received emails from many settlement support workers whose job is to help international students transition into North American schools and host families. Some of them expressed a desperate need for help to understand Chinese students' "behavioral problems," such as not respecting host family' house rules, refusing to share house chores, and having minimal interaction and communication with their host family. I have learned that many of the conflicts and tensions were caused by misunderstanding and miscommunication between individuals from drastically different cultures. However, an extreme case that happened in California in 2015 made me wonder about the extent to which the traditional Chinese emphasis on moral teaching has been neglected in China today.

In this case in Los Angeles, an 18-year-old girl from China, Liu Yiyan, was brutally tortured at a park for five hours by a group of Chinese teens, all "parachute kids" who were attending American high schools and whose parents remained in China. The victim suffered severe physical and psychological harm, and three of the assailants were sentenced to 6 – 13 years in California prisons on counts of kidnapping and assault by means of force. The direct cause of the attack was an unpaid dinner bill. However, the purported underlying social and psychological conditions of the violent attack, according to the journalistic reports, were the parachute kids' lack of parental supervision and loneliness. "I'm sure they suffer from loneliness," said Rayford Fountain, the attorney of one of the assailants, "So they bond with other kids in the small Chinese circles with no supervision, no one to turn to for assistance. So these things can get out of control" (Chang, 2016). During the initial hearings, California Superior Court Judge Thomas C. Falls likened the case to Lord of the Flies, a 1954 novel by William Golding about a group of British school boys who were stranded on a remote and uninhabited island, isolated from civilization and bereft of adult supervision, who created their own society for self-governance, but eventually descended into savagery.

Obviously, teenagers who live in a new country without parental supervision are subject to a range of social, emotional, and behavioral challenges such as feelings of fear, loneliness, dependency on peers, and even substance abuse. However, actively participating in a violent and prolonged attack such as in the above case suggests a lack of moral consideration, legal knowledge, and an erosion of empathy in the assailants. After all, Los Angeles is not the remote, uncivilized, and helpless island in Lord of the Flies, nor were the assailants (all 18 or older at the time of the assault) as young as the pre-adolescent children in Golding's novel. Recognizing that this is an extreme case should not prevent us from asking a broader educational question: how can educators prepare children, from a young age, to make independent moral, legal, and ethical decisions? Further, what social, moral, and ethical principles may provide guidance for children to make responsible decisions both in their own country and in countries where they are newcomers? To answer these questions, it is helpful to introduce the major contemporary theories in Western psychology that explain how children develop their social and moral thinking based on principles that are arguably valued by all human societies.

How to Raise Good Children? Western Theories of Moral and Social Development

The Confucian emphasis of teaching children how to be human is closest to the concerns of moral development and education in Western psychology. "To educate a person in the mind but not in morals is to educate a menace to society," said Theodore Roosevelt famously. Educating children in morals is to help them develop the capacity and acquire the virtues that will help them live good lives and become contributing members of their communities. Similar to the Confucian tradition of cultivating in children the virtues of benevolence (仁), righteousness (义) etiquette (礼), wisdom (智) and sincerity (信), Western traditional approaches to moral education also sought to instill values and virtues with an emphasis on doing good deeds. But the question is: whose values, morals, and virtues? In other words, who defines the moral ideals that members of society should all strive to achieve? Cultures differ in values. For example, Western societies often prioritize individual rights and freedom over group needs, whereas traditional Eastern societies often emphasize community and divinity over individual autonomy as the guiding principles of moral judgment and decision (Shredder, 1997). Taking a pragmatic perspective, the philosopher John Dewey (1916) has argued that moral ideals should change as the needs in society change.

Moral ideals have indeed changed in China. In 2003, moral education in Chinese schools was reformed to include the teaching of individualism, consumerism, pro-social behaviors, and humanistic values (Lu & Gao, 2004; Zhu & Liu, 2004). Understandably, the co-existence of individualist and collectivist values in Chinese society leads to conflicts and confusion in adults' moral teaching and children's moral thinking. As a result, young people in China refer to values from different sources to justify their behavior, as long as those moral values conveniently fit with their needs and goals (Yan, 2009; Zhao & Selman, 2019). How to reconcile confusing and even contradictory social and moral values is a developmental task facing Chinese children today, especially those who will travel between China and Western society as international students or immigrants. Therefore, it is important for children to learn about moral ideals and values such as individual dignity, personal responsibility, and mutual support that are emphasized by Chinese tradition and arguably shared by all modern societies. It is also critical for Chinese educators to equip children with the *capacity* to use these principles for making moral judgments in social situations that are new to them. What does the capacity involve? How can educators cultivate a habit of moral deliberation and social perspective-taking in children? Here the cognitive-developmental approach to moral education in Western psychology, represented by the theories of Laurence Kohlberg and Robert Selman, are particularly helpful.

The Development of Justice Reasoning

Moral education in North America has been profoundly influenced by Kohlberg's theory on the development of justice reasoning. Here I provide the part of his theory that I believe has important implications for educational practice in China. Kohlberg's theorization of moral development is based on the moral philosophy of Immanuel Kant and the moral development theory of Jean Piaget. For Kant, morality is a standard of reasoning that is based on a fundamental, objective, and unconditional principle. That is, the respect of individuals' equal rights to life, liberty and property. According to Piaget, cognitive development involves structural changes in children's understanding of basic concepts such as time, space, and causality. In the moral domain, Piaget observed that young children's reasoning is often based on the consequences of an act (e. g. , punishment), and only older children are able to take into account the actor's intentions. Bringing these two theoretical traditions together, Kohlberg (1981, 1984) argued that the psychological study of morality should also be grounded on *universalizable* principles of judgment such as welfare, respect, and justice. He developed moral dilemmas, including whether it would be permissible for a poor man to steal medicine for his dying wife, and used the dilemmas to interview more than 70 boys.

Following his 15 years of research, Kohlberg (1981, 1984) described three levels of moral judgment. Level 1 is *pre-conventional morality*. At this level, children, mostly younger than 9, consider what is good and bad based on adults' standards and the consequences of following or breaking adults' rules. In other words, moral authority is outside of the child and reasoning is based on the physical consequences of actions. Level 2 is *conventional morality*. At this level, older children begin to internalize the moral standards of the adults they admire. That is, authority is internalized but not questioned, and reasoning is based on the norms of the group to which one belongs. Level 3 is *post-conventional morality*. At this level, a person's moral judgment is based on self-chosen principles such as individual rights and justice. Kohlberg emphasized that the transition from one level to a higher one is not due to the direct impact of learning more about social rules, but due to changes in cognitive structure as a result of interactions between the individual and his or her environment. Even though Kohlberg's theory is challenged by both philosophers and psychologists for being based solely on research with white male participants and for treating emotion as secondary (e. g., Noddings, 2002), his theory may help Chinese educators consider the direction of children's moral development in relation to their age and the impact of the social environment.

The Capacity to Take Social Perspectives

In the social domain, Robert Selman, also influenced by Piaget, argued that the development of children's psychosocial competence involves changes in three components: their capacity to understand the logic of relationship (knowledge), their social skills and ability to resolve conflicts and deepen a relationship (strategy), and their motivation and capacity to be deeply connected with others (valuing). Underlying these competencies is a core capacity — children's developing ability to consider a situation from a different point of view and coordinate different social perspectives. While young children are unable to differentiate other people's perspectives from their own (e. g., young children believe if they like ice cream, everybody likes ice cream), older children are more able to differentiate, understand, and finally coordinate different perspectives (Selman, 2007). Selman argued that the development of this core capacity and its three components are influenced by nature (biological predispositions) and nurture (family, school, and society). To promote young children's perspective-taking ability, adults can talk with children about how they themselves and other people, in real life and in stories, think and feel about a hypothesized or real-life situation (see Selman's articles in this volume).

Moral Development as the Primary Goal of Education

The key contribution of the theories of Kohlberg and Selman to the literature of social and moral development lies in their description of the developmental trajectories of individuals' justice reasoning and their capacity for social perspective-taking. In this sense, their theories are scientific descriptions of the links between children's biological maturation and their moral and social thinking in the social and cultural context of North American society. It can also be argued that both Kohlberg and Selman are philosophers before they are developmental scientists. Their theories are not value-neutral, but firmly based on what they believe to be universally valued principles: the principle of justice in Kohlberg's theory, and the commitment to coordinating different point of views and maintaining social engagement in Selman's. What extent do these theories reflect children's social and moral development in China?

The above question is not only a developmental one, but also sociological, historical, and existential. Our recent research in China using social and moral dilemmas (e. g., whether to help a new student being teased by others) to prompt interviews and focus groups, found that not only did urban and rural Chinese children differ in their moral judgment and choices, urban children attending different schools and coming from different family backgrounds also had different perceptions of the same social or moral issue (Zhao, Haste, Selman, & Luan, 2014; Zhao, 2015; Zhao & Selman, 2019). In general, however, younger Chinese children (grade 8) often explained their moral choices by referring to values such as kindness, empathy, and helping others; in contrast, older children (grade 11) were more likely to emphasize the importance of self-protection (e. g., avoid trouble). Older adolescents also showed less interest in public issues (e. g., pollution and food safety) and less motivation to help others. The sole focus of their life was on gaining a competitive edge in academic competition in order to go to a good university, as every day they were told by their parents and teachers that this was the "social reality" they face (Zhao, 2015). Yet social reality is constructed by a society's systems and institutions, by individuals' belief systems, and by their evaluation, acceptance, and resistance of societal pressure. I argue that only when moral development is considered the primary goal of education and children are supported to develop the capacity for justice reasoning and perspective-taking can a society have a future as a healthy, wealthy, and happy community for all.

How to Raise Children Who Will Succeed in Global Job Markets? Twenty-First Century Skills

Becoming a good person by itself does not seem to be good enough as an educational goal in today's world. Understandably, all parents want schools to teach their children skills for their future career success. What are these skills? In the 1980s, Chinese children were all familiar with a saying with rhyming Chinese words, "Work hard on math, physics, and chemistry to trot across the world without fear" (学好数理化，走遍天下都不怕). With the technological boom of the 1990s, STEM (Science, Technology, Engineering and Math) education has been increasingly emphasized globally, in both developed and developing countries. STEM education is considered as vital not only to the success of individual students, but also to the success of entire nations (e. g., NSTC, 2018). In the United States, where the emphasis of STEM education is often placed in secondary education, it has been argued that effective science and mathematics instruction must begin in the early grades in order to ensure long-term success in these subjects (Swift & Watkins, 2004).

However, putting STEM at the center of education has been considered an over-simplification of the situation even by people from within the technological fields. It has been argued that STEM education is necessary but not enough; education and workforce development in the 21st century requires the incorporation of a very high cognitive level of scientific and technical knowledge with a deep understanding of human wants, needs, and behaviors (Hill, 2019). This argument is confirmed by research conducted by Google, a corporation that most identifies with STEM (Strauss, 2017). In a project called *Project Oxygen*, Google researchers studied the hiring, firing, and promotion processes since the company's founding in 1998 to understand what qualities characterize the most successful employees. Their conclusion shocked everyone. Among the eight most important qualities of Google's top employees, STEM skills came in dead last. The most valuable skills that Google now looks for in job candidates include:

1. Being a good coach
2. Communicating and listening well
3. Possessing insights into others (social awareness)
4. Empathy and support toward colleagues
5. Critical thinking
6. Problem solving
7. Drawing conclusions by connecting complex ideas

Further, in a follow-up study named *Project Aristotle*, Google researchers looked into the characteristics of their best teams. Again, their finding is surprising: the best and most productive ideas have not come from the teams consisting of members with the most specialized knowledge, but the teams that exhibited a range of soft skills including equality, generosity, curiosity toward the ideas of others, empathy, and emotional intelligence. Most importantly, to succeed, a team must make each and every member feel confident to speak up, make mistakes, and feel they are being heard. The *Washington Post* article reporting the study concluded, "What helps you thrive in a changing world isn't rocket science. It may just well be social science, and, yes, even the humanities and the arts that contribute to making you not just workforce ready but world ready." What are the educational implications of these findings from the workplace? What can teachers and parents do to prepare their young children to be workforce *and* world ready, mentally and emotionally?

The Eight Cs

In his book *Creative schools: The grassroots revolution that is transforming education*, the British educationalist Sir Ken Robinson sums up eight important qualities that schools should try to foster in children (Robinson & Aronica, 2015). They include: curiosity, creativity, criticism, communication, collaboration, compassion, composure, and citizenship. Sir Robinson has been a strong critic of the modern educational system for being mechanistic and generating compliance and conformity. He believes schools across the world should strive to foster the eight qualities in children, and it is my view that these eight qualities should be emphasized in Chinese education. My research with Chinese children and parents in China and North America in the past 15 years has led me to the realization that Chinese children need extra support in exactly the same areas. When educators (teachers and parents) fail to understand children's need to develop these qualities, and the pressure for compliance and conformity is high (often in the form of a singular emphasis on children's performance on standardized tests), boredom, anxiety, and even more severe physical and mental health problems occur. I therefore briefly introduce the eight Cs defined by Sir Ken Robinson and summarize his arguments about the implications for classroom teaching.

1. *Curiosity*: *The ability to ask questions and explore how the world works*

In the classroom, instead of asking children to keep quiet, teachers need to encourage children to ask questions and help them engage in the topic being discussed.

2. *Creativity*: *The ability to generate new ideas and to apply them in practice*

Creativity is the fruit of imagination in arts, science, and technology. As much as they can, teachers need to let children explore, allow them to be wrong, and encourage them to express their own ideas, without rushing to correct them.

3. *Criticism*: *The ability to analyze information and ideas and to form reasoned arguments and judgments*

In the classroom, teachers need to focus more on helping children critically analyze information rather than on introducing new information. Teachers need to help children learn how to make use of information, how to incorporate it correctly in their lives, and how to determine truth from falsehood.

4. *Communication*: *The ability to express thoughts and feelings clearly and confidently in a range of media and forms*

Teachers need to encourage children and provide a safe environment for them to communicate their thoughts and express their feelings. Teachers also need to provide opportunities for children to communicate not just in written and verbal forms but also through arts, dance, and theater.

5. *Collaboration*: *The ability to work constructively with others*

Instead of encouraging children to compete with each other, teachers can invite children to work and play with others, in pairs or groups, and to solve problems together. Teachers also help children learn how to share ideas, listen to others with respect, and take others' perspectives into account in their activities.

6. *Compassion*: *The ability to empathize with others and act accordingly*

Compassion is rooted in empathy, and empathy is the ability to take others' perspectives. Schools need to build a culture of compassion and inclusion. Teachers should communicate the importance of being sensitive to others' plights and help children understand what behaviors count as bullying and prejudice. They also need to demonstrate sensitivity in their own responses to children, especially those in distress.

7. *Composure*: *The ability to connect with the inner life of feeling*

and develop a sense of personal harmony and balance

Composure is the ability to understand oneself and to be centered in oneself. Teachers need to help children understand and connect with their own thoughts and feelings and encourage them to accept, express, and control their feelings when necessary.

8. *Citizenship: The ability to engage constructively with society and to participate in the processes that sustain it*

Teachers can inform and help children understand what is going on in society and their own roles as future citizens.

Two More Cs: Promoting Chinese Children's Long-term Positive Development

Informed by my research with Chinese children and parents, I add two more Cs to Sir Roberson's list: choice and confidence. These two traits are among the soft skills identified by the Google studies introduced above as important for both individual success and good team work. However, it is through our own my research with Chinese children that we realized children's ability to make choices and their confidence in their own judgment are the basic conditions for achieving the eight Cs in Ken Robinson's list. Our research shows that, influenced by Western psychological and educational ideas, urban middle-and upper-class adults in China are increasingly aware of the need to respect the intention, desire, and will of children as separate individuals (Zhao, Selman, & Luke, 2018). Many parents allow and encourage their young children to make their own choices about food, clothes, toys, and books, and later about school and career options, and at the same time they set necessary boundaries and provide needed guidance. However, it is still very common for Chinese adults to consider children, even teenagers, too young to make decisions for themselves, and common for them to make all plans and arrangements for their children.

This parental practice seems to be related to several factors, including, (1) traditional Chinese beliefs about education, (2) the low level of economic development in China before the 1990s when the majority of today's parents were children themselves, and (3) the current social and educational policies in China. Traditionally, Chinese adults see the primary task of socialization as helping children develop the capacity for controlling personal desires and emotions (Desjarlais, Eisenberg, Good, & Kleinman, 1995). Chinese children are often encouraged to be aware of other people's needs rather than express their own desires and preferences. Further, when the majority of current generations of parents were growing up, a lack of resources made it costly or impossible to make choices about clothes, toys, and books. Understandably, this generation raises their children in the same way they were raised, giving their children the best they have but less autonomy to make their own decisions and mistakes. Furthermore, stress from work and home and anxiety about their children's school performance in a competition-and test-based education system also prevent many parents from giving their children the opportunity and time to make choices.

Due to the combination of these cultural and socio-economic influences, many Chinese parents in their 30s and 40s had to go through a deep, long process of self-examination to understand their own and their parents' behaviors in parenting. In my research, some reflective parents mentioned that as adults they often found it difficult to make choices in situations as mundane as grocery and clothes shopping. They attributed this problem to their childhood experience of not having the opportunity to express their desires and make their own choices, and later a lack of trust in their own desires and judgments when making choices and decisions. As a consequence, they often filled their refrigerator and closet with food and clothes they did not need.

Another way that anxious adults deprive children of the opportunity to explore and undermine children's confidence and their long-term mental health is through inculcating in children what I call a linear and reductionist logic about life. Adults do this by repeatedly telling children something like, "if you fail this task/test, you won't go to a good elementary/high school, and you won't go to a good college and have a good job, and your life would be a total failure." This logic works to make children afraid of making mistakes and avoid taking risks. It prevents them from exploring and discovering their interests and potential. In the short term, children motivated by fear may comply with adults' wills and successfully achieve the goals adults want them to; in the long term, however, they carry the risk of developing anxiety and depression, feeling as though a life scripted by others and by the expectations of those around them is not worth living.

Conclusion

What should educators and parents do to raise good, happy, and successful children? This is also a question about what adults should *not* do to prevent children from becoming good, happy and successful individuals. Bertrand Russell, the famous British philosopher, mathematician, historian, and Nobel Laureate, observed that children's vitality tends to be diminished by education. He argued that, since authority in education is to some extent unavoidable, adults must be filled through and through with the spirit of reverence. Instead of trying to mold children, adults must feel something "sacred, indefinable, unlimited, individual, and strangely precious" in each child (Russell, 1971). In my view, this suggests an educational philosophy and related practices that are radically different from the common practice of comparing children across a very narrow spectrum of achievement areas and making judgments about who among them are winners and losers, comparisons and judgments that are made implicitly or explicitly, consciously or unconsciously, culturally or structurally. Educators need to ask themselves - at each level of education, and in the contexts of family, school, and the broader society - how we can support each of our children to develop as a unique individual. Fear and anxiety are never the paths to a successful and happy life nor a healthy society. To raise good, happy and successful children, the primary goal of education in China and elsewhere should continue to be about how to help each child to *be human* (做人). To achieve this goal, education should aim to support children in achieving desirable human qualities such as the 10 Cs through reflection *and* action in the context of social interaction and dialogues between teachers and students and among students themselves, rather than singularly focusing on the pursuit of high test scores, prestigious credentials, and enviable income levels in a mad race that leads to isolation, anxiety and depression in the long term. Ultimately, the goal of education is to enable children to find and achieve their own potential, engage and connect with others, and make unique contributions to the world. In this way, they will be able to live through the vicissitudes of life and continue to find it worth living.

References

Butterfield, F. (1981). https://www.nytimes.com/1981/01/05/style/how-china-raises-its-well-behaved-children.html.

Cameron, L., Erkal, N., Gangadharan, L., and Meng, X. (2013). Little Emperors: Behavioral Impacts of China's One-Child Policy. Science, 339 (6122), 953 - 957.

Chang, C. (2016). Sentenced to prison for assault, teenage 'parachute kids' deliver warning to adults in China. LA Times. February 17, 2016. https://www.latimes.com/local/lanow/la-me-ln-parachute-kids-sentencing-20160217-story.html.

Chen, X., Wang, L., & Wang, Z. (2009). Shyness-sensitivity and social, school, and psychological adjustment in rural migrant and urban children in China. Child Development, 80, 1499 - 1513.

Dewey, J. (1916). Democracy and education. New York: Dover Publications.

Desjarlais, R., Eisenberg, L., Good, B., & Kleinman, A. (1995). World mental health: Problems and priorities in low-income countries. New York, NY: Oxford University Press.

Hill, C. (2019). STEM Is Not Enough: Education for Success in the Post-Scientific Society.

Journal of Science Education and Technology, 28, 69. https://doi.org/10.1007/s10956-018-9745-1.

Kohlberg, L. (1981). The philosophy of moral development: moral stages and the idea of justice (1st ed.). San Francisco: Harper & Row.

Kohlberg, L. (1984). The psychology of moral development: the nature and validity of moral stages (1st ed.). San Francisco: Harper & Row.

Lu, J., & Gao, D. (2004). New directions in the moral education curriculum in Chinese primary schools. Journal of Moral Education, 33(4), 495 - 510.

National Science and Technology Council (NSTC) (2018). Chartering a course for success: America's strategy for STEM education.

https://www.whitehouse.gov/wp-content/uploads/2018/12/STEM-Education-Strategic-Plan-2018.pdf

Noddings, N. (2002). Educating moral people. New York and London.: Teachers College, Columbia University.

Russell, B. (1971). Principles of Social Construction. New York, Routledge.

Swift, T. M., & Watkins, S. E. (2004). An engineering primer for outreach to K-4 education. Journal of STEM Education: Innovations and Research, 5 (3/4), 67-76. http://www.greenframingham.org/stem/research/item2_engr_k4_outreach.pdf.

Roberson, K. & Aronica, L. (2015). Creative schools: The grassroots revolution that is transforming education. London, UK: Penguin.

Selman, R. L. (2007). The promotion of social awareness: Powerful lessons from the partnership of developmental theory and classroom practice. New York: Russell Sage.

Strauss, V. (2017). The surprising thing Google learned about its employees — and what it means for today's students. Washington Post, December 20, 2017. https://www.washingtonpost.com/news/answer-sheet/wp/2017/12/20/the-surprising-thing-google-learned-about-its-employees-and-what-it-means-for-todays-students/?utm_term=.d038a6160904

Yan, Y. (2009), The Individualization of Chinese Society, vol. 77, Oxford: Berg.

Shweder, R. A., Much, N. C., Mahapatra, M., & Park, L. (1997). The "Big Three" of morality (autonomy, community, divinity) and the "Big Three" explanations of suffering. In A. Brandt, & P. Rozin (Eds.), Morality and Health, 119-172. New York: Routledge.

Yang, Y. (2016). The 'Lord of the Flies' bullying case that's sending three Chinese 'parachute kids' to Calif. Prison. Washington Post, February 18, 2016. https://www.washingtonpost.com/news/morning-mix/wp/2016/02/18/the-lord-of-the-flies-bullying-case-thats-sending-three-chinese-parachute-kids-to-calif-prison/?noredirect=on&utm_term=.690051115e52.

Zhao, X. (2015). Competition and compassion in Chinese secondary education. New York: Palgrave MacMillan.

Zhao, X., Haste, H., Selman, R. L., & Luan, Z. (2014). Compliant, cynical, or critical: Chinese adolescents' explanations of social problems and individual civic responsibility. Youth & Society, 49(8), 1123-1148. doi: 10.1177/0044118X14559504.

Zhao, X., Selman, R. L., & Luke, A. (2018). Academic competition and parental practice: Habitus and change. In M. Mu, K. Dooley, & A. Luke

(Eds.), Bourdieu and Chinese Education (pp. 144 – 174). NY: Routledge.

Zhao, X. , & Selman, R. L. (2019). Bystanders' responsibilities in a situation of teasing: A Dual Dynamic Analysis approach for understanding culture, context, and youth moral development. Qualitative Psychology.

Zhu, X. , & Liu, C. (2004). Teacher training for moral education in China. Journal of Moral Education, 33(4), 481 – 494. doi: 10.1080/0305724042000315608.

Jing Zhou

Deputy Dean and Professor of College of Preschool and Special Education of East China Normal University;

Director of ESEC Children's Language Research Center of East China Normal University;

Chairman of World Preschool Education Association of China;

Education Professional Committee of Self-taught Higher Education Examinations Steering Committee of Ministry of Education;

Council Member of Goldian and Harvard Professors' Educational Research and Practice Center.

9. On Early Childhood English Education in China

Jing Zhou

East China Normal University

Since the 1990s, early childhood English education in China has raised great attention from the academia. Up to this moment, no consensus has been reached. As is shown in real life, irrespective of the divergences of opinions concerning this heated topic, there has been an increase in the number of parents who appeal for English education in kindergartens, of English classes that are introduced into kindergartens, and of amateur English training sessions that go to great lengths to attract parents and children with fancy and irresistible slogans. As educators that work with young children, it is our unshirkable responsibility to pay attention to and follow up with such a phenomenon by in-depth research. In this sense, simple comments are no longer sufficient to this emerging theme in early childhood education in China.

Before we contemplate on the great popularity of English in China, we have to step back and start with a thorough analysis of the social and cultural environment lying under this phenomenon. The past few years have witnessed the rapid development of science and technology as well as the implementation of the policy of reform and opening-up. As a result, tremendous changes have been made in the economic, social and cultural life of the Chinese people. With the economic globalization, the trend of multiculturalism is marching towards developing countries whose economy is growing at a staggering rate. As the leading economic power in Asia, China has turned into a multicultural society whose development draws global attention. Therefore, the research on early childhood English education in China has to take into consideration the Chinese society that evolves over time .

As is known to all, evidently, a multicultural society features language diversity. Immersed in a social environment with different demographic groups and cultures, people have to rely on more than one language for the purpose of communication. A common language that is shared by people all over the world is of special significance in this sense. In recent years, there has been a growing number of people who pay attention to the propensity of language diversity in China or some other Asian countries and regions. The status of English in China and other developing multicultural societies has been elevated from time to time. In this sense, it suffices to say that English learning during the early childhood period in China can be attributed to the social development and change in China, as well as the development of a multicultural society in China. From now on to the next few years, the phenomenon that parents send young children to learn English and require English education in kindergartens may not be reversed or changed by disputes over this issue or certain mandatory measures. As for Chinese educators, what is worth serious consideration is how to position early childhood English learning in the Chinese culture, how to guide our children to learn English in an active and effective way, and how to guarantee that the second language children acquire will not affect or even facilitate its mother tongue.

We hold the belief that there is a basic principle for English learning during early childhood in China, which is "**Do not learn English unless you are able to learn Mandarin well**".

In a multicultural society, any language apart from one's mother tongue may become a second language for people to learn. In this sense, while we are probing into early childhood English education, we are also exploring the significance of early second language learning in China, which, from the perspective of linguistics, falls under the category of bilingual learning and bilingual education. Pursuant to some research, early childhood is a critical period for the learning of oral native language. If one misses this critical period, his language development will be irreparably affected. However, second language learning does not have a special critical period of development as one's mother tongue (Snow, 2002). Over the years, various studies have shown that children who learn a second or foreign language during early childhood may not have more advantages than those who learn English at a later age in terms of syntax, semantics and pragmatics, with phonetics as an exception. Meanwhile, research also tells us that second language learning can promote human development to some extent. For example, human language development is inextricably related to cognitive and social development. Correspondingly, for those who have the opportunity to learn a second language, it will also be beneficial to their cognitive and social development (Gleason, 2001). Hence, we acknowledge the value of English for children's language development and other aspects of development, in the hope that its significance will not be hyped up blindly.

Given the characteristics of a developing multicultural society, we need to confirm that there is no "balanced" bilingual learning or bilingual education environment in China for the time being. For the sake of the holistic development of children in China, the learning of Mandarin should be undoubtedly given top priority in language education. Early childhood educators in China have to bear in mind that any second language education plan that affects the development of children's mother tongue may lead to negative results. As for certain educational arrangements that run counter to the language education policy in China, not only are they deemed as a sign of ignorance, but they may also do great harm to children's lifelong development. To illustrate, the so-called "all-English schools" that have sprung up in some developed areas have deliberately constructed an "educational environment" in which English is the first language and isolates children from the natural mother tongue learning environment. This phenomenon not only violates the basic law of children's development, but also deviates from China's educational policies and strategies. In this sense, some monitoring and supervision have to come in. To provide a multicultural language environment for children where they can learn English after they have displayed the ability to learn their mother tongue well—this is our primary point of view for this chapter.

Based on the afore-mentioned information, we believe that the objectives of English education for preschool children can be recapitulated as follows:

Firstly, we should cultivate children's interest in English learning and guide them to play a more proactive role in using various languages to communicate. Research on child language development has identified children's purpose of learning as their major motivation to learn a new language. Indeed, children are motivated to learn their mother tongue in a natural and spontaneous way; as for second language learning, it may need to be stimulated by environmental factors in most cases. For preschool children, the best motivation is their interest—when they are interested, they are inclined to learn actively and use the language for communication. Preschool children are usually very confident when using a second language and will not feel embarrassed about their mistakes—this is exactly what we have to make full use of, with a view to providing an English learning environment that generates and maintains their interest. We would like to see that they find English learning exciting, joyful and intriguing and that they feel exhilarated, happy and inspired in the process of learning English, without getting bored. Interest in English learning, together with the purpose of interaction, will have an important impact on their future second language learning.

Secondly, we should help children establish a preliminary sense of English phonetics and increase their language sensitivity. As mentioned earlier, people's phonetic awareness comes into being in the stage of early childhood. The phonetic awareness for a second language can also be acquired relatively more easily in this period. Early childhood English learning should have its own distinct characteristics. For example, by teaching children to sing, read or speak English, educators will find that they have naturally acquired a sense of English phonetics as well as an increased sensitivity to a language differing from their mother tongue. Such language sensitivity established in the critical period of early language acquisition will help children distinguish the phonetics of various languages, and identify the differences between languages. With regard to preschool English learning, children should not be required to learn as many words and sentence patterns as possible, or take the acquisition of international phonetic symbols as a priority. On the contrary, their main task should simply be their exposure to the English language. All they have to do is to feel what is means to speak English, so that their sensitivity to languages can be formed, which in fact, will exert a subtle impact on the brain of the child and play a positive role in first or second language learning.

Thirdly, we should provide opportunities for children to experience different cultures by using English so that they can acquire the basic concept of cultural diversity from an early age. Judging from the booming multicultural society in China nowadays, flowing under the large number of parents who provide English learning opportunities for children and of English courses kept being introduced into kindergartens is the mentality that they have to prepare their children to adapt to an evolving multicultural society. It is because any language in the world is inseparable from the culture from which it emerges. So it suffices to say that in the process of learning a language, the child is also learning unconsciously its cultural implications. In the preschool phase, it is by interacting with adults and peers that children gradually form their perception of culture. Therefore, we should guide children to acquire English skills through a diversity of activities such as original English nurseries, stories, games, dramas. In that way, realization will gradually descend upon them that people or things from different cultures have their own characteristics. Looking through the lens of English, children are able to stare into the distance and give free rein to their imagination of a different world, which will foster in them the basic concept of cultural diversity from an early age.

Considering the positioning of early childhood English education, set against the backdrop of the current Chinese society, we hold that kindergartens which have access to pertinent resources can regard English learning as a component of language education. While striving to develop the Mandarin skills of children, we should set aside a little time and foster a fun environment for English learning so that children can happily get to know what is "English", and prepare themselves for future learning.

After the discussion of the basic positioning of early childhood English education in China, we need to further consider the existing problems of English learning in kindergartens. Over the past decade, as Chinese early childhood educators observe, there have emerged, all of a sudden, a multitude of English textbooks in the market. Educators have to adapt themselves to the new challenges, select teaching materials with great prudence and organize effective teaching sessions. In what way are we able to choose from an abundance of teaching materials the ones that suit children the best? How to develop an appropriate pedagogical methodology to ensure an effective learning experience for our children? In the following paragraphs, I would like to refer to some fundamental principles to which educators have to adhere.

The early childhood educational reform in the 1990s in China once informed us of the basic "whole language" principles in language education for kindergarteners. It should be noted that irrespective of some special rules stemming from second language learning, from the perspective of language education, there is no difference in the basic concepts of mother tongue and bilingual education. In consequence, it is imperative to remind preschool educators of the importance to adhere to the six "whole language" principles in the process of English teaching.

Firstly, children's language learning is per se a holistic process. On the foundation of the achievements of contemporary child language studies, researchers have come to the conclusion that since birth, children are equipped with all that is needed for learning any kind of human language. As child language development is a comprehensive process, so is the cognitive learning of language. In the early stage of language education, not only shall we pay attention to the development of children's listening and speaking abilities, but we also have to stretch every sinew to create an environment facilitating the improvement of their reading and writing skills.

Secondly, children's language learning is a natural process. Advocates for "whole language" principles attach great importance to the rules of child language development. They believe that it is through the interaction with others that children learn how to use languages. In the meantime, they will take the initiative to understand the meaning behind languages. Hence, early education institutions should provide children with opportunities and resources to learn a wide range of languages, surrounding them with an ample amount of linguistic information. Additionally, it is advised that "natural learning mode" be adopted for language education, which consists of four parts: exemplification, participation, practice or role-playing, and creative expression (Holdaway, 1986).

Thirdly, children's language learning is both effective and useful. The study finds that as a link between personal experience and social learning, effective language learning is neither "correct" nor "standard". For young children, only when their language learning shows some effect or when they are able to communicate in the very language that they acquire can we say that this process of learning is meaningful. They will concentrate on the topic of discussion, while trying to gather relevant linguistic information from the words of interlocutors or the books they read. The moment they begin to express what they have learned by speaking or writing, children turn into learners who seek and make meaningful communication. Educators should, consequently, make every effort to guide children to learn a language in various situations, which is of special importance to their language learning (Harste, et al. 1985).

Fourthly, children's language learning is a process of integration. The new concept of whole language education indicates that the process of learning is actually tantamount to the acquisition of symbols. From the perspective of early language education, the system of language symbols is de facto constitutive of two functions: one of the learning objectives as well as tools for children. Whole language researchers have adopted Vygotsky's theory, arguing that the principles concerning the learning of any symbol system are per se correlated to each other. As a result of which, it is suggested that different symbol systems should be employed in the process of learning. For example, one can inject arts, drama, music and dance symbols into language learning and goes beyond the disciplinary limitations, which is beneficial not only to children's cognitive learning of language, but also to the learning of other related fields (Goodman & Kenneth, 1986; Fisher, 1991).

Fifthly, children's language learning is an open and equal process. With regard to whole-language-based education concepts, teachers and children are working together to form a pleasant learning process. As for teachers, they enjoy, in relative terms, much professional autonomy, which is mainly demonstrated in their knowledge of learning and teaching theories, their experience of curriculum design and teaching material selection, and their organization of educational activities based on the needs of students. With respect to children, they work with their teachers as equal partners, not as their subordinates (Goodman, 1986). Teachers' responsibility is to create an optimal and non-competitive language learning community for children. In particular, we have to realize that when children have the right to make their own choices, the learning effect will be the best (Fisher, 1991).

Lastly, children's language learning is a creative process. Language learning and application can be both conservative and innovative. By "conservative", it means that language is the product of social conventions, and that people tend to make the same definition of a certain language that they share and use in a social and cultural environment. Nevertheless, language is also the product of constant innovation. As for all language researchers, there are no "mistakes" in child language learning process, but only " attempts " and "innovations". Only by trying can children know how to make things right the next time. Attempt is the prelude and only way leading to innovation. Educators should fully acknowledge and encourage children's innovative spirit in language learning (Harste, 1984). In some kindergartens that endorse the whole language approach, teachers regard children as young readers and writers. They give children sufficient space to practice and build their language ability. Teachers do not care if they make mistakes, or if their expressions are perfect; instead, looking forward to their progress, teachers will welcome and appreciate children's desire to demonstrate their language skills (Raines & Canady, 1990).

If we are going to set early childhood English education in China against the yardstick of the afore-mentioned principles and standards, we will realize that there are some basic problems, as reflected in the following two aspects, in our practice which we have to take note of:

Language inputs during the teaching process: language inputs from teachers have always been a key factor in second language learning, needless to say in early childhood English learning. As far as the language inputs from preschool English teachers in China are concerned, it is summarized that (1) there is a lack of English inputs, which can be partially attributed to the limited level of teachers' English proficiency. Consequently, many teachers are unable to interact with children naturally in English. In addition, pedagogical concepts and methods can also be one of the causes for insufficient inputs. To take one example, many teaching materials that enjoy a cult following among teachers and learners actually are greatly influenced by conventional pedagogy. Students are asked to read one sentence or a few words repetitively. Lying under such mechanical exercises and repetitions is a serious destitution of English inputs. (2) The quality of teachers' English inputs is not that ideal. Due to the limited English proficiency of teachers or teaching materials of low quality, chances are that the English that is taught in classrooms is not standard enough, particularly when it comes to phonetics and pragmatics. Some phenomena concerning "Chinglish", which was often ridiculed in comedies or farces in the past, still prevail among Chinese English learners. However, it does not mean that there will be no problem at all if students are taught by foreign teachers, whose teaching methods and language proficiency may also vary greatly from person to person due to their various cultural and educational backgrounds.

The employment of language during the learning process: the use of a certain language is the driving force of language education, which directly affects their learning effect in the entire process. This is especially true for second language learning. As for young English learners, whether they will have the chance to use the language that matches the language inputs they receive determines effect of English learning and motivation of continuous learning. Early childhood English learning in China is confronted with three main problems: (a) Children do not really have enough opportunities to use the language they learn. Even for English classes with better inputs, there still exists a phenomenon in which the teacher speaks more than the students. (b) Children are restricted to only a few ways of using the language. As the class is mainly teacher-directed, children are more expected to answer questions instead of taking the initiative to speak or use different types of language. (c) Children do not have much chance to socially interact with other people in the language they acquire. In most cases, the English learning environment in China tends to focus more on collective activities, ignoring the creation of opportunities for individual or group interaction. Such English learning activities lack the opportunity for children to practice the language they have learned and communicate with others.

In order to resolve the problems mentioned above, we believe that English teaching for Chinese children should take into consideration what we call the "optimal condition" (Snow, 2002). It is suggested that educators take the following measures:

1. Selecting teaching materials in line with the new educational concepts, carefully examining whether pedagogical methodologies are in conformity to the current curriculum reform in China, making every effort to integrate English and Chinese courses during the early childhood period, with a view to turning the teaching of both languages into an integral part of the curriculum as a whole and making sure that children's English learning is effective and caters to the needs of the whole language development.

2. Using English CD, audio-visual clips and other teaching aids of relatively high quality to create a standard and natural English learning environment for children, and offering sufficient high-quality language

inputs during English teaching.

3. Actively carrying out different forms of English teacher training activities, with a focus on the concept and methodology of English education, at the same time, offering to teachers oral English training, choosing English teaching institutions with the presence of licensed foreign teachers who are able to demonstrate their English proficiency and professionalism.

Children's learning process entails many aspects that are interrelated to each other. In consequence, when it comes to early childhood English education in China, there is no way that we can separate it from the curricula of kindergartens. We have to further discuss this topic and think about the relationship between English education and the daily learning experience of children, from the perspective of curriculum. Only by incorporating English learning into the curriculum as an effective part of all the courses in kindergartens can English teaching lead to fruitful results.

Then, in specific terms, how are we going to make it all happen? To take one example, a bunch of first-grade students in a kindergarten are going to attend a course called "Play House" in the next semester. Predicted upon the core content of the course, we provide children with learning materials aligned with their life experience, and propose a few criteria concerning the various abilities the students are expected to develop. We incline to construct and improve children's learning through games and activities. Next, we can introduce the English lesson of "My Family", with a strong emphasis on the concepts of "家-family" and "我家-my family", for it is also related to the Chinese curriculum. By analyzing both the English and Chinese lessons which are independent of and complementary for each other, we may find that: (1) In the process of learning English, the children's understanding of interpersonal relationship, affection and love in the family is consistent with their response to the Chinese course. Therefore, what the children gain from the Chinese version of "Play House" can support their English learning. It is also certain that if one combines the English lesson with other similar courses, it can also evoke similar or relevant learning experience from children. (2) When it comes to teachers' requirements, they will ask for a relatively lower level of expression in English than in Chinese. By contrast, the cognitive level during the learning process is the same. Their level of comprehension and conception of English is equivalent to that of Chinese. (3) We should also be convinced that children are able to feel the phonetics, intonations and rhythm of English by singing English ballads, grasp basic words and sentence patterns by listening to English stories, and try to use the language to express and communicate through playing games in English. Children can naturally acquire their ability to express themselves in English.

Consequently, in light of theories on children language learning, second language learning, children's development and education, it is in our sincere hope that three connections can be formed during early childhood English education:

The first is the connection between English and Chinese learning. Regardless of the number of languages a person acquires, it is through the cognitive system that he/she realizes the symbolization of concepts. In fact, this also concerns the representation of the same concept by different linguistic symbols. In terms of the situation in China, when children learn

English, the level of their mother tongue is much higher than that of their second language. Accordingly, the kind of connection between native and second language learning will be beneficial to children's understanding and application of the English content, and help them gain twice the result with half the effort. Hypothetically, today children have learnt the Chinese fairy tale "Three Butterflies". If they are also going to learn an English song called "Butterfly", then we can assume that they will master the song very fast.

The second is the connection between English learning and life experience. Language learning is inseparable from social life. Also, it is social interaction that makes language learning happen. This very fact is also applicable to child English learning. Effective and useful English learning must be related to children's life experience. Educators engaged in preschool English teaching need to pay close attention to life experience of their children and try to utilize it in the process of teaching. If English teaching is independent of children's life and asks only for monotonous recitation, there is no way it can lay a positive impact on the young English learners.

The third is the connection between English learning and a comprehensive curriculum. Incorporating English teaching into the comprehensive curriculum in kindergartens will also be conducive to the resolution of the previous two questions as well as to the promotion of the whole language approach. As a result, preschool educational institutions need to pay attention to the connection between children's Chinese and English education, and concentrate on the integration of the English content into the Chinese curriculum, so that the two can compensate for each other and strive for mutual development. Even if some kindergartens lack the kind of human resources that are able to integrate the Chinese and English curricula, it is still advised that English teachers pay attention to this issue and do their utmost to coordinate the English content with the current curriculum.

In summary, early childhood English education in China is still in the phase of exploration and experiment. Because of this, we hope to see an increasing number of scholars who will make concerted effort to launch research in this thematic area, with a view to resolving the problems concerning early childhood education that emerge in the society and providing a better learning environment conducive to the holistic and harmonious development of children.

References

Gleason, J. B. (Ed.) (2001). The development of language. (5th ed.) MA: Allyn & Bacon.

Fisher, B. (1991). Joyful learning — A whole language kindergarten. Porstmouth, NH: Heinemann

Goodman, K. (1986). What's whole in whole language? Porstmouth, NH: Heinemann

Harste, J. C., Woodward, V. A. & Burke, C. L. (1985). Language stories and literacy lessons. Porstmouth, NH: Heinemann

Holdaway, D. (1986). The structure of natural learning as a basis for literacy instruction. In Sampson, M. (ed.). The pursuit of literacy: Early reading and writing. Dubuque, IA: Kendall/Hunt

Raines, S. C & Canady, R. J. (1990). The whole language kindergarten. NY: Teachers College Press

Snow, C. E. (2002). Looking Closely at Second Language Learning, Unpublished interview in HGSE News, Harvard Graduate School of Education, USA

10. Early Childhood Language and Brain Development Research

Jing Zhou, Chuanjiang Li, Yibin Zhang

East China Normal University

The past half-century has witnessed a series of fruitful research results in the domain of early childhood language acquisition and development, which can be attributed to generations of linguists and psychologists. A general consensus has been reached among different schools that language acquisition during early childhood must be predicated on the physiological basis of the brain and will develop gradually with the interaction with the environment. However, how does the interactive process of child language formation and development come into being? In other words, what is the intrinsic relationship between child language acquisition and brain development? This very question has always been a "black box" for researchers. In the 21st century, with the rapid development of non-invasive neuroimaging technology and methods, various studies on children have gone beyond the original observation and speculation of external behavior, allowing us to establish neurophysiological links between genes and behaviors [1], which has led to more sensitive and effective research paradigms. Therefore, the "black box" concerning the mechanism of early childhood language development and neural development of the brain has gradually opened up, ushering into a new era with more breakthroughs to come. This chapter aims to review the research progress in this field in recent years, and tries to respond to some relevant issues of significance in the academia, with a view to promoting in-depth discussion of language development and early childhood education in China.

1. Physiology of the Brain as Basis for Child Language Development

Since the inception of the research on children's language, it is generally believed that language is a trait unique to human beings, who are equipped with a brain of more complication and sophistication. Early studies have found that it is the left cerebral hemisphere that is mainly responsible for human language, with what we call an "irreversible determinism". Researchers of neonatal language processing [2] found that children's left brain is inclined to process complex speech sounds, indicative of the fact that language is processed on the left side of the brain since birth. Studies on children with brain damage have also suggested that children whose left brains are severed encounter severe language dysfunction while tackling syntactic tasks. These findings have further aroused people's curiosity. What is the mechanism of brain physiology for child language development? Which parts of the brain are more closely related to child language development?

First of all, according to recent research, the left cerebral hemisphere does not assume the sole responsibility for the comprehension and production of language when the human brain processes language. As a matter of fact, both sides of the brain work closely together in this very process. Relevant studies have discovered that in some language activities, young children display the same brain regions activated as adults, especially in the classic Broca's area and superior temporal gyrus, known for being closely related to speech production. The intensity of activation in their left brains is significantly higher than that in the right brains [4]. Monolingual and bilingual children have experienced similar activations in these brain regions, such as the activation of superior temporal gyrus for the processing of speech sounds and that of the left inferior frontal gyrus for the processing of words [5,6]. However, many studies have shown that even though most of the language-related brain activity is likely to occur on the left side of the brain, it does not mean that the right brain has no part to play. When it comes to syntactic processing, phonetic and semantic analysis, the right hemisphere is also activated [7,8]. Classical linguistic and cognitive brain areas (anterior cingulate cortex, dorsolateral prefrontal cortex) are activated when bilingual children are switching between languages [9,10]. In the process of paragraph and sentence comprehension, human beings will constantly mobilize the semantic maps in the brain, which are reflected in both hemispheres. This further demonstrates that both sides of the brain are responsible for human language activities [11].

Secondly, recent studies have proposed the notion of neural network structure in language acquisition. Conventional theories hold that most of the language areas in the brain for children's language development are monolingual. For example: (1) Eloquent Cortex, which is located in the posterior inferior frontal gyrus (areas 44 and 45, also known as Broca's Area); (2) Auditory Speech Center, which is located in the cortex of areas 42 and 22 of the superior temporal gyrus. This region is able to receive auditory information and to interpret it into a series of processes; (3) Visual Language Center, which is located in the angular gyrus of inferior parietal lobule. This area plays the role of understanding the symbols that people see and the meaning of words; (4) Application Center, which is situated in the supramarginal gyrus of the inferior parietal lobule, i. e. area 40. This area is in charge of the meticulous task of coordination; (5) Writing Center, which is situated in areas 6 and 8 in the posterior middle frontal gyrus, or in other words, the front of the central anterior gyrus. In the past, our understanding of the neurological aspect of language was that language was a simple model composed of Broca's Area, Wernicke's Area as well as Arcuate Fasciculus that connect the former two. With the development of neuroscience and cognitive neuroscience, researchers [12] have come to realize that all kinds of psychological activities, especially some sophisticated and complicated cognitive activities, such as the production of language, are completed by neural networks constituted of various brain regions. The development of the cortex of the individual language network can be divided into two stages. In the first stage (from birth to 3 years old), linguistic brain regions of young children follow a bottom-up development path, accompanied by the rapid development of both temporal lobes. In the second stage (from 3 years old to adulthood), the development path gradually goes top-down, with the growth of the functional selection and structural connectivity of the left forehead. More recent neuroscience studies, such as imaging studies of aphasia, diffusion tensor imaging studies, functional magnetic resonance imaging studies, electrophysiological studies of cortical and subcutaneous tissues have enhanced the understanding of the complexity of language neural networks in the brain. Fujii and other researchers [13] have asserted that language is processed through two different pathways—dorsal stream and ventral stream. The core of dorsal pathway is the arcuate fasciculus, which is closely related to speech processing, while semantic processing is primarily related to the ventral pathway (mainly including the inferior fronto-occipital fasciculus and the internal network of temporal bones). In addition, they have found frontal aslant tract, which connects the supplementary motor area and Broca's area, and plays a pivotal role in the formation and motivation of language. Due to the immature brain network analysis technology and the insufficient collection and knowledge of multimodal data, further study is still needed on ways to integrate the network model of language brain structure and function, and to elucidate the corresponding production and development of language. It is fair to say that the traditional theories concerning language brain regions has not yet been completely replaced.

Furthermore, recent studies suggest that brain development of young children can predict their future language development. In recent years, a series of studies have focused on the relationship between the development of brain structure of young children and the future development of their linguistic and cognitive ability. The researchers [14] have used functional magnetic resonance imaging (fMRI) technology to launch their studies and found that the right amygdala volume of normal children at the age of six months is correlated with the receptive and expressive language skills of children between two to four years old, but it is not correlated with language abilities when children reach 12 months of age. As a result, it is believed that the amygdala tissue will be mobilized to process language information generated from the environment during the first six months since birth. At the age of one, other brain regions of young children will be involved more in language activities. The amygdala structure plays a vital role in language acquisition of young children. Some research on children with autism has drawn similar conclusions. The larger the left amygdala is, the better the child's language ability turns out to be; the opposite is true of the right amygdala [15]. Therefore, it is concluded that the amygdala volume during the early childhood period is strongly correlated with one's future language ability. In addition, a series of studies have found that a baby's brain activity level of phonetic learning can predict his language ability at the age of 14 to 30 months [16]; the language activity level of a baby's brain can predict its language development at five years old as well as its pre-reading and pre-writing ability [17]; the brain language processing image during infancy can also predict a child's language ability and cognitive level at eight years old [18]. Some studies [19] have also shown that the EEG level of word processing of two-year-old autistic children can predict their receptive language ability, cognitive ability and adaptive behavior at the age of four to six. The extent to which the brain has developed during early childhood period can predict the language proficiency of a child. In consequence, researchers continue to commit themselves to exploring susceptibility genes for dyslexia by observing early childhood brain activities. Under the auspices of neuroimaging research, they are also devoted to confirming the different functions of those genes, as well as neuronal migration and axonal growth which may trigger abnormal cerebral development in the early phase. They are also making efforts to identify children prone to dyslexia and to provide evidence for accurate diagnosis, so as to take preemptive measures to help children with developmental dyslexia, which account for 5% to 17% of the students in the United States [20].

The research on the neurophysiological mechanism concerning children's brain and language development shows that early childhood brain development has a great impact on children's language development and education, whose significance cannot be overemphasized and which deserves the attention of researchers and educators.

2. Critical Period of Language Acquisition and Window of Opportunity for Brain Development for Children

The concept of critical period of children's language development was officially proposed in *the Biological Basis of Language* written by Lenneberg [21], and was universally recognized by the linguistic research on child language in the 20th century. The main point of view on the critical period of language development is that the early childhood is a period in which language acquisition is much easier than at any other time of life. Evidence for critical periods of language development, on the one hand, comes from neurophysiological findings at that time, which hold that human evolution determines the fact that a child is equipped with language learning mechanism since birth, while the Broca's Area and Wernicke's Area in the human brain, which are responsible for language learning, are highly sensitive from 4 to 12 years old. The language stored at that time will be deemed as "mother tongue", and consequently, it can be acquired in a rather quick fashion and employed in a flexible way. On the other hand, the critical period theory of language development is based on a series of studies on children who are linguistically disadvantaged. For example, the study on the relationship between brain injuries of children and the recovery of their language competences has found that after a certain point, the rehabilitation of language is very difficult to realize. A study on the speech acts of children deprived of the environment for language development reveals that without any exposure to language, children missed the chance to learn languages during childhood and that their future language development was seriously affected. Studies on second language acquisition of children from immigrant families have confirmed over and over again that early childhood is the key stage for child language development.

Research on brain development in early childhood reveals the rapid development process since infancy, which is accompanied by the rapid development of neurons. Indicative of the proliferation and rapid emergence of synapses, the development of synapses in cerebral cortex also means that preschool children are experiencing the most optimal period of cerebral nerve cells development [22]. At the same time, the research also shows that in this very developmental process, the nerve cells of various functions develop at different rates, which may correspond to different areas of child development. During the development of the brain, there exist various "Windows of Opportunity" for young children—the very period that witnesses the rapid connection and myelination of nerve cells [23]. The Window of Opportunity is there equally for each and every child. One of the main conditions for the development of a child is to give him/her the kind of positive stimuli needed in a proper period of window of opportunity, so as to guarantee his/her development in certain respects.

Based on the studies on the Window of Opportunity for brain development, we believe that in the field of children's language development, the Window of Opportunity witnesses the rapid connection and myelination of language neurons, the fact of which leads to the reconsideration of critical period of child language acquisition.

Firstly, the Window of Opportunity for child brain development corresponds to the sensitive period of different aspects of language development. Although existing studies are not able to keep track of the exact period of development of a certain linguistic element, linguistic studies on children's brain activities have shown that various parts of children's language development, such as phonetic, semantic and syntactic acquisition differ in terms of critical periods. The study [24] has found that the critical period of children's phonetic learning occurs within the first year since birth, specifically within six to 12 months. The critical period for syntactic acquisition of mother tongue is from 18 to 36 months, during which children are capable of picking up various syntactic elements rather quickly. The window of opportunity for vocabulary development is

18 months, which witnesses a giant leap in a child's corpus. However, it should be noted that in light of the research, the vocabulary of a child develops in a sustained way. Individuals are able to amass new words at any age and this process is not entirely influenced by age.

Kuhl [25] holds that from the perspective of early phonetic learning, the development of children's language depends on two conditions which coexist and interact with each other during this process: learning during the window of opportunity and the neurological conditions for mother tongues. For instance, within six months after birth, the development of their brain neural circuits and overall structure allows them to absorb the phonetic and rhythmic patterns from their surroundings. Phonetic learning during the window of opportunity will exert its influence on children's speech perception and change their future language learning proficiency. Offer young children the chance to learn in various windows of opportunity, and the neural networks that reflect natural language inputs will be formed in them. Those preliminary neural networks will also lay an impact on the learning of a new language [26]. We need to realize that there is a certain window of opportunity for children's language development and to understand that language environment and experience matter to the rapid growth of neural synapses and neural networks during the entire early childhood, especially before the age of one. Accordingly, we need to provide appropriate language stimuli and a proper environment for children so that their language proficiency can be enhanced in this sensitive period. As shown in Figure 1 [27], the development of nervous tissues for language was linear and fast eight months ago, reaching its peak in approximately the eighth month; the development of advanced cognitive neurons reached its peak at about one year old and then it started to stabilize and decline.

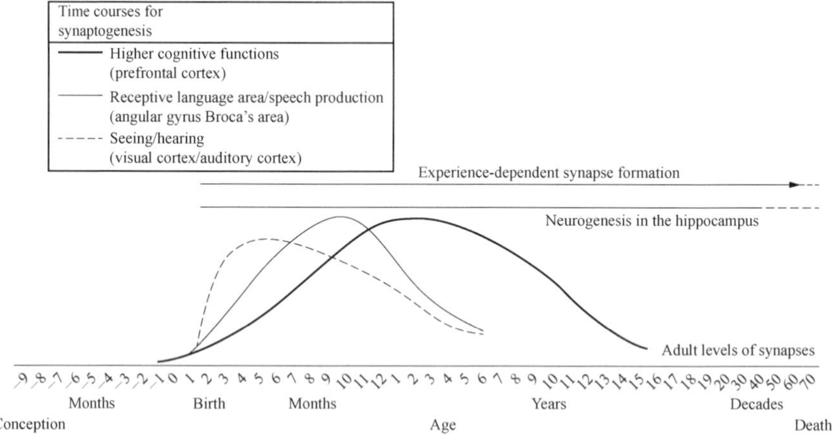

Figure 1 The Development of Human Brain

Secondly, the malleability of children's brain allows complementary development at critical stages of language development. The malleability of the brain indicates its capability of structural and functional changes as it is shaped by experience. A series of linguistic research on children with special needs points out that early language learning experience will have an impact on the anatomical structure of the brain, thus compensating for the original disadvantages of language development. Mayberry et al. [28] have studied the acquisition of sign language (which, in this case, is the first language) among people with hearing impairment from birth to 14 years old using fMRI. They have discovered that the age of sign language acquisition is in linear negative correlation with the activation level of the anterior language area in the brain, and in positive correlation with the activation level of the visual area. For some hearing-impaired children, early reading and writing learning may change the structure of their brain and level of cerebral activation. Reading and writing will develop phonetic awareness, oral ability and promote speech processing. Through reading acquisition, specific brain areas (left posterior temporal cortex, an area for visual word formation) can respond to the orthographic stimulus of the acquired text. Dehaene et al. [29] have also found, with the help of fMRI technology, that reading and writing can enhance the activity level of the brain. Firstly, it enhances the organization of visual cortex, especially the left posterior temporal cortex and vision-related occipital cortex. Secondly, sentence writing activities activates the spoken language network of the entire left hemisphere, or in other words, promotes the development of speech through reading. Thirdly, reading and writing improve the processing of spoken language by pushing forward the development of the speech area (planum temporale). Further studies [30] indicate that children gaining experience can lead to changes in brain structures and functions, and that task-related brain areas will be strengthened after training, while brain areas which are not related with tasks will gradually weaken in terms of activation level. Brain is not an entity that changes not. Modern neuroscience has revealed that it will change with the growth of children, and more importantly, it will vary according to environmental inputs and learners' experience. Hence, educational support plays an important role in the development of children's brain [31]. However, it should be noted that some studies [32] have pointed out that learning during the window of opportunity and critical period of language development is of critical importance. To illustrate, with respect to sign language acquisition of different ages, when observing the change in the density of occipital cortex related to language processing, the researchers have found that the ages of sign language acquisition have exerted various effects on it. Therefore, we need to clarify that it is very important to make use of the window of opportunity for children's brain, to provide special support to children's language development in the critical period and to help children reshape the development of brain and language.

3. Children's Bilingual Learning and Bilingual Brain Development

In recent years, an increasing number of studies have focused on children's bilingual learning. Studies [33] have shown that children's second language learning is not in sync with the critical period of language development, for even after the sensitive period of second language learning, the brain is still, to a certain degree, malleable. However, more studies have revealed that bilingual learning in early childhood can influence the functional activities or even the structure of the brain. Thus, we take it as our duty to respond to the statements directly.

First of all, we have to answer whether bilingualism is beneficial to children's brain development.

The research on the relation between cerebral growth and "cognitive advantages of bilingualism" has, in recent years, aroused heated discussion among scholars specializing in child language development. Many behavioral experiments have found that bilingual children perform better than monolingual ones in some verbal and nonverbal cognitive tasks, especially in the execution of functional tasks—this is what we call "cognitive advantages of bilingualism" [34, 35]. With regard to the specific manifestations of the influence that bilingualism exerts on child brain development, studies over the past decade have found that it is mainly reflected in the changes of executive functions as well as their structures. It is also discovered that bilingualism enables the area of executive functions to keep being activated, as a result of which, its cognitive control and flexibility are reinforced in children. Kovelman et al. [36] have concluded, from a semantic test, that the dorsolateral prefrontal lobe and inferior frontal gyrus of bilingual children are more activated than monolinguals, even though there has been no difference in terms of the performance between the two groups of children. The dorsolateral prefrontal lobe is related to cognitive functions such as working memory and inhibitory control. Pursuant to the research outcomes, the cognitive control and flexibility of the brain can be strengthened by bilingual experience.

Many studies have focused on the effects of bilingualism on children's brain structure. By means of high-resolution magnetic resonance imaging, some researchers [37] have noticed that when it comes to the inferior parietal lobe, the density of gray matter in multilingual children is significantly higher than that in monolinguals. Other studies [38] also indicate that basal nuclei, caudate nuclei in particular, are also influenced by bilingual experience, for the latter plays an indispensable role in language conversion. Accordingly, researchers [39] have identified a remarkably higher grey matter density in left caudate nuclei of bilinguals than those of monolinguals. A report written by Hosoda et al. [40] states that after some second language vocabulary training, the gray matter volume in the caudate nuclei of bilinguals tends to increase notably in comparison with other brain regions.

Secondly, we have to return to the relationship between early bilingual learning and child brain development. Pertinent studies have raised the question as to whether bilingual brains are the same as monolingual ones, trying to explore the relationship between language and cognitive mechanism in children in an attempt to find out if early bilingual experience can change the brain, which has been heatedly discussed. These studies start with the discussion as to in what way the age of the preliminary second language acquisition influences the activation of language neurons. Some researchers [41] have tried to divide normal children aged from seven to ten years old into two groups: bilingual and monolingual ones. Comparison has been made between children and adults of the same groups, in order to observe the activation level of various regions in the brain as candidates of different ages and language experience process sentences. The bilingual children group includes both early bilinguals (born into a second-language environment) and late bilinguals (those exposed to a second-language environment since four to six years old). As for both bilingual children and adults, the activation level of classical language areas on the left side has been greatly elevated. More importantly, we come to the realization that early bilingual children process bilingual sentences by mobilizing the classical language areas, while late bilingual children change the brain areas of advanced executive functions to process sentences, with prefrontal lobes even more activated.

Further research has endeavored to explore whether early language learning experience affects the growth of nervous system related to reading, and to prove whether the latter varies from monolingual to bilingual children. Jasiska et al. [42] have utilized the brain imaging technology to compare the brain activation patterns of children aged from six to seven, children aged from eight to ten as well as adults in the process of reading. They have noticed that classical language areas, such as the left inferior frontal gyrus (LIFG) and superior temporal gyrus (STG), will change with age, and the activation level of LIFG, STG and cognitive areas on both sides (such as dorsolateral prefrontal lobes) is higher with bilingual children. This kind of bilingual "neural signature" indicates that early second language learning experience can change children's reading nervous system and promote the development of their reading ability.

Recent neuroimaging studies show that not only do bilinguals excel in language tasks in comparison with monolinguals, but they are also able to employ cognitive control networks in a more effective way with a better performance [43]. Arredondo et al. [44] have discovered that early bilingual experience can change the attentional control of prefrontal cortex. When dealing with tasks that require attentional control, monolinguals tend to activate and use the right frontal lobe more; in contrast, bilingual children activate the left frontal lobe more, especially the left inferior frontal gyrus, indicative of the fact that bilingual children have the propensity to mobilize language brain areas in general tasks linked with attentional control. They believe that bilingual experience and the growth and impact of early cognitive interaction have altered the function of the left prefrontal lobe in the brain. Abutalebi et al. [45] have compared the performance of monolinguals and bilinguals in nonverbal conflict monitoring tasks, and found that both of them have activated the anterior cingulate gyrus—a brain area involved in cognitive control; nevertheless, bilinguals have turned out to be efficient, as in conflict monitoring tasks of the same level, they require a lower level of brain activation.

And now, we still have to answer the question as to why bilingual learning brings benefits to child brain development. Mainstream studies suggest that bilinguals have a competitive edge when it comes to functional behavioral tasks, which can be attributed to the additional or excessive inhibitory control training they obtain. Constant inhibition stems from the stimuli and reactions that interfere in language. This is mainly because, as many psychological and behavioral studies have found, when bilinguals use only one language, both languages are activated and compete with each other. Brain science interprets the "bilingual cognitive advantages" from the perspective of intrinsic neural mechanism, and holds that we need to pay attention to whether language selection, control mechanism and cognitive control mechanism depend on similar neural networks. It is found that the dorsolateral prefrontal cortex will be activated when individuals convert or control two languages [10,46]. The dorsolateral prefrontal cortex, which is the core area of executive functions, will also be activated when individuals tackle functional tasks [47]. Studies have also shown that basal nuclei play an important role in language selection [48], as well as in executive functions [38]. To summarize, researchers often use the paradigms of language conversion to study bilingual language control mechanisms. They discover that the left inferior frontal gyrus, bilateral dorsal prefrontal lobe, anterior cingulate gyrus, caudate nucleus and so forth seem to be related to the inhibitory function of bilingual vocabulary competition [49]. Cognitive control is part of executive functions. Some researchers [9] believe that it is mainly responsible for five important brain areas: left dorsolateral prefrontal lobe, anterior cingulate gyrus, caudate nucleus and supramarginal gyrus or inferior parietal lobule.

Studies [50,51] show that the advantages of bilinguals come from the super exercise given to their brains via language learning. When two languages are competing against each other, the brain regions and neural networks of individuals who have fulfilled tasks of executive control, tend to generate multiple levels of activation, so that the brain area for executive functions can be actively involved. Bilingual learners and users switch between two languages and by doing that, the area of executive functions is constantly activated, which ensures a better control. In light of neurophysiology, the advantages of executive functions of bilinguals benefit from bilingual language selection and the competition mechanism.

On the relationship between bilingual learning and brain development in children, there is another key issue that we need to resolve in reality: what is the optimal time to start bilingual learning?

In order to respond to this question, it is of paramount importance that we pay attention to the research on the critical period of children's language development and the window of opportunity for brain development. Furthermore, we also have to take into consideration the research which asserts that the critical period may not necessarily exist for second language learning. More studies demonstrate that the time of first contact with a second language, or the age of exposure to a bilingual environment affects children's bilingual development [52]. Some researchers hold that [53,54], the best time to ensure bilingual development is to engage in bilingualism before the age of five. At the same time, it is imperative to make sure if there exist a large number of systematic and multi-channel bilingual factors, which a good second language learning environment features, in the ambience, community and family of bilingual learning. Kovelman et al. [55] put forward the notion that "one pair of gloves is not suitable for everyone". In the meantime, they stressed that the whole language environment approach suits more those who are exposed to bilingualism before the age of three and that it can effectively improve their language and reading abilities. If three-or four-year-olds are exposed to a second language for the first time, it is advised that educators take into account the combination of the whole language environment and phonics, so as to ensure a better development of children's decoding and reading abilities. In addition, we also have to refer to the degree of bilingual proficiency that children may acquire through learning and consequently its impact on their development. In accordance with some studies [56], bilingual proficiency regulates children's performance in executing control tasks—the more proficient they are in second language, the better their performance is in controlling. Mechelli et al. [57] have found that the more proficient bilingual children are in second language, the higher their gray matter density is in the left inferior parietal lobe is. These studies also show that bilingual learning is beneficial to the development of children's brain. When and how to learn will growingly influence the effect of malleability of children's brain, which deserves our careful attention.

4. Child Language and "Social Brain" Development

In the study of children's language development and brain development, researchers [58] have found that even for very young infants, the change of their perception of language is greatly affected by the frequency distribution of all the sounds that surround them. When babies learn languages, they demonstrate the amazing ability to distinguish phonetic factors and intonations in the language environment and gradually acquire phonetic elements and vocabulary by using the analytical models accumulated from social interactions. Therefore, adults who interact with babies in the early stage can give their babies plenty of positive linguistic stimuli, which will help them develop their language and support the growth of a "social brain" [59].

Studies suggest that babies no more than six months old can be called "cosmopolitans" because they can distinguish different sounds of all the languages in the world, while the language learning of babies between 10 to 14 months of age have already been influenced by sociocultural factors. A study by Kuhl et al. [60] focused on social interaction and language learning of 9-month-old infants in the United States. The candidates targeted were divided into four groups: for one of the groups, teachers would read and play with the babies on the floor in Mandarin; for the other two groups, babies would watch videos in Mandarin and listen to audio clips in Mandarin; for the fourth group, which was the contrast group, babies would not be exposed to Mandarin. Instead, an American postgraduate student would read the same book and play the same toys with them in English. The results showcased that: (1) subsequent to 12 activities that take place in one month, American infants who listened to Mandarin spoken to them by real persons learned to identify the various phonemes of Mandarin, and their listening capability of Mandarin reached the level of babies of 11 months old who were immersed in a purely Chinese environment; (2) infants exposed to Mandarin through television or audio recordings did not fully acquire the phonemes of Mandarin, and their ability to identify phonemes was tantamount to that of the contrast group; (3) the infants in the contrast group were not exposed to Mandarin at all. Naturally, there is no difference in their ability to distinguish phonemes before or after the research. This experiment fully demonstrates that only language interaction in natural situations can promote the formation and learning of language. The interaction between adults and infants in mother tongue determines infants' sensitivity to their native language.

Social interactive learning determines the growth of children's "social brain" as well as language development. Which parts of social interaction can better support children's language learning as their "social brain" grows with their language [61]? This is a new direction of research. Suggestions that may appear effective for readers are recapitulated as follows:

Firstly, to provide children with positive social interaction experience, and to use language so as to construct a positive interactive process. Some researchers have found that parents need to foster a warm social interaction environment. When adults read picture books and play toys with their babies, babies cast their looks at different places according to their parents' words, and also change their performance according to their parents' eye movements [62,63]. Brooks et al. [64] claim that in the first two years after birth, children who can follow where adult are looking will have more vocabulary than children who cannot track eye movements of adults. According to the study, the correlation between gaze and speech in social interaction is very crucial. Parents and children need close contact but not passive interaction via digital media. With regard to the studies launched by Kemp [65], by reading stories aloud to their children, parents can effectively promote the development of children's brain and language. As for those children, whose parents read stories to them a lot at home, interact with them frequently, or who are exposed to books very often at home, the semantic processing area in their brain is more active. This area is crucial for language development of and the ability to read on one's own. The study also shows that image-related brain regions are activated, which enables children to "see the stories" and shores up the previous theories concerning the importance of visualization to story comprehension and reading skills. Therefore, in the social interaction between parents and children, parent-child reading is regarded as an effective way to establish the relationship between "social brain" and language.

Secondly, social games designed for children are the best practice for the simultaneous development of their language and social brain. Recent studies demonstrate that the role of games lies in the activation of neurons in the brain, which help the brain to establish connections between neurons during the critical window of development and formulate a good cerebral growth map. The new game theories associate playing with brain development and explore the relationship between play-based activities and brain development, as in, the impact of brain activity on the playing process or the promotion of brain development by games [66]. The study [67] proves that children actively participate in games, which forms a mutually reinforcing process of brain activity, similar to self-guided brain remodeling. Game experts [68] believe that there is a mutually beneficial relationship between games, brain development and a highly interactive environment. They also opine that games are a magical, flexible, unpredictable and evolutionary form of force that evokes creative responses. They can enhance the malleability of children's brain and its connection with the reality by means of rich environmental factors. Therefore, we can draw the conclusion that game playing is an important way for children to learn, which has been further confirmed by the research of brain science. When we pay attention to children's language development and "social brain" development, we know that in social games, children need to experience and practice the various abilities that adults teach them via scaffolding. Children need to follow the rules of the game when playing with dolls. They need to discuss the play house game plans with their peers. They need to remember their roles. In the course of the game, they need to pay attention to what each of the characters does and add in a plot that everyone is interested in. These seemingly fun games, however, are both educational and entertaining in nature and require effective application of the languages as well as the "social brain" experience that children have accumulated.

Thirdly, this essay will illustrate the creation of an environment of language and "social brain" development for the sake of effective learning. The concept of children's "social brain" is actually linked with the society, school, family environment, as well as the influence of social and economic situation on children's brain and holistic development. Up to the present times, all studies have reached a consensus that a negative environment for the growth of "social brain" will be detrimental to the brain and holistic development of children. We could attribute the environment to economic factors but we have to realize that economy does not have the absolute call. The National Advisory Committee on Child Development Sciences (NCSDS) of the United States has proposed three categories of stress affecting children's brain development [69]. The study points out that there are three kinds of stress that influence children's development in real life: positive, tolerable and toxic ones. In this framework, "stress" refers to the physiological performance of the stress response system, rather than the nature of stimuli or the kind of pressure that is measured or acquired objectively. Although many studies are still in the middle of exploring stress mechanisms, there have already emerged several concepts on the basis of biology. Positive stress refers to the kind of moderate and short-term increase in heart rhythm, blood pressure and hormone levels related to stress. Tolerable stress denotes a physiological state in which it may potentially damage the brain structure, but it can be buffered by supportive environments, simulative and adaptive interactions. Toxic stress indicates the adverse effects of intense, frequent or prolonged lack of adult support for or buffer against children's neurological response system [70]. As far as language and "social brain" growth are concerned, we hope that our readers will carefully examine the environment where the children grow, avert toxic stress, provide positive pressure, and truly create a positive and effective learning and development environment for children.

In conclusion, we need to support children's language development, as well as the healthy development of children's brain—this is the most important task and greatest challenge of early childhood education.

References

[1] Braver TS, Cole MW, Yarkoni T. Vive les differences! Individual variation in neural mechanisms of executive control [J]. Curr Opin Neurobiol, 2010, 20(2): 242-250.

[2] Hellige JB. Hemispheric asymmetry: what's right and what's left [M]. Cambridge Harvard University Press, 1993.

[3] Day PS, Ulatowska HK. Perceptual, cognitive, and linguistic development after early hemispherectomy: two case studies [J]. Brain Lang, 1979, 7(1): 17-33.

[4] Petitto LA. Cortical images of early language and phonetic development using near infrared spectroscopy [J]. Educ Brain, 2010: 213-231.

[5] Petitto LA. Revolutions in brain, language and education [R]. Vatican City Pontifical Academy of Sciences, 2003.

[6] Petitto LA, Baker S, Baird A, et al. Near-infrared spectroscopy studies of children and adults during language processing [C]. Cambridge International Workshop on Near-Infrared Spectroscopy, 2004.

[7] Beeman MJ, Bowden EM, Gernsbacher MA. Right and left hemisphere cooperation for drawing predictive and coherence inferences during normal story comprehension [J]. Brain Lang, 2000, 71(2): 310-336.

[8] Vigneau M, Beaucousin V, Hervé PY, et al. What is right-hemisphere contribution to phonological, lexico-semantic, and sentence processing? Insights from a meta-analysis [J]. Neuroimage, 2011, 54(1): 577-593.

[9] Abutalebi J, Green D. Bilingual language production the neurocognition of language representation and control [J]. J Neurolinguistics, 2007, 20(3): 242-275.

[10] Buchweitz A, Prat C. The bilingual brain flexibility and control in the human cortex [J] . Phys Life Rev, 2013, 10(4): 428 - 443.

[11] Huth AG, de Heer WA, Griffiths TL, et al. Natural speech reveals the semantic maps that tile human cerebral cortex [J] . Nature, 2016, 532 (7600): 453 - 458.

[12] Skeide MA, Friederici AD. The ontogeny of the cortical language network [J] . Nat Rev Neurosci, 2016, 17(5): 323 - 332.

[13] Fujii M, Maesawa S, Ishiai S, et al. Neural basis of language an overview of an evolving model [J] . Neurol Med Chir (Tokyo), 2016, 56(7): 379 - 386.

[14] Ortiz-Mantilla S, Choe MS, Flax J, et al. Associations between the size of the amygdala in infancy and language abilities during the preschool years in normally developing children [J] . Neuroimage, 2010, 49 (3): 2791 - 2799.

[15] Munson J, Dawson G, Abbott R, et al. Amygdalar volume and behavioral development in autism [J] . Arch Gen Psychiatry, 2006, 63 (6): 686 - 693.

[16] Kuhl P, Rivera-Gaxiola M. Neural substrates of language acquisition [J] . Annu Rev Neurosci, 2008, 31: 511-534.

[17] Cardillo GC. Predicting the predictors: individual differences in longitudinal relationships between infant phonetic perception, toddler vocabulary, and preschooler language and phonological awareness [D] . Seattle University of Washington, 2010.

[18] Molfese DL. Predicting dyslexia at 8 years of age using neonatal brain responses [J] . Brain Lang, 2000, 72(3): 238 - 245.

[19] Kuhl PK, Coffey-Corina S, Padden D, et al. Brain responses to words in 2-year-olds with autism predict developmental outcomes at age 6 [J] . PLoS One, 2013, 8(5): e64967.

[20] Ozernov-Palchik O, Gaab N. Tackling the 'dyslexia paradox' reading brain and behavior for early markers of developmental dyslexia [J] . Wiley Interdiscip Rev Cogn Sci, 2016, 7(2): 156 - 176.

[21] Lenneberg EH, Chomsky N, Marx O. Biological foundations of language [M] . New York Wiley, 1967.

[22] Huttenlocher PR, Dabholkar AS. Regional differences in synaptogenesis in human cerebral cortex [J] . J Comp Neurol, 1997, 387(2): 167 - 178.

[23] Schiller P. Early brain development research review and update [J] . Exchange, 2010(11): 26 - 30.

[24] Kuhl PK. Brain mechanisms in early language acquisition [J] . Neuron,

2010, 67(5): 713 - 727.
[25] Kuhl PK. Early language acquisition cracking the speech code [J] . Nat Rev Neurosci, 2004, 5(11): 831-843.
[26] Kuhl PK, Conboy BT, Padden D, et al. Early speech perception and later language development implications for the "critical period" [J] . Lang Learn Dev, 2005, 1(3): 237 - 264.
[27] Shonkoff JP, Phillips DA. From neurons to neighborhoods the science of early childhood development [M] . Washington, D. C. National Academies Press, 2000: 188.
[28] Mayberry RI, Chen JK, Witcher P, et al. Age of acquisition effects on the functional organization of language in the adult brain [J] . Brain Lang, 2011, 119(1): 16 - 29.
[29] Dehaene S, Pegado F, Braga LW, et al. How learning to read changes the cortical networks for vision and language [J] . Science, 2010, 330 (6009): 1359 - 1364.
[30] Casey BJ, Tottenham N, Liston C, et al. Imaging the developing brain what have we learned about cognitive development [J] . Trends Cogn Sci, 2005, 9(3): 104 - 110.
[31] Sousa DA. 周加仙，译. 心智、脑与教育：教育神经科学对课堂教学的启示 [M] . 上海：华东师范大学出版社，2012。
[32] Pénicaud S, Klein D, Zatorre RJ, et al. Structural brain changes linked to delayed first language acquisition in congenitally deaf individuals [J] . Neuroimage, 2013(66): 42 - 49.
[33] Li P, Legault J, Litcofsky KA. Neuroplasticity as a function of second language learning anatomical changes in the human brain [J] . Cortex, 2014(58): 301 - 324.
[34] Costa A, Sebastián-Gallés N. How does the bilingual experience sculpt the brain? [J] . Nat Rev Neurosci, 2014, 15(5): 336 - 345.
[35] Calvo A, Bialystok E. Independent effects of bilingualism and socioeconomic status on language ability and executive functioning [J] . Cognition, 2014, 130(3): 278 - 288.
[36] Kovelman I, Baker SA, Petitto LA. Bilingual and monolingual brains compared a functional magnetic resonance imaging investigation of syntactic processing and a possible "neural signature" of bilingualism [J] . J Cogn Neurosci, 2008, 20(1): 153 - 169.
[37] Della Rosa PA, Videsott G, Borsa VM, et al. A neural interactive location for multilingual talent [J] . Cortex, 2013, 49 (2): 605 - 608.

[38] Stocco A, Yamasaki B, Natalenko R, et al. Bilingual brain training a neurobiological framework of how bilingual experience improves executive function [J] . Int J Bilingua, 2012, 18(1): 67 - 92.

[39] Zou L, Abutalebi J, Zinszer B, et al. Second language experience modulates functional brain network for the native language production in bimodal bilinguals [J] . Neuroimage, 2012, 62(3): 1367 - 1375.

[40] Hosoda C, Tanaka K, Nariai T, et al. Dynamic neural network reorganization associated with second language vocabulary acquisition a multimodal imaging study [J] . J Neurosci, 2013, 33 (34): 13663 - 13672.

[41] Jasińska KK, Petitto LA. Age of bilingual exposure predicts distinct contributions of phonological and semantic knowledge to successful reading development [R] . Seattle Society for Research in Child, 2013.

[42] Jasińska KK, Petitto LA. Development of neural systems for reading in the monolingual and bilingual brain new insights from functional near infrared spectroscopy neuroimaging [J] . Dev Neuropsychol, 2014, 39 (6): 421 - 439.

[43] Kroll JF, Bobb SC, Hoshino N. Two languages in mind bilingualism as a tool to investigate language, cognition, and the brain [J] . Curr Dir Psychol Sci, 2014, 23(3): 159 - 163.

[44] Arredondo MM, Hu XS, Satterfield T, et al. Bilingualism alters children's frontal lobe functioning for attentional control [J] . Dev Sci, 2016 Jan 6. [Epub ahead of print] .

[45] Abutalebi J, Della Rosa PA, Green DW, et al. Bilingualism tunes the anterior cingulate cortex for conflict monitoring [J] . Cereb Cortex, 2012, 22(9): 2076 - 2086.

[46] Rodriguez-Fornells A, De Diego Balaguer R, Münte TF. Executive control in bilingual language processing [J] . Lang Learn, 2006, 56 (S1): 133 - 190.

[47] 倪媛媛，李红. 从生理机制探讨心理理论与执行功能的关系 [J] . 西南师范大学学报自然科学版，2010，35(5)：75 - 79.

[48] Ullman MT. The neural basis of lexicon and grammar in first and second language the declarative/procedural model [J] . Bilingualism, 2001, 4 (2): 105 - 122.

[49] Abutalebi J. Neural aspects of second language representation and language control [J] . Acta Psychol Amst, 2008, 128(3): 466 - 478.

[50] Abutalebi J, Green DW. Neuroimaging of language control in bilinguals neural adaptation and reserve [J] . Bilingualism, 2016, 1 (4):

689 – 698.

[51] Weissberger GH, Gollan TH, Bondi MW, et al. Language and task switching in the bilingual brain bilinguals are staying, not switching, experts [J] . Neuropsychologia, 2015(66): 193 – 203.

[52] Petitto LA. New discoveries from the bilingual brain and mind across the life span: Implications for education [J] . Mind Brain Educ, 2009, 3(4): 185 – 197.

[53] Petitto LA, Kovelman I. The bilingual paradox how signing-speaking bilingual children help us to resolve it and teach us about the brain's mechanisms underlying all language acquisition [J] . Learn Lang, 2003, 8(3): 5 – 19.

[54] Petitto LA, Kovelman I, Harasymowycz U. Bilingual language development learning the new damage [R] . Ann Arbor Society for Research in Child Development, 2003.

[55] Kovelman I, Salahuddin M, Berens MS, et al. "One glove does not fit all" in bilingual reading acquisition using the age of first bilingual language exposure to understand optimal contexts for reading success [J] . Cogent Educ, 2015, 2(1): 1006504.

[56] Thomas-Sunesson D, Hakuta K, Bialystok E. Degree of bilingualism modifies executive control in Hispanic children in the USA [J] . Int J Biling Educ Biling, 2016.

[57] Mechelli A, Crinion JT, Noppeney U, et al. Neurolinguistics structural plasticity in the bilingual brain [J] . Nature, 2004, 431(7010): 757 – 757.

[58] Maye J, Werker JF, Gerken L. Infant sensitivity to distributional information can affect phonetic discrimination [J] . Cognition, 2002, 82(3): B101-B111.

[59] Kuhl PK. Early language learning and the social brain [C] //Cold Spring Harbor symposia on quantitative biology. New York Cold Spring Harbor Laboratory Press, 2014: 211 – 220.

[60] Kuhl PK, Tsao FM, Liu HM. Foreign-language experience in infancy effects of short-term exposure and social interaction on phonetic learning [J] . Proc Natl Acad Sci USA, 2003, 100(15): 9096 – 9101.

[61] Meltzoff AN, Kuhl PK, Movellan J, et al. Foundations for a new science of learning [J] . Science, 2009, 325(5938): 284 – 288.

[62] Brooks R, Meltzoff AN. The importance of eyes how infants interpret adult looking behavior [J] . Dev Psychol, 2002, 38(6): 958 – 966.

[63] Brooks R, Meltzoff AN. Connecting the dots from infancy to childhood a

longitudinal study connecting gaze following, language, and explicit theory of mind [J] . J Exp Child Psychol, 2015(130): 67－78.

[64] Brooks R, Meltzoff AN. The development of gaze following and its relation to language [J] . Dev Sci, 2005, 8(6): 535－543.

[65] Kemp C. MRI shows association between reading to young children and brain activity [N] . APP News, 2015－04－25(4).

[66] McFadden D, Train K. Mixed MNL models for discrete response [J] . J Appl Econometrics, 2000, 15(5): 447－470.

[67] Konner M. The evolution of childhood relationships, emotion, mind [M] . Cambridge Harvard University Press, 2010.

[68] Sutton-Smith B. The ambiguity of play [M] . Cambridge Harvard University Press, 1997.

[69] Shonkoff JP, Boyce WT, McEwen BS. Neuroscience, molecular biology, and the childhood roots of health disparities building a new framework for health promotion and disease prevention [J] . JAMA, 2009, 301(21): 2252－2259.

[70] 周兢，陈思. 建立儿童学习的脑科学交管系统——脑执行功能理论对学前儿童发展与教育的启示 [J] . 全球教育展望，2011，40(6): 28—33.

Acknowledgement

Dr. Robert Selman and Dr. Catherine E. Snow would like to thank Qianhui Sun, Shuangchen Yu, Yue Wang, Jingyu Li, Yixuan Wang and Haiqing He for their contribution to the work that is the basis for the Chapter one and Chapter two. The authors are grateful to Si Chen, Ziwen Mei, Yi Zhao, Siwei (Wendy) He, Yitong Hu, Kunlei He, Zhuo Feng, Skyler Yin and Chloe Chen of the CEREC Lab for their translation and proofreading. Dr. Selman also thanks Haiqing He and Lucheng Wang for their additional translation work.

Epilogue

Manyuen Kou

After three years of accumulation and ten months of preparation, the book, *International Working Group's Research on Early Childhood Education-A volume contributed by Harvard University*, *the University of Calgary*, *East China Normal University* (herein referred to as *International Working Group's Research on ECE*), is finally ready to meet its readers. I would like to avail myself of this opportunity to express my heartfelt gratitude to the four world-renowned professors who have contributed ten high-quality essays to the volume, the scholars who have taken time out of their busy schedule to write prefaces for the book, the teachers and students from Harvard University and the University of Calgary who have helped proofread the translated versions of all the essays, all the directors and editors from the "Goldian Group ECE R&D Center" and the publishing company who have provided much assistance to the completion of the volume as well as all the friends who care about the publication of the book.

Well goes an ancient Chinese verse, "It takes ten months to give birth to a new life and three years to breastfeed a baby. A mother is always ready to toil and moil for the well-being of her child." In a similar way, the four professors from Harvard University, the University of Calgary, East China Normal University have dedicated themselves to bringing into existence this newborn – *International Working Group's Research on ECE*, with the decades of knowledge and expertise they have accumulated in the academia as well as their unremitting passion for the cause of early childhood education. From selecting books to read with young children to early childhood language and brain development research, the volume covers ten themes that are of significance to education. We hope that parents, early childhood teachers, administrators, and education specialists who read this book will find it enlightening and edifying, and that the volume could equip them with better knowledge to cultivate caring, capable and responsible global citizens. After finishing reading the book, I was immersed in deep contemplation and reflection–I think every adult should ask himself after he reads the book what we can learn from children, rather than what we can teach them.

Goldian's engagement in education has de facto commenced many years ago. In March, 2014, Goldian Group participated in the 34th annual international conference of WFUCA held at the UNHQ in New York and the award of World Peace Builder was conferred on it. In July, Goldian Group was invited to the 2014 Asia Europe Forum of Education (AEFE) in Changchun and awarded "Outstanding Contributor of World

Multicultural Exchanges" by WFUCA. In order to introduce more advanced global educational resources and boost the development of quality early childhood education, Goldian Group established the "Goldian Group ECE R&D Center" in 2015 and "Goldian and Harvard Professors' Educational Research and Practice Center" in 2016.

We hold that the essence of education is to make positive influence on children's life. To nurture a seed with great care and help it grow into a blossom of humanity and vitality that will make the world a better place -this is the ultimate purpose of the book.

On the occasion of the completion of this volume, I would like to have a chance to "revisit" the speech I made during the 2014 AEFE. May we all stand in solidarity for the cause of education.

British royal etiquette courses

To build a home of humanities by absorbing the essence of diverse cultures

—Message delivered on the occasion of Asia Europe Forum of Education (AEFE) in 2014

Your Excellencies,

Ladies and gentlemen,

Dear teachers and students,

Good morning!

All that are present today are professors, scholars or academicians. I got a feeling that I am once again back to school. That is why I am both a bit nervous and greatly honored right now. Please accept my deepest congratulations on the convocation of the Asia Europe Forum of Education (AEFE).

To start with, my heartfelt thanks go to China Federation of UNESCO Clubs, Centers and Associations, the organizing committee of the forum, for having me. On behalf of Goldian Group, the only enterprise representative that has been invited, I would like to say that it is our distinct privilege to participate in the 2014 AEFE and present the World Multicultural Education Center with Haïmalong, an artwork which symbolizes the fusion of Eastern and Western cultures.

You may be curious and ask what is Haïmalong? What is its implication or origin? In response to your questions, I would like to tell you a story. In the 15th century, a young prince—the nephew of Chinese emperor Yongli, was fascinated by Marco Polo. Keen to retrace Marco Polo's steps along the Silk Road, he decided to embark on a journey to the West, eventually ending up in France where he was able to demonstrate his marvelous talent and artistic attainment and became the goldsmith to King Charles VI. He also encountered the love of his life. As a lasting tribute to their love, the young prince set about the task of sculpting a mystic animal, which was imbued with the attributes of a seahorse and a dragon. The former represents the chariot driven by Poseidon; the latter is the sign of majesty in the oriental culture. He called it Haïmalong, for it stands for the fusion of the East and West, symbolizing peace, tolerance and wisdom. Not only did the young prince win the heart of his love, he also won the respect of the people.

To me, this is not just a legend of love; rather, it is more of a dream. The theme for today's forum is "promoting multicultural communication and advocating international education". As an enterprise with a strong sense of social responsibility, we have to play an active role in multicultural and educational exchanges by adhering to our corporate culture. Goldian Group was awarded "World Peace Builder" at the United Nations Headquarters in March, 2014. On behalf of the delegation of China Federation of UNESCO Clubs, Centers and Associations,

Goldian Group presented to the United Nations a collection of cultural and artistic treasures that represent peace, tolerance and wisdom—Haïmalong and Peace Seal. As a global pioneer of humanistic real estate in China, Goldian Group has indeed stepped forward in the cause of civic diplomacy and shown to the world a real China.

Dear friends, I believe you must have witnessed quite a lot of world-famous architectures in the world, be it Schloss Schönbrunn in Austria, New Swan Stone Castle in Germany, Kremlin in Russia, or Louvre in France. One of the reasons that made them stand the test of time is the fact that they absorbed the quintessence of various cultures. Inspired by the same idea, Goldian Group is committed to cultural exchange and fusion on the path to humanistic real estate. We have assimilated a diversity of architectural cultures, evidenced by the communities as well as facilities we built. To illustrate, the charitable Anna Chan Chennault Peace Garden has been erected to commemorate the legendary love story between Anna Chan Chennault, the first female war correspondent from China, and General Claire Lee Chennault, an American military aviator best known for his advocate for peace and leadership of the "Flying Tigers". The Garden is also home to the Anna Chan Chennault Humanities Hall and Exhibition, which symbolize their efforts to boost the communication between the East and West. The three true love humanistic and artistic treasures of our design—Peace Irene, Haïmalong, and Haïmafong, add a touch of vivacity and gracefulness into the garden. The spirit of "peace, harmony and beauty" that they convey can be applied to various humanistic sectors of our livelihood, such as education, culture, architecture, etc.

Nowadays, there is a growing global trend towards multicultural education that is people-centered, family- or community-based. Accordingly, we have to follow this trend by introducing international schools, providing education- and culture-related information for communities, offering international trainings and mobilizing all sorts of resources to elevate the education standards in communities.

What is lying under the culture is the conscience of a nation—not only do we have to hold close to our hearts what has been passed down upon us, but we also have to break free from the yoke of the past and bring innovation. As to me, this is exactly the kind of responsibility that is expected of us in this very forum; it is also the mission and objective of us entrepreneurs.

I have two eight-year-old girls at home. Once, they stood between the Peace Wishing Fountain and a 15-meter-high statue of Peace Irene. Palms pressed together, the girls made a prayer. I asked my younger daughter what kind of wish they made. She paused a bit and then said, "we hope that we will not fight ever again."

What a touching moment it is! Absence of fight, pursuit of peace, inclusiveness and mutual love, tolerance and harmony… If the entire world becomes as innocent as young children, we believe that we can definitely construct a peaceful, harmonious and beautiful future!

Thank you for your attention.

(Manyuen Kou: President of Goldian Group)

Little angels making a wish in front of the peace fountain and the statue of Irene

Photo Caption:

1. **A stimulating learning environment offering a diversity of facilities**

   Square of Yulong Kindergarten

   Heart-shaped Gesture of "9 · 9 True Love"

   Outdoor rainbow playground of Yulong Kindergarten, with a natural lawn

   Playground for children

   Professional basketball court and tennis court

2. **Curricula geared to international standards cultivating confident future global citizens**

   British royal etiquette courses

   Afternoon tea in Yulong palace

   Equestrian lessons in Anna Chan Chennault Peace Royal Garden

   Skylight Swimming Pool in Yulong Palace

3. **Unique humanistic and artistic treasures radiating charm and charisma**

   Premiere of three humanistic and artistic treasures in the United Nations: Haïmalong, Haïmafong and Irene

   9 · 9 gallery of celebrities

   Little angels making a wish in front of the peace fountain and the statue of Irene

图书在版编目(CIP)数据

国际教育专家论"早教":来自哈佛大学、卡尔加里大学、华东师范大学的研究/高迪安&哈佛大学教授国际合作教育科研中心主编. —上海:上海三联书店,2020.7
ISBN 978-7-5426-6906-3

Ⅰ.①国… Ⅱ.①高… Ⅲ.①早期教育—研究 Ⅳ.①G61

中国版本图书馆CIP数据核字(2020)第140865号

国际教育专家论"早教":来自哈佛大学、卡尔加里大学、华东师范大学的研究

主　　编 / 高迪安 & 哈佛大学教授国际合作教育科研中心

责任编辑 / 殷亚平
装帧设计 / 徐　徐
监　　制 / 姚　军
责任校对 / 张大伟　王凌霄

出版发行 / 上海三联书店
(200030)中国上海市漕溪北路331号A座6楼
邮购电话 / 021-22895540
印　　刷 / 上海新岛印刷有限公司

版　　次 / 2020年7月第1版
印　　次 / 2020年7月第1次印刷
开　　本 / 640×960　1/16
字　　数 / 350千字
印　　张 / 26.5
书　　号 / ISBN 978-7-5426-6906-3/G·1550
定　　价 / 99.00元